ROUTLEDGE LIBRARY EDITIONS:
DEVELOPMENT

FACTORS IN ECONOMIC DEVELOPMENT

FACTORS IN ECONOMIC DEVELOPMENT

A. K. CAIRNCROSS

Volume 30

Routledge
Taylor & Francis Group
LONDON AND NEW YORK

First published in 1962

This edition first published in 2011
by Routledge
2 Park Square, Milton Park, Abingdon, Oxon, OX14 4RN

Simultaneously published in the USA and Canada
by Routledge
711 Third Avenue, New York, NY 10017

Routledge is an imprint of the Taylor & Francis Group, an informa business

First issued in paperback 2013

British Library Cataloguing in Publication Data
A catalogue record for this book is available from the British Library

ISBN 13: 978-0-415-58414-2 (Set)
eISBN 13: 978-0-203-84035-1 (Set)
ISBN 13: 978-0-415-59357-1 (hbk Volume 30)
ISBN 13: 978-0-415-84759-9 (pbk Volume 30)
eISBN 13: 978-0-203-83854-9 (Volume 30)

Publisher's Note
The publisher has gone to great lengths to ensure the quality of this reprint but points out that some imperfections in the original copies may be apparent.

Disclaimer
The publisher has made every effort to trace copyright holders and welcomes correspondence from those they have been unable to contact.

A. K. CAIRNCROSS

Factors in Economic Development

LONDON
GEORGE ALLEN & UNWIN LTD.
Ruskin House Museum Street

FIRST PUBLISHED IN 1962
SECOND IMPRESSION 1963
THIRD IMPRESSION 1964

TO MARY

Nec ad vitam anima
Satis sit dimidia

PREFACE

THIS volume is intended as a kind of gladiatorial salute by one on the point of academic death and is addressed not so much to a professional audience as to that larger assembly of informed onlookers for whose attention and favour applied economists like to contend. As a gesture to such onlookers it is no doubt a little clumsy: the score of articles and essays selected for inclusion were written for different types of occasion, are reprinted virtually as they were originally delivered or published, and are, at times, obscured from the layman by a thick varnish of jargon and technical detail. Some have been written, as it were, in the margin of other occupations, without leisure to reconsider style, form or content as they took shape. Yet whatever their defects, on which my mind is concentrated wonderfully by an increasing awareness that it is too late to remedy them, they have the merit of dealing for the most part with issues of public importance in terms that are as a rule within the reach of public understanding.

In deciding what to include in this volume I did not aim deliberately at continuity of theme. I discarded anything more than ten years old, anything I thought relatively accessible, and anything that seemed too topical, esoteric or local in interest. This implied, for example, the exclusion of any article published in a British Bank Review. It also implied the exclusion of any analysis of Scottish economic problems. What remained after this process of winnowing, in which I was greatly assisted by the good judgment of Mr J. R. Parkinson, was the present collection of essays, guesses and addresses. Seven of them, as I write, are still unpublished, although of this seven all but one—my address on 'The Work of the Economic Development Institute'—are likely to appear while this volume is in the press. The items selected have been drawn from a dozen different journals and half-a-dozen symposia and have been published in five different countries.

This sprawl of publications might seem to destroy any prospect of coherence in the subject-matter. But in fact the collection turns out to be more than an anthology and to reflect a preoccupation with a limited range of related topics, all of them associated in some way with economic development.

These topics are listed in the headings to the successive parts: investment and technical progress; trade; administration and planning. To this list might be added education, the importance of which for economic development is repeatedly emphasized, even if there is no extended treatment of the interconnection between the two. The successive chapters do not outline any systematic theory of economic development or any specific strategy that might be followed by governments trying to force the pace. Nor are they devised so as to carry forward the treatment of a single theme from one aspect to the next. But they may serve to remind the reader by the very multiplicity of the factors that are introduced of the many facets to economic development, the variety of possible approaches to it, and the complexity of the elements by which it is governed.

If I set out again to discuss the causes of economic growth I should certainly say different things and say them in a different way. In dealing with capital investment, I should probably concede more willingly the importance of its rôle, particularly in under-developed countries. I should still put most emphasis on innovation in its widest sense, and argue the need to study far more attentively the social and economic forces to which innovation responds: not just scientific research but the incentives to seek out and employ new knowledge at the risk of loss. I should want also to stress that development in one country takes place in the presence of simultaneous development in others and that few countries can deliberately shut out external forces and enforce a calculus of action that takes no account of alternative locations abroad. But it is perhaps the final section that I should find least satisfactory. It does not get to grips with the rôle of government either in planning economic activity or in strengthening individual incentives. It has nothing to say about the behaviour of social classes, a subject which cannot be dismissed merely because Marx oversimplified it. There is also very little about the influence of a changing industrial structure and changing social relationships on the motives to, and opportunities for, economic advancement. At best, the reader may find a clue here and there to these largely neglected topics.

Of my intellectual debts in the writing of these essays

something may be guessed from the footnotes to them. But they are far heavier and more extensive than is ever explicitly stated. If I have retained any claim to originality it must be because I have not always had time to familiarize myself with my colleagues' contributions and have had to work out for myself what they, no doubt, have already said. It is, however, other debts of which I am most conscious when I look back over the years during which these essays were written. There were five solid reasons in the Cairncross household against writing any of them and if these obstacles to the development of the volume did not prevail it was thanks to the influence of a still more powerful factor noted in the dedication.

No one, I hope, will suppose that this volume is intended to reflect the views of Her Majesty's Government. It had already gone to press before I took up my official duties as Economic Adviser.

A.K.C.

Glasgow
12.5.1961

CONTENTS

PART I: THE SETTING

CHAPTER 1

The Poverty of Nations[1]

I

Two hundred years ago, when Adam Smith was trying to systematize his ideas about economic development, he chose as the title of his exposition *The Wealth of Nations*. Today, if he were expounding the same theme, he would be more likely to include in the title a reference to poverty as well as wealth. The most challenging problem confronting economists remains what it was in his time: to bring to light the forces that determine the economic growth and development of nations. But it would now be more natural than it was in 1776 to look at the problem in comparative terms and ask why growth should be faster in one country than another, whether the gap in standards of living between rich countries and poor is likely to widen or narrow and what might be done to promote a greater measure of international equality.

There are many reasons for this shift in emphasis. It does not result solely from the facts of poverty and inequality on the international plane for these facts have been with us from time immemorial. Even in Adam Smith's time there was a perceptible and growing difference in the levels of economic achievement in different parts of Europe and between Western Europe and most of the Continent of Asia. But it was impossible, in the absence of statistics, to measure these differences or to detect any systematic foundation for them. A few centuries earlier Europe had not been conspicuously prosperous and in a few centuries' time the lead might pass

[1] One of the Stevenson lectures delivered in the University of Glasgow, in February 1961.

to other continents. The fortunes of nations might revolve in a vast cycle in obedience to the laws of nature and society: they certainly did not move forward ineluctably from one generation to the next. Progress was a merry-go-round, not a railway train. If economists speculated on the reasons for those phases of the cycle when the forces of growth were in the ascendency they hesitated to assume that the cycle had been broken and that society had entered an indefinite period of cumulative and self-sustaining growth. On the contrary, long after Adam Smith, the literature of economics is strewn with prophecies of a stationary state in which growth would finally cease under the influence of some limiting factor such as population growth, the law of diminishing returns, a fuel shortage or a chronic tendency to over-save.[1] It would be very difficult to point to any economist in the nineteenth century or even the first forty years of the twentieth who embraced the view that the gap between rich countries and poor was destined to go on widening without any foreseeable limit.

Even when this gap had already become far too large to escape attention, economists could still treat it as a temporary affair. Having seen one country after another follow in Britain's wake and begin to overhaul her, they tended to adopt the optimistic view that it was only a matter of time before the whole world economy would be in movement and that once movement began it was at least as likely to be an advantage as a disadvantage to be a late starter. In any event, there were problems enough in the advanced countries without any compulsion to give thought to what was going on in those that remained backward; and there were few economists in backward countries capable of challenging the views of western economists and forcing them to re-examine the special obstacles to development that backwardness imposes.

The main shift in opinion did not take place until the war and post-war years. Largely because of the setting up of new international organizations with world-wide economic responsibilities, economists became much more knowledgeable about the problems of under-developed countries, more alive to the importance of these problems and more fascinated by

[1] H. W. Singer, *Recent Trends in Economic Thought on Under-developed Countries* (mimeographed, Nov. 1960).

their intellectual challenge. A constant stream of statistics poured from the United Nations and its associated institutions, and a long series of economic surveys, reports of missions, and special studies provided ample background for the interpretation of the statistics. It became possible for the first time to measure with some degree of precision the scale and pace of economic advance in the under-developed countries, to map out its predominant features and to understand the economic and social forces controlling it. Attention was focused as never before on economic development. Just as the statisticians who studied the life and labour of the poor towards the end of last century aroused the public conscience and gave it direction in dealing with poverty, so the statisticians of today have brought home the poverty of nations and the need to do something about it. The under-developed countries are the slums of the world economy, and slumming has become the fashion again.

The flow of statistics and reports is not the only reason for the growing consciousness that something must and can be done. As more and more of the under-developed countries gain political independence their ambitions become increasingly centred on economic independence and on the freedom which comes from greater wealth. Their poverty stands out more starkly when it can no longer be blamed on colonial rule. It is felt to be less excusable the more rapidly other countries draw ahead of them, including countries like Japan and Russia which only recently were almost equally poor. Above all, the very fact that nearly all of them are now undergoing perceptible development sharpens their consciousness of backwardness, brings home the attainability of more rapid progress and with the perversity of human appetite makes it grow by what it feeds on.

Nor is it only the less advanced countries that have been roused from apathy; the richer countries are more concerned to help them. The nearer they approach a solution of their own economic problems, the more intolerable seem the misfortunes of others and the easier it is to indulge the ordinary obligations of humanity. Just as in our own country it was difficult to campaign against poverty so long as it was part of the accepted order of things and its inevitability was demonstrated by moralists and economists alike, so it has only been since the economic backwardness of other nations ceased to appear inevitable that deliberate efforts have been made to assist them. No doubt these efforts have been quickened by a sense of the attractions that Communism offers to countries seeking a short-cut to industrialization. No doubt also we are still far from any sense of unity in a single world economy in which national aspirations have to give place to duties to our international neighbours. But already it has come to be accepted that, in international as in national affairs, the economically backward have a moral right to look for assistance to the economically advanced.

This was not so even at the end of the last war. The colonial powers usually recognized an obligation to promote the development of their colonies and this sometimes involved them in outright financial grants. But such grants were always on a purely bilateral basis and any international participation would have been strenuously resisted. In Britain the Colonial Development and Welfare Fund was still not in existence; and in the United States, aid for the under-developed countries was dismissed as 'feeding the Hottentots'. We have travelled a long way since then.

Curiously enough, one of the most decisive steps had no apparent relationship to the under-developed countries. The Marshall Aid Programme so triumphantly demonstrated the possibilities of international aid that it left behind a great fund of goodwill for similar experiments in other continents. By an expenditure of $13,000 m., or about 4 per cent of its income for one year, the United States succeeded beyond all expectations in helping the economies of Western Europe to recover from the destruction and dislocation of war. After only two and a half years industrial production was 40 per cent and agricultural production 20 per cent higher than in the best pre-war years. It is natural to feel that if the resources of all the industrial countries were mobilized and a similar effort of collaboration went to the promotion of world-wide economic development, the results might be equally spectacular. It was no doubt some such hope that inspired Mr Kennedy's declaration in his Inaugural Address:

'To those new states . . . of half the globe struggling to break the bonds of mass misery, we pledge our best efforts to help them help themselves, for whatever period is required. . . . If the free society cannot help the many who are poor, it can never save the few who are rich.'

II

We cannot hope to form any satisfactory judgment of the help that might be given to the under-developed countries without some knowledge of their circumstances. Since each country is unique we must limit ourselves to broad generalizations applicable to most of them without dwelling too much on the exceptions, however important.

First of all, nearly all the most backward countries are in three continents: Asia, Africa and Latin America. Of these three, Asia is by far the largest in population since every second human being lives there. Africa and Latin America both have a population slightly larger than that of the United States. Some countries in these continents, such as Japan and South Africa, are relatively advanced, just as some European countries are still relatively backward. But the broad division is accurate for most purposes.

This means, secondly, that the under-developed countries are those that lie closest to the equator. This would be even more true if we were willing to leave out Japan (which is no longer one of the poorer countries), China (which used to be one of the most advanced) and Argentine, Uruguay and Chile (all of which are among the most prosperous of the less advanced countries). It is more accurate to contrast the tropical with the temperate countries than the countries of the northern half of the world with those of the southern half (as Sir Oliver Franks has suggested), all the more as the countries of Asia lie almost entirely to the north of the equator.

If, thirdly, we take average income per head as a broad measure of the difference between rich countries and poor, we find a small group of countries at one extreme with per capita incomes of $1,000 or over. Britain just scrapes into this group which also includes North America, Australia, New Zealand and some of the Scandinavian countries. At the other extreme is a long list of countries, which together make up over half the population of the world, with per capita incomes of $100 or less. Even if we allow for all the ambiguities that such comparisons involve, there is no reason to doubt that between the poorer half of humanity and the top tenth the disparity in living standards is at least of the order of 1:10.

We know, moreover, that most of this disparity is the product of the last hundred years or so. In many of the richer countries real incomes have risen at least fivefold within the past century while in the under-developed countries it is inconceivable that incomes should ever have been so far below their present level and quite possible that in some of them incomes have fallen rather than risen.

There is also no doubt that the gap in standards of living is a growing one. Even if the under-developed countries were able to improve their incomes ten times as fast as the most advanced countries, the gap would still widen. A 10 per cent annual increase in per capita incomes would add less than $10 to the average, while in the United States a 1 per cent increase would add $20. It is not impossible that the United States might achieve a rate of growth that would add more every year to her average income per head than the entire income per head available in some of the under-developed countries.

While the absolute size of the gap is undoubtedly growing, it is not so certain that the more advanced countries are showing a faster *rate* of growth than the under-developed countries. Many of the Latin American countries in particular have maintained remarkably high rates of growth over the past decade—rates well in excess of those recorded in the United States or the United Kingdom. On the other hand, some countries like Indonesia have shown very little change. The scatter is so wide that to take an average and make comparisons with the corresponding average for advanced countries is not only seriously misleading but yields different results at different hands. Some distinguished economists go on repeating with increasing emphasis that it is the advanced countries that are growing faster, while others, no less distinguished, produce statistics that suggest the contrary. Whatever the difference, it is not uniform, and it is consistent with widespread improvement at a rate which, by nineteenth century standards, is far from disappointing, however much contemporary expectations may have risen. But it still leaves three-quarters of the world's population in conditions of extreme poverty and without hope of any radical transformation in these conditions within the next decade or two.

The basis of livelihood in nearly all the under-developed countries lies in primary production. Their citizens are for the most part peasants, farming small plots of ground by primitive methods, often on an insecure tenure and encumbered by debt. Sometimes there are extensive mineral deposits, including oil, which make it very much easier to earn foreign exchange. But these deposits, which are a matter of luck, do little to enrich the mass of the population or provide them with employment. It is agriculture that is the staple activity. Manufacturing, on the other hand, is under-developed.

Nor are these two circumstances unconnected. For since agriculture tends to be backward and the cultivators are poor, the market for manufactured goods is limited and more easily supplied from abroad. Apart from all the other difficulties of introducing modern factories, the scale on which production for the domestic market could be undertaken is often insufficient to allow the use of specialized equipment at full capacity. Thus the typical under-developed country exports primary produce exclusively, and obtains manufactures in return from the more advanced countries to which its exports are directed. They are in this sense dependent economies, meeting the overspill of demand from foreign economies and to some extent limited in their development by the pace set for them by industrial expansion in other countries.

For most of them international trade is of the greatest importance. To take an extreme example, 40 per cent of the income of Ceylon is derived from production for export, nearly twice as high a proportion as applies to Great Britain. The more they are drawn from purely subsistence activities to produce for sale against money the higher tends to be the relative size of the export sector and the greater their dependence on foreign demand. The range of exports which they can make is usually extremely limited while the imports which they require are highly diversified. The list of products which, collectively, they supply is also an extremely limited one so that they are usually brought into keen competition with one another; and as world markets for these products tend to be highly inelastic and to expand relatively slowly, their power to enlarge their export earnings without damage to the economies of other under-developed countries is correspondingly restricted.

Yet the picture of primary producing countries specializing heavily on individual products and dependent on the industrial countries for nearly all the manufactures which they can afford to buy is one that must obviously be qualified. Most of what they grow they consume themselves and if they could grow more to meet their own needs they would have no need to wait on world markets for an incentive to expand. What the world buys from them relieves their poverty because it presumably offers a better return than production for their own requirements. But if the world market is limited this does not put a stop to agricultural improvement. The poorer they are, the more urgent is an enlargement of food production to supply the domestic market and meet domestic needs.

Similarly, it is an oversimplification to imagine that all their manufactures are imported. Many of them have already a thriving industrial sector. As we know to our cost, now that we are a net importer of cotton textiles, the textile industry in particular has a firm footing in under-developed countries all over the world and some of these countries have emerged as large exporters. India is almost unique among them in deriving half her export earnings from manufactures. But there are many others that are at least capable of meeting most of their domestic requirements of consumer goods. Taking the under-developed countries as a group, we cannot be far wrong in assuming that they manufacture about half as much as they import. Naturally this proportion varies greatly from country to country. It is also very much less for machinery than for consumer goods: a circumstance of particular importance when the under-developed countries try to force the pace in industrializing themselves and are obliged to finance the importation of most of the necessary capital equipment out of their limited and inelastic export earnings.

Finally, we must take account of the fact that whatever the inequalities *between* countries in the world economy these inequalities are repeated, often far more strikingly, *within* the under-developed countries themselves. There are great inequalities in wealth and social conditions; and these inequalities tend to be aggravated in the early stages of growth, since it is often the rich who either respond to the opportunities that development offers or win uncovenanted benefits when it takes place. We need only think of some of the Arab oil-producers or of many of the countries of Latin America to remind ourselves of the magnitude of these inequalities and of the strains and stresses in the social and political fabric which they occasion. The problem of reconciling economic development with entrenched inequalities is not the least of the difficulties confronting those who would like to contribute from the outside to the elimination of poverty and backwardness.

There is another sense in which the major problem is one of inequality *within* the under-developed countries. Again and again we find within them an astonishing spread between the primitive and the modern. In technology they may display the whole gamut of human progress from the Stone Age to the latest advances in medical science. Even in Japan one finds side by side a brand-new steel works and a workshop almost unchanged since mediaeval times. One can read of Arab sheikhs arriving on a camel to continue their journey by Comet. In Latin America there are villages where the only major change since the arrival of the Spaniards has been the introduction of the wheel and not far off are great ports equipped to handle Transatlantic liners. Alongside towns that rival or surpass the cities of our own country are the miserable shanty towns in which the human overspill collects; and in the hinterland, the mass of the population are housed in conditions that may be more picturesque and less squalid but conceal still greater poverty.

These juxtapositions are a vivid reminder that there are always two sides to development: the initial innovation and its subsequent dissemination. The main current that sweeps us forward is a current of thought: rising from those distant landmarks where modern science has its source and flowing in an ever broadening stream of experiment and discovery. The current cannot be confined within the boundaries of national states: men of all countries can draw from it and add to it. But if the body of scientific knowledge is universal and trans-national, its application in new productive techniques need not be. Each new discovery is local: it does not spread instantaneously but takes time to become known and made use of. There is always a lag, therefore, while the process of dissemination takes place: an inequality between the centre of discovery and the periphery towards which it spreads. The lag may be prolonged by indifference to new ideas as such or to the discovery itself: by habits of mind hostile to scientific thinking or unable to come to terms with it: by incapacity to grasp the relevance of the new discovery: by inability to adapt it to a different set of circumstances: or by powerlessness to take advantage of it. All these influences are at work in the under-developed countries to delay the transmission to them of advances in science and technology occurring elsewhere and to delay still further the dissemination within them of what is known and applied at their points of contact with other countries. Their stock of unabsorbed technology is therefore far larger than in the countries where innovations most commonly originate or where the process of diffusion is made more rapid and effective by better education, wider experience and a keener sense of commercial advantage.

Put in this way, it might seem that the problem of offering assistance to the under-developed countries was a relatively straightforward one. The greater the technological lag, the greater the scope for adopting or adapting techniques already well tried in other countries and using them in order to raise the level of production. But the transfer of technology is by no means a straightforward affair nor is the low diffusion rate of technological knowledge the only obstacle to more rapid development. As anyone who has ever taken part in a programme of technical assistance knows only too well, the problem is not one of supplying information in a seller's market, but of overcoming a whole series of obstacles among which poverty and ignorance take a prominent place.

Consider, for example, what can be done to improve agricultural output. In advanced countries a system of advisory services has been created and no doubt contributes to the more rapid adoption of new techniques (although I am told that the Archers have done more to kindle interest in them than all the experts in the counties). In the less developed countries governments may have difficulty in financing similar services; the experts themselves may be poorly trained or impossible to find; the peasants may remain apathetic towards them or have no capital to profit from the advice they are offered or fear that if they are successful they will merely have their rents put up. Very often, progress is made only when pressure of market demand brings in a new group of farmers who do not hesitate to experiment because they know that the returns are high and that they can affaord to make mistakes so long as their total output is expanded. Once their success is established, example proves more powerful than precept and their neighbours follow suit. As in other countries, agricultural improvement is fastest in the vicinity of growing towns under the stimulus of an expanding market and in periods when favourable prices encourage heavier investment. But agriculture itself is rarely the dynamic centre from which economic growth radiates throughout the economy. Far more commonly it is the dependent variable responding to development in other sectors of the economy or to the growth of demand in foreign markets.

Even if this is so, it does not justify inaction. It would be impossible to leave aside the staple industry (and often the most backward one) in any programme of development. It might be thought that the Soviet Union proves the contrary and that so long as the peasants can be forced to part with food for the towns it does not matter very much whether they produce more food or not. But Russia was a large exporter of her own staple foodstuffs when she embarked on industrialization—resembling in this as in so many other respects the United States rather than the typical underdeveloped country—and she could divert to home use the crops which, before the Revolution were sold abroad. An example much more relevant is that of Japan where crop yields a hundred years ago were no higher than they are now in other parts of Asia and were doubled within a few decades, long before industrialization was complete.

Whatever the difficulties in raising agricultural productivity, they are no less in manufacturing. It might be supposed that with the advantage of cheap labour the underdeveloped countries would have little difficulty in competing with the more advanced countries and that they should be able to follow rapidly along the path already taken by those countries. But in most though by no means all industries they are usually high-cost not low-cost manufacturers. Unskilled labour is a relatively small element in most branches of modern industry and what matters far more is a wide range of skills, including the skills of supervision and management. The under-developed countries lack the supervisory staff that we take for granted: the experienced foreman, the skilled man who has been to night school, the draughtsman, toolmaker and others. They lack also the skilled administrator, the industrialist who knows how to organize a large business, the entrepreneur with the courage and self-confidence to take the long view that is born of previous experience. Their business enterprises tend to be more isolated, less able to draw on the network of services, sub-contractors and specialized suppliers of components that forms part of the industrial structure in advanced countries.

Yet even these difficulties are not insuperable as long as there is assurance of continuing access to a large and expanding market. Puerto Rico and Hong Kong provide standing examples of what can be done when the simpler kinds of manufactured goods are admitted to foreign markets; and the more familiar example of Japan demonstrates that once industry has won a footing in world markets it acquires a momentum that carries it from simpler to more complicated manufactures and begins to generate innovations of its own. Development is not easy; but it is possible, and it is taking place.

III

Given the circumstances of the under-developed countries, what could we most usefully do to help them?

It is not necessary for us to ask *whether* we should help them because we are already doing so on an expanding scale. In grants alone the under-developed countries receive annually about $1,500 m. and in loans in one form or another at least $4,000 m. more. These totals have grown all through the fifties and show no sign of dropping. The main source of funds, both by way of grants and of loans, has been the United States, with France taking second place some way behind. The Communist bloc provided about $2,000 m. over the five years 1954–58, almost entirely in the form of low-interest loans. The United Kingdom's contribution consists partly of private investment, mainly within the Commonwealth, and partly of grants and loans through government agencies: the total amount of aid provided to the underdeveloped countries in these ways is now of the order of £150 m. per annum, or not far short of the 1 per cent of the British national income often suggested as a target.

In considering what more we might do we cannot disregard the difficulties in which additional aid might involve us. If, for example, it took the form of larger grants we should be adding correspondingly to our own tax burden and if it took the form of loans we should be obliged to reduce correspondingly the investment that we could carry out within the United Kingdom. In either event we should also be adding to the difficulty of balancing our international accounts unless we made it a condition of aid that the proceeds should be expended in sterling on British goods. To make such a condition would not only detract from the value of the aid but would set a precedent for other countries which we might later have cause to regret. On the other hand, to make no condition at all would expose the balance of payments to additional hazards when our freedom of action is seriously limited by the risks we already run.

These are not negligible difficulties. It would be reasonable to us to insist that we did not act alone. But it is also important that we should not take a purely self-centred attitude and content ourselves with examining what we can spare, however unselfish our mood. We should try instead to make up our minds what we hope to accomplish in the underdeveloped countries and decide what we might usefully offer that would at the same time prove acceptable. We may, after all, be mistaken in taking the Marshall Plan as a prototype and assuming that all that is required is the voting of larger sums for transfer in the form of grants or loans to the underdeveloped countries.

It is, in fact, abundantly clear that what these countries do not want—and certainly what they ought not to have—is a kind of perpetual dole. They want eventually to stand on their own feet with a fully developed economy capable of yielding them a tolerable standard of living and one that can be expected to go on improving in parallel with the standard in other countries. If loans or grants can help them to achieve this end, well and good. But they may not. Grants may do no more than postpone the evil day if devoted to the consumption of things that are beyond the means of the recipient and do nothing to enhance productive power. They may serve to encourage expensive appetites: even the offer of cheap wheat may in the long run be a disservice if it develops the taste for a relatively expensive form of starch. The benefits may fall to limited groups through misappropriation or monopoly. The government may feel that, even if no strings are attached, its subsequent freedom of manoeuvre is prejudiced. Similarly, loans, particularly if made at rates that reflect, however vaguely, the risks involved, encumber the economy with external debts that may not prove easy to discharge and can absorb quite a high proportion of current export earnings.

It is also clear enough that there are many things that must be done by the country itself and that cannot be undertaken from without. Development is not just a matter of having plenty of money nor is it purely an economic phenomenon. It embraces all aspects of social behaviour: the establishment of law and order, scrupulousness in business dealings including dealings with the revenue authorities, relationships within the family, literacy, familiarity with mechanical gadgets, and so on. The more emphasis we place on factors of this kind and the more independent of economic influences they seem, the more powerless are we to assist development. Social change is more difficult to control than economic change, particularly from the outside; and there is a great danger, all too readily neglected, that in our anxiety to promote economic change we may disregard both the social obstacles that frustrate it and the social disintegration to which it so often gives rise.

Accepting all this, we are left with three main lines of action: financial assistance, technical assistance, and freer trade. Of these three, the first has up till now made the greatest demands on the developed countries. Its principal contribution is towards an increase in the rate of capital formation. As is obvious enough even to a casual visitor, the under-developed countries are often strikingly deficient in real capital assets such as an adequate transport network, sources of power, warehouses, factories and so on. This is a deficiency which, given their poverty, these countries are powerless to remove quickly out of domestic savings. The possibilities of additional taxation are usually limited, so that the central government has not enough command over resources to devote a large proportion to capital purposes; and many of the projects that would most effectively promote development cannot be financed because the arrangements for mobilizing domestic capital are themselves under-developed. Loans and grants by foreign countries can enlarge the resources available and help towards a more rapid rate of capital accumulation at the points in the system where the shortage is most severe.

Financial assistance may, secondly, help towards a more intangible but sometimes more important form of capital accumulation by contributing to the budgetary cost of education, health and other services. This social investment creates a better trained and healthier labour force, extends the working life, and makes the population more adaptable and receptive to new ways of doing things.

A third contribution of external finance is to cover any deficit in the balance of payments. It is not uncommon in under-developed countries—and indeed in others as well—for recurrent crises in the balance of payments to restrict the programmes that governments can carry through. They are particularly likely to get into difficulties because of their dependence on imported capital goods but if these goods can be paid for out of foreign grants and loans, the difficulties can be avoided.

Given the stage that we have now reached, it is at least as important to guarantee the continuity of financial assistance on its present scale as to add to it. The under-developed countries receive assistance through a variety of channels and for a variety of purposes, but they cannot tell from year to year what they will receive nor from whom. The practice of extending public aid has grown up *ad hoc* without any settled basis on which to decide how it should be shared between the recipients and how different national and international agencies might best participate. Most of the aid, for easily understood reasons, passes along bilateral channels and there is no necessary co-ordination of the aid programmes of different countries. Some that are deserving may receive little and some that are not may receive much. The burden of providing aid is shared with equally little regard for equity.

We cannot be surprised that this should be so since each country clings to its sovereignty and is free to take what view it likes of its international responsibilities. But it would make not only for more equity but for greater effectiveness if aid programmes followed more closely the model of the Marshall Plan, with the recipient countries working out comprehensive development programmes, showing in what way it was proposed to co-ordinate external assistance with domestic development. It would also be an advantage if more of the aid could be channelled through international agencies like the International Bank which have had long experience in grappling with the problems of economic development in backward countries.

On the importance of technical assistance I have already insisted. The more we are inclined to view the lag in development as a technological one, the more natural it is to try, by an improvement in human communications, to cut down the lag. This can never by itself be enough. Professor Blackett told us some years ago that 'the sending of experts to poor countries without the capital to carry out their plans could be as irritating as to send a trained cook to a family unable to pay the baker'; and although this seems to me to misconceive the true reasons why foreign experts are often ineffective Professor Blackett is entirely right in insisting that there is a great deal more to development plans than technical advice in their preparation. It is often not so much ideas that are lacking as the appetite for new ideas, open-mindedness, willingness to experiment, and pertinacity. Very often, too, the business of the expert is not to recommend heavier expenditure but expenditure to better purpose: to insist that something is not worth doing or not so valuable as something else that would cost less.

The major difficulties in the way of effective technical assistance are human. The best technical experts may not be willing to go to under-developed countries for long enough to accomplish anything; they are placed in situations where expertise may be the least of the assets they require; they may offer their advice when it is out-of-date, or to the wrong man, or without backing it up later or leaving anyone behind who fully understands it; or it may be disregarded for all sorts of reasons. There is undoubtedly great waste in much of the expenditure on technical assistance that goes on. On the other hand, it is one of the most effective ways of helping the under-developed countries. Ideas are cheap and if some advice goes to waste the return on the rest is often out of all proportion to its cost.

I turn finally to the contribution that might be made by freer trade. It is not so long ago since we ourselves made use of the slogan 'Trade not Aid' and we cannot complain if the same slogan is now made use of by other countries. Nor can European countries join issue over the importance of a wide market in which all are free to compete when they are busy with the setting up of a Common Market and a Free Trade Association. It is part of the professed object of the countries so engaged to help the under-developed countries with which they have political affiliations.

Yet if we look at the freedom currently enjoyed by the under-developed countries to compete in the markets of the advanced countries we may have difficulty in reconciling profession with reality. It is true that the agricultural protectionism in which nearly every European country indulges deals a heavier blow at producers in temperate than in tropical latitudes. It is countries like Australia and New Zealand, not countries like Burma and Ghana, that are hardest hit. The price of butter, for example, is held at twice or thrice its world level in France and Germany and the price of wheat in Switzerland at thrice the price received by farmers in Canada and Australia. But there are tropical products that are penalized almost as heavily, not necessarily for protective reasons. The duties on coffee in Germany, France and Italy are all in excess of 70 per cent (and their rates are not the highest) and on tea the levies in Germany reach nearly 100 per cent. The countries of the European Economic Community will levy in due course a common tariff on sugar of 80 per cent.

In a sense tariffs are the least of the problem. Far more restrictive are the quotas by which a ceiling can be placed on imports and all power to raise trade to a higher level destroyed. This is of particular importance in the case of manufactures. If Western Europe's imports of manufactures from the under-developed countries are almost negligible this is not because these countries are unable to compete but because they are only too able to compete. Tariffs being powerless to keep such imports out, the guillotine is applied in the form of quotas. Alternatively, a gentleman's agreement is come to—Britain being the pioneer among gentlemen—for quotas to be applied 'voluntarily' at the other end.

The British record in relation to imports from the under-developed countries is one of which, with minor reservations, we have no reason to be ashamed. The British market is, by tradition, open to the primary producers of all countries and although that tradition was abandoned at Ottawa in 1931 the principle of free entry for Commonwealth goods was maintained, as it has been maintained ever since. Not only do the under-developed countries of the Commonwealth enjoy tariff-free entry into the British market for their primary produce but they have greater freedom from quotas on their manufactured goods than in almost any other market except, perhaps, the United States. Against non-Commonwealth countries, however—and notably Japan—the British market is far from open.

If the under-developed countries are to be offered freer markets it is obviously desirable for a large number of the industrial countries to take collective action. If their fears of being flooded with cheap goods prove to be justified, the wave will be less formidable if it can be allowed to spend itself on a wider front; and if, as happened when imports from the United States were liberalized with equal trepidation, their fears prove to be unjustified they will at least have taken the sting out of what may become an increasing source of grievance.

We do well to recall that there is another group of countries only too anxious to do business with the under-developed countries and in a very favourable position to do so. The Communist countries are not likely to show any hurry to ad mit the cheaper sort of manufactures. But they might find it highly advantageous to open their markets to tropical products like sugar and cotton both of which the USSR, for example, produces at high cost. In terms of the engineering products that she might manufacture instead and the sugar and cotton that she might buy from Cuba and Egypt with those products, it would pay the USSR to trade more freely, apart altogether from any political advantages that she might derive.

We can have no quarrel with a greater volume of such trade if it will help to lift the people of Cuba and Egypt a little way out of their poverty and take them a little further on the road to a developed economy. But we should not allow ourselves to be left behind nor have it thrown in our teeth that we buy primary produce but not manufactures because we want to keep our suppliers dependent and poor. We of all countries know what trade can contribute to a nation's development: that where there is a market, capital will never be lacking and improvements in technique will not pass unnoticed. Let us not forget these truths in our commercial policy towards the under-developed countries.

IV

In the last resort the problem of international poverty is only superficially an economic one: in a deeper sense it is an educational one. The poverty that has to be destroyed is far less a deficiency in the external assets of modern industrial society than in its intellectual and spiritual endowment. Where men have the attributes that such a society requires—knowledge and experience, skill and self-discipline, the power to take a long view, willingness to be guided by reason and observation, readiness to look for new and better ways of doing things, responsiveness to opportunity and adaptability to change—they usually find a way to create the assets they need. Development may be impossible without building the physical apparatus of advanced countries; but it is still more impossible if it does not take place in the minds of the men who build. The apparatus can be donated or foreign enterprise may create it; but the development of *men* is another matter. They have to be free, like children, to broaden their experience, to make mistakes and learn from their mistakes. They have to be educated.

No country can count itself developed in which education in the ways of industrial civilization has not taken place. Peasants have to be brought within the monetary economy not left to pursue subsistence-farming; workers have to become used to working fixed hours in factories for wage-payments; towns have to grow, and banks and business enterprises; the fruits of science have to be applied throughout the economy. Above all there must emerge, as a continuing element in the life of the country, a group of business administrative and political leaders who can be depended upon to maintain the momentum of development by constant innovation.

Education is not, as we are sometimes tempted to think, something that goes on exclusively in schools and universities. Indeed, what goes on in these places may yield educational results that actively interfere with economic development. But our experience in Britain strongly suggests that a good educational system is closely linked with rapid development and that investment in schools and universities may offer large returns in economic terms, apart from any other merits by which it may be justified. If this is true of Britain, how much more true it is likely to be of under-developed countries.

Moreover, if education is of such strategic importance does it not follow that there is a fourth way in which advanced countries can help and in which they have been helping all along? Are not our universities one of our principal contributions to the development of the less advanced countries? Might we not, by making ampler provision for the students of the less advanced countries, do still more? Let us not in casting around for ways in which we might help overlook a weapon that lies immediately to our hand. Let us remember that we are not the only country in which student numbers are rising and more provision for new branches of study and research is required.

CHAPTER 2

The Economics of 1984[1]

'MANKIND,' said Keynes in 1930, looking forward over the next century, 'is solving its economic problem. . . . I think with dread of the readjustment of the habits and instincts of the ordinary man, bred into him for countless generations, which he may be asked to discard within a few decades. . . . I see us free . . . to return to some of the most sure and certain principles of religion and traditional virtue—that avarice is a vice, that the exaction of usury is a misdemeanour, and the love of money is detestable. . . . It will all happen gradually, not as a catastrophe. Indeed it has begun already.' 'But beware!' he added. 'The time for all this is not yet. . . . It will remain reasonable to be economically purposive for others after it has ceased to be reasonable for oneself.'[2]

Economists in 1957 count chickens for their grandchildren more systematically and confidently than in 1930; but when they put their slide rules away, and do not busy themselves too much with percentages, they are likely to find fewer signs than Keynes of a weakening of economic incentives, an eventual surfeit of capital and a return to effort adequate to meet all ordinary requirements. They can point to no reduction in hours of labour over the past twenty years, no diminished appetite for money, no let-up in the pressure to save and accumulate. They have almost persuaded themselves that there will be none in the next twenty years. Neither the rise of 50 per cent in income per head that has already occurred nor the rise of 50 per cent that is predicted in twenty years is taken as evidence that the economic problem is on the way to solution. On the contrary, any faltering in the upward trend in income is an occasion for heart-searching and dismay. The cry is for more rapid growth, for still higher productivity, for

[1] From *Problems of United States Economic Development*, Vol. I, pp. 67–74, Committee for Economic Development, New York, 1958.

[2] 'Economic Possibilities for our Grandchildren', *The Nation and Athenaeum*, October 11 and 18, 1930.

a demonstration of the superiority, not of the American way of life but of its technical prowess. The pursuit of higher incomes is becoming a matter of religion rather than of 'habits and instincts' and is giving to economic activity an unwholesome dominance over the thinking and energies of mankind. For these higher incomes go increasingly with less, not more, leisure; with a more anxious, not a more relaxed, existence; with the direction of human imagination and skill to the creation of means rather than ends of action.

Yet surely Keynes was right to warn us to prepare for abundance. The next twenty years cannot be like the last if there is to be any hope for the human race. Unless destruction is to be utter and complete, there can be no world war; and there must be some limit to expenditure on deterrents once those already at hand are overwhelming. For these and other reasons, it may be far less necessary to appeal to economic incentives and to struggle with a chronic shortage of capital. On the other hand, the ordinary man may continue to seek the servitude of economic necessity. There will then emerge a contradiction between the social need for effort and thrift and the settled preference of the public, almost independently of their consuming habits, to occupy themselves in the daily grind and to build economic security out of their savings.

Such a contradiction need not issue in unemployment and frustration but could be a great opportunity, which only governments could seize, of exploiting the idea in Keynes's aside that 'it will remain reasonable to be economically purposive for others after it has ceased to be reasonable for oneself'. Indeed the system of taxation that has already come into existence rests on this very idea. Income tax obliges the taxpayer to use a dual reckoning, gross of tax and net of tax, in comparing the value of his work with the spendable income that he earns from it. Whether he likes it or not, he must remain 'economically purposive for others' as well as for himself.

Who are those 'others' in whose favour the State might redistribute income that would either remain unspent or be spent on items of diminishing real significance to human enjoyment? There are many claimants inside the United States —the sick and the aged, for example. But it is the claimants outside, to whom the United States owes nothing except what her own interests dictate, to whom special thought should be given over the next twenty years. The greatest economic problem facing the United States is not how she can raise her own standard of living but how she can harmonize her economic development with the worldwide process of growth.

This problem would exist even if the United States were not in a specially favourable position to offer assistance to her neighbours. But, just as it arises in large measure out of the very disparity between American incomes and incomes elsewhere, so its solution should be facilitated by that disparity. By parting with a relatively limited amount of purchasing power, the United States can—or so experience with the Marshall Plan appeared to demonstrate—give a quite disproportionate impulse to the development of other countries.

First of all, the very fact of rapid progress in a country already in a dominant position in the world economy creates difficulties for her neighbours. So long as nearly half the world's industrial output is concentrated in the United States, the rest of the world is almost forced to dance to an American tune. It cannot escape major fluctuations originating there; and its requirements of American goods and services tend to rise more steeply than its power to make sales in the American market. Secondly, the economic success of the United States charges the feelings of less fortunate countries with that ambivalence that is so often aroused by great wealth; on the one hand, they feel drawn to copy her, and on the other, they feel envious and frustrated because of the gulf that separates them from their model. Thirdly, if the United States were to profess herself indifferent to what was happening elsewhere in the world, and offered no rescue or relief from the storms which her own actions unwittingly let loose, her power and influence would rapidly dwindle and the ideas for which she stands would be supplanted.

One may indeed go further and question whether, for twenty years to come, national sovereignty can survive and each country be left free to decide for itself when to make use of all the powers of destruction at its disposal. Are we not bound to steer, however gently, towards a union of all and seek to create the institutions of world government? In such a union, the world would form a single economic unit, in which common policies would have to be devised to meet common ends. The leadership that has been thrust upon the United

States over the past twenty years would undergo a sea-change, but she would still have to bear heavy responsibilities in the preparation of such policies.

Of the various economic problems that will face the United States in her dealings with the rest of the world, none are likely to be of greater importance than the problem of the under-developed countries. To them more than in any other direction does Keynes's final sentence apply. If the economic problem becomes less urgent in the United States and there is no diminished preference for work and saving, here is a fruitful resolution of the dilemma; the application of some of this surplus zeal to rescue the under-developed countries from stultification and endow them with the means of economic growth. If, at the same time, a way is to be cleared for peaceful union of all nations, what better beginning than a common attack on poverty and backwardness?

Easier said than done. For ten years there has been plenty of talk about speeding-up development by international aid but only a trickle of loans and grants, nearly all financed by the United States, has flowed to the under-developed countries. The annual inflow of capital in the past few years has been of the order of $1,200–$1,500 m. compared with a rate of net capital formation of some $10,000 m. The under-developed countries have gained immensely more from the boom in primary produce in the war and post-war world; but the boom is over and it is unlikely that conditions in the next twenty years will be so uniformly favourable. Thus from now on, aid may have to be supplied against, not with, the tide. When exports are bounding upwards, it is easy to justify projects of development; but when they begin to droop, and cause every other sector of the economy to droop, it is more difficult to summon confidence and persevere with capital expenditure that no longer shows a profit.

Suppose that the United States stands ready to offer large-scale aid. On what footing could she best supply it? By stepping up bilateral aid or by channelling it through some international agency? The first alternative is bound to be by far the most attractive to Congress since it allows the United States to decide which of her friends she will help and on what conditions, whereas the second would involve her in surrendering control and yet supplying the bulk of the money internationally administered. For the present, there can be no escape from reliance primarily on bilateral aid; but a beginning ought to be made with international aid on a modest scale, with the intention of expanding it if it can be made truly international and if experience shows its value.

Such a beginning might take the form of an International Development Fund along the lines proposed for SUNFED, with a capital of $250 m. subscribed by the members of the International Bank and administered by the Bank. This capital would be used initially to assist two specific objects of expenditure: transport and education. Preference would be given to road transport in the one case, and to technical and higher education in the other. This is a rather arbitrary selection but it can be defended on the grounds that these are the points in most under-developed countries at which external economies are largest. The International Bank already makes loans for road-building, and so also does the Export-Import Bank, but the current rate of road-building is far below what rapid world development would require.

It would obviously be futile to provide capital from the Fund on the same terms as it is already available from the International Bank. It would have to be the clear intention to subsidize the use of capital in the under-developed countries, either by grants or by loans at low rates of interest. The Fund might be used, for example, to reduce the service charge on loans contracted with the International Bank in the usual way and at the usual rate of interest. This could be accomplished by letting the Fund participate in Bank loans just as a commercial bank does at present but forgoing all or part of the interest on its share of the loan.

There is another direction that policy might take. The rising standard of living in the United States is to a large extent traceable to organized scientific research—a phenomenon hardly a generation old and likely in another generation to have a still more tremendous impact on the economy. But the fruits of this research are either slow in reaching other countries or are incapable of adoption by them without elaborate and costly modifications. Moreover, some part of scientific research is directed towards finding methods of producing in the laboratory (and subsequently in the factory) what normally occurs in nature or is cultivated or mined by human labour. These researches, although they may, as in the case of fertilizers, enhance the productivity of the soil, have a marked tendency to render land and those who work on the land redundant. They frequently provide a capital-intensive substitute for the products of the under-developed countries so that they strike at the exports of those countries without offering them an alternative outlet for their resources. If, for example, it were possible to synthesize coffee from a cheap carbohydrate, the livelihood of innumerable communities would disappear and an important economic activity would gravitate to an entirely new location.

Commonsense suggests, however, that scientific progress need not and, on balance, probably does not operate to depress the standard of living of the peasants of the under-developed world. The Technical Assistance Programme already seeks to cut down the lag in scientific knowledge. But is there not also room for efforts to adapt western inventions to the needs of under-developed countries? These inventions have tended on the whole to increase the size of plant (in terms of output) in which the most modern practice could be realized. This has frequently put such plants well over the limits of the market that they could hope to supply in under-developed countries. Could more development effort go into scaling-down the technical optimum, so bringing it within the reach of those countries (and, incidentally, contributing to a more competitive system of production in the United States)?

This is not, after all, such a fanciful idea. The rise of consumers' durables represents just such an effort of development and has brought with it, in the capital and horse-power that durables embody, a conversion of the average American house into something almost indistinguishable from a factory. The 'Do-it-yourself' movement represents a similar step towards a small-scale, household unit of production. Under-developed countries have, as a rule, hardly progressed beyond the household stage. Is it possible that, in the next twenty years, the emerging household economy of the United States may pioneer those techniques and instruments that, reproduced on a sufficient scale, could enable cottage industries and small factories and workshops to revolutionize the standard of living of the rest of the world?

PART II: INVESTMENT, TECHNICAL PROGRESS AND DEVELOPMENT

CHAPTER 3

The Contribution of Foreign and Domestic Capital to Economic Development[1]

I

OUR thinking about the rôle of indigenous and foreign investment in the development of relatively backward economies is necessarily coloured by the conclusions we draw from past experience. I propose, therefore, to begin by reviewing that experience, if only to show that it is much less relevant to present-day problems than is generally imagined.

One feature of nineteenth-century international capital flows that has impressed itself strongly on the popular mind is their scale. It is a common belief that capital transfers were once a larger element in the international economy than at present and made a more significant contribution to world economic development. This belief seems to derive from a contrast between British investment fifty years ago and American investment today and from a further contrast between the apparent ease with which the countries that have succeeded in industrializing themselves obtained the necessary finance and the difficulty in raising capital abroad experienced by countries that are now seeking to industrialize themselves.

The first of these contrasts is well founded so long as our attention is confined to the proportion of domestic savings invested abroad by Britain and the United States, without regard to the investment opportunities to which the flow of capital was a response. In the forty years between 1875 and 1914 about two-fifths of all additions to the stock of capital

[1] From *International Journal of Agrarian Affairs*, April 1961.

owned in the United Kingdom consisted of investments abroad.[1] There were years when more than half of current British savings went to the finance of foreign assets. It is unimaginable that what was then true of the United Kingdom could now apply to the United States. To yield such a result, the flow of investment from the United States would require the entire Marshall Plan to be carried out at least thrice a year.

If instead of comparing the leading creditor countries in the two periods we compare the flow of capital with the flow of trade, there is less reason to suppose that foreign investment (although it may have altered in character) is now on a relatively smaller scale. World trade, to take visible items only, has grown fivefold since 1913 (at current prices) and international investment, including grants and all capital transfers other than repayments, has probably grown in roughly the same proportion. British foreign investment in 1913 came to roughly $1 billion and other countries may have been investing, at a guess, a further $1 billion. In 1958 the balance of payments of the non-industrial countries (as defined by GATT so as to exclude the Communist bloc, the main petroleum exporters and most of the overseas members of the French Community but to include Australia, New Zealand and the Union of South Africa) showed a deficit of nearly $6 billion on income account.[2] There was in addition considerable investment in some of the industrial countries such as Canada, and the non-industrial countries excluded from GATT's total. We cannot be very far out if we put the current flow of international investment (including aid) at $10 billion. This would give a fivefold increase since 1913 (if the guess for non-British investment is reasonable), or exactly the same as the increase in trade.

More significant, however, is the change that has taken place in the flow of capital to the less-advanced countries. International investment before 1914 was heavily concentrated in countries that were either already regarded as advanced or would not be reckoned today as 'less advanced'. Relatively little British capital, for example, went to Asia (India, China and Malaya apart) or to Africa (with the ex-

[1] A. K. Cairncross, *Home and Foreign Investment*, 1870–1913 (Cambridge, 1953), p. 4.

[2] *International Trade* 1959 (Geneva, 1960), p. 42.

ception of Egypt and South Africa); other capital-exporting countries also tended to avoid those continents. Even if we include Latin America, it is unlikely that the less-advanced countries as a group obtained more than about $500 m. a year in foreign capital in the decade before 1914 when the international flow of capital was at its tide. Whatever the exact figure, it was plainly far below the current rate of capital transfer to those countries today.

Nor is it true that over the past two centuries heavy recourse to foreign borrowing has been a normal, or indeed an inevitable, feature of the transition from a pre-industrial to an industrial society. The contribution made by foreign capital to the economic development of different countries shows great diversity. In general, however, this contribution has been, if not negligible, far smaller in amount than the contribution made by domestic savings. Although it is rarely possible to make exact comparisons, there is little doubt 'the great bulk of the savings needed for growth and industrialization were generated inside each country'.[1]

The United Kingdom, for example, although possibly assisted at first by some Dutch investment in government stock, was a net exporter of capital from the late eighteenth century onwards. France and Germany borrowed abroad in the early stages of industrialization but not on any large scale and mainly to finance railway-building. There was also some direct investment, especially by British entrepreneurs, in these and other European countries, but this investment, although of importance because of its impact on local industry, did not give rise to any large-scale transfer of capital. Of the Scandinavian countries, Finland borrowed little, Denmark only changed from being a net lender to a net borrower after industrialization was already well advanced, Swedish borrowing, although heavier and extending over a longer period, also came relatively late, and Norway borrowed most of all. The Norwegian Government issued bonds abroad from the middle of the century onwards, first for the modernization of agriculture and later for railway-building, while private investment moved into mining, pulp and paper and

[1] K. Berrill, *Foreign Capital and Take-off*, p. 2. (Paper delivered at the Conference of the International Economic Association at Konstanz, September 1960.)

hydroelectric schemes. The largest borrower in Europe was Russia; like most continental countries she imported capital for railway-building—mainly in the sixties and seventies—while later investment tended to be in industry, including textiles, mining, steel and oil.[1]

All these countries, except perhaps Norway and Russia, generated within themselves nearly the whole of the savings needed for their industrialization. It was probably exceptional in Europe for foreign borrowing to exceed, for even a few years, one-fifth of net domestic investment. This does not mean that foreign investment did little to change the course of events; its significance lay not so much in the proportionate addition to domestic savings which it yielded as in its impact on the sectors of the economy that were critical to further growth.

Transport took the lion's share of foreign capital, and transport was often difficult to finance through domestic financial institutions. A reduction in transport costs through railway-building widened the domestic market, improved mobility and assisted that permeation of the economy with modern ideas that lies at the root of continuing development. Similarly in industry, foreign enterprises provided a model to be copied and improved upon, a market to be supplied and a training ground for labour and management alike. The external economies flowing from these investments, and the changes in production functions to which they led, were of a different order of importance from the direct returns on the investments themselves. They jolted the economy on to a new path which it would not otherwise have followed.

In other continents there was just as great diversity in the part played by foreign investments as in Europe. The United States was by 1914 the largest single debtor in the world; but in comparison with her own enormous resources her debts were almost negligible, and within the space of the First World War, although herself a belligerent, she became a net creditor. In the early stages of industrialization in the nineteenth century she imported comparatively little capital and even when the inflow was at its peak in the railway building after the Civil War it never amounted to more than a small fraction of total investment. Japanese foreign borrowing was

[1] For a useful summary, on which I have drawn above, see Berrill, op. cit.

insignificant throughout, apart from a short burst after 1903 mainly to pay for the war with Russia. In Canada, Australia and New Zealand, on the other hand, foreign capital played a much larger part and there were times when, as happened in Canada just before the First World War, it financed half the net domestic capital formation. Even in those thinly populated countries, however, the *average* contribution made by foreign capital over the years of railway-building was much lower.

While foreign investment undoubtedly speeded up the development of those countries, it is more accurate to think of it as accompanying and reinforcing their growth than as preliminary to it. There were bursts of heavy investment, especially in railways, when the economy was expanding, and this investment contributed to further growth. But the foreign investor did not usually join in until comparatively late in the day, lagging behind rather than running in front. Railway networks, for example, were not built at one go, but were enlarged and articulated in spurts when conditions were propitious: when existing line capacity was under pressure, rolling stock was insufficient, extensions and new branch lines seemed likely to pay, and the foreign investor was in a confident mood. As one might expect, it was a rapid growth in output, more than anything else, that created a shortage of capital—including public utility capital—and made it necessary to have recourse to foreign borrowing.

The countries that made most use of foreign capital in those days were in many ways an unusual group. They were either newly settled countries—chiefly in the Western Hemisphere or in Australasia—or countries well above the level of subsistence—like those of Western Europe in the early stages of industrialization—or very large countries—like Russia, China and India. Most of the capital invested was transferred from European countries to countries inhabited or governed by Europeans. There were large and obvious investment opportunities; these opportunities could easily be conveyed to foreign investors; and usually, although by no means invariably, the confidence of those investors was not seriously weakened by the nationality of the borrower.

The newly settled countries had particularly large requirements for capital; but they could offer excellent security in the shape of a rapidly expanding market in the very country from which they were most anxious to borrow. They had little need to trouble over possible transfer difficulties or about convincing the investor that they were genuine low-cost areas; the British investor had only to study the trade returns to satisfy himself on both points. He was well aware after 1870 of the large cost-differentials in agriculture in favour of the areas in which he was investing, of the power of railway transport to revolutionize an economy—at least two-thirds of British foreign investments went directly or indirectly into railways—and of the increasing needs of the British market for imports of primary produce. The harmony of interests between lender and borrower could hardly have been closer.

In Western Europe this harmony was less pronounced. Whether one looks at the investments made by continental countries outside the area or at the investments which they made in each other, the interrelation of capital and commodity flows was less close and the stimulus to primary production less conspicuous. Some of the investments—e.g. those made by France in Russia—had a marked political flavour. Others were more akin to modern direct investment in foreign subsidiaries.

On the Continent as in most of the newer countries the borrowing country generally shared the outlook and institutions of the lending country, or was at least not widely separated by a different social and political tradition. It may be true that capital tended to flow from the more-advanced to the less-advanced countries; but the difference in levels of development was far narrower and more exclusively economic than it is today between industrial countries and those that have hardly begun to industrialize themselves. This meant, amongst other things, that indigenous investment was far from negligible, that financial institutions for the mobilization of domestic savings either already existed or could easily be created, and that the organizational and entrepreneurial obstacles to development were easily surmounted. It was also possible to predict with fair confidence that the path of development would be roughly parallel to that followed in the leading country, not only in respect of industrial growth, urbanization, the emergence of a wage-system and so on, but also in much more far-reaching directions such as the movement of birth rates and savings ratios, the evolution of tax policies and the behaviour of governments.

There were other important peculiarities of foreign investment in those years. It was almost entirely financed by private investors or financial institutions, very rarely by governments.[1] Thus it was controlled by the private advantages which it offered in the form of interest, dividends and security of capital, not, as a rule, by considerations of national policy. It was financed through the capital market rather than through the reinvestment of profits, the acquisition of subsidiary companies and other forms of direct investment; and what passed into the portfolio of investors usually consisted of bonds issued by governments or public utilities, particularly railways. The international capital market was adapted to the handling of large bond issues by known borrowers; this meant in practice either governments or large public utilities rather than borrowers from agriculture, industry and commerce. The amounts required by the latter group were too small, the reputation of the borrower too local, and the variability of the return too great to allow of large bond issues in a foreign capital market. Then, as now, the individual firm in those sectors depended mainly on domestic capital, whether raised on the Stock Exchange or from institutional lenders or accumulated out of past profits.

It has been estimated, for example, that out of total British foreign investments of £4,000 million in 1913, some £500 million consisted of direct investments (tea and rubber plantations, tramway undertakings, branches of British firms, etc.). On the other hand, of total private US foreign investments of $44·8 billion in 1959, no less than $30·0 billion represented direct investments. Portfolio investment by private investors has lost its former importance and has changed in character, far more of the holdings of investors being in foreign equities rather than in bonds. At the same time, the capital required by public utilities has tended to be supplied to a much greater extent by governments or by international agencies such as the World Bank. Direct investments, on the other hand, have been principally in industry and have risen

[1] Except perhaps in Africa where of the total capital invested from 1870 to 1936 nearly one-half was supplied by governments or public authorities (S. H. Frankel, *The Economic Impact on Under-developed Societies* (Oxford, 1953), p. 131).

largely through the reinvestment of profits by the branches of foreign concerns. Thus transport and power are financed either from local sources, from grants and governmental loans, or by the World Bank, while industry has been increasingly financed from abroad as a result of the emergence of the international firm. The typical (private) foreign investment of the nineteenth century was in railway bonds, while the typical (private) foreign investment of the twentieth century is in the shares of a large oil company with assets overseas.

II

If we look back on nineteenth-century experience we cannot help being struck far more by the contrasts than by the parallels with the present day. The under-developed countries of the modern world—or at least in Asia and Africa—are quite unlike the under-developed countries that attracted most of the foreign capital in the nineteenth century. In the first place, their capital requirements in relation to the size of the world economy are much smaller. It is true that in terms of population they are far larger: Asia alone has half the world's population. But they are a great deal poorer; their own savings are correspondingly low—no more than a few dollars per head on the average; and the trade which they sustain is relatively small in amount and limited in variety. Few of them (outside Latin America and the petroleum exporters) have ever attracted private foreign investment on a large scale, and there is no reason to suppose that they are attracting less today than in the past.

This failure to attract large-scale investment is due principally to a further contrast in circumstances. Investment opportunities in the newly settled countries were associated with resource development on the grand scale. In 1913 no less than 40 per cent of world exports of primary produce originated in the Western Hemisphere or Australasia[1]—a proportion which has since increased rather than fallen—and this enormous volume of trade was the fruit of earlier investment in which foreign capital played a critical part. In large measure it was the outcome of agricultural development based on im-

[1] P. Lamartine Yates, *Forty Years of Foreign Trade* (London, 1959), p. 231.

proved transport and wide differences in production costs. Food and agricultural materials represented all but a small fraction of the primary produce exported from the newly settled areas, minerals (including petroleum) forming not much more than 10 per cent. Thus whatever form the investment took, it rested ultimately on an expansion of agriculture on virgin soils and on a displacement of European (particularly British) agriculture through large-scale movements of food.

There exists no similar scope for commercial investment in the under-developed countries of Asia and Africa. They cannot compete in the range of foodstuffs exported from temperate latitudes and are largely confined to tropical foodstuffs and mineral products. But the market for the former, although growing, is relatively inelastic, while investment in the latter meets with many obstacles and is apt to be denounced as the creation of an enclave of no permanent value to the debtor country.

It is sometimes said that one of the functions that foreign capital can perform is the building up of an infrastructure of social overhead capital that will permit of more rapid economic development. There is no doubt that historically this has been the most outstanding contribution of foreign investment, especially in newly settled countries. But the use of the word 'infrastructure' implies that a structure will come into existence. In the older under-developed countries this does not happen nearly so readily as in the countries settled from abroad. The main reason for this lies in the special difficulty of resource development when there is no striking cost difference to exploit and when agricultural change is retarded by the tenures, practices and attitudes of an already settled country. The same factors that made it so much easier to finance the infrastructure of the newer countries ensured the building of an industrial structure on top of it; but in older countries, as experience has shown over and over again, an infrastructure is not enough.

The process of industrialization has always required, and has very often been preceded by, an expansion of agricultural output. It is this expansion that has enabled the domestic market to grow, specialization to take hold and industry to reach a scale that allowed mechanical methods to be employed. Even where external demand for foodstuffs does little to furnish the initial impulse, therefore, there cannot be much question of the overwhelming need to improve agricultural methods in under-developed countries; and the extent to which additional capital could contribute to this is a question which I shall discuss later.

If we leave agriculture aside for the moment, the next biggest sector in consumption is clothing, and for this reason alone the development of a modern textile industry is bound to be of outstanding importance in an under-developed country. It happens that it is one of the easiest industries to mechanize; that the minimum scale of efficient production is relatively low; and that both the raw materials and finished products are very light in relation to their value so that production can be widely dispersed without great loss. In the absence of a decisive cost advantage in agriculture, it is conceivable that a country could develop a marked advantage (in labour costs at least) in textiles. Not only is it conceivable but this is precisely what many countries have done in the early stages of industrialization. In Scotland, for example, there were more workers in the textiles, leather and clothing group of industries in 1851 than in the whole of agriculture, forestry and fishing, and nearly thrice as many as in all other manufacturing industries put together; much the same was true of England and Wales. As late as 1900 nearly half Britain's exports of manufactures still consisted of textiles. For many other European countries the ratio was not much lower, and for Japan it was, and long remained, appreciably higher.

Here, too, we are faced with a contrast. The under-developed countries of the modern world cannot so easily use the textile industries as a springboard to industrialization, even if they can establish a cost advantage. The international specialization of the nineteenth century allowed one group of countries to make full use of their advantages as food producers and another to turn to equal account their advantages as textile manufacturers. Trade grew very rapidly in consequence of the structural shifts that increasing specialization involved. But just as the under-developed countries of Asia and Africa cannot now displace the great producers of non-tropical foodstuffs from their dominant position and are obliged by the facts of geography to concentrate on a narrow range of tropical products and minerals, so they are also prevented from displacing the great textile exporters because they have entered the international market late in the day, and can offer only the low-grade textiles of which they were themselves, until recently, the major importers. They have also to reckon with strong protectionist forces, which although not new, operate more through quotas than tariffs and so impose a ceiling on trade which was previously absent. World trade in textiles, once so large a proportion of total trade in manufactures, has now shrunk to the point at which it accounts, not for one-third as in 1900, but for one-seventh or less.

Textiles are illustrative of a further point of contrast. In the countries between which the major flows of capital took place in the nineteenth century, there was, as a rule, no great difference in income-levels. This meant that the importing countries had a large domestic market for manufactures which provided a natural base for industrialization. It was not necessary for governments to force the pace, although by tariffs and in other ways they did attempt to do so: the market was a sufficient engine of growth. Moreover, the kind of manufactures in demand was similar to the kind entering into trade, if only because a high proportion was in fact imported. But in the less-advanced countries of today the difference in income-levels not only narrows the domestic market but is apt to create a gap between the products of indigenous industry and the products that might be sold abroad. Manufactures are necessarily adapted to the needs of a poorer consuming public and not easily marketed in the richer countries that account for over half the trade of the world.

III

When we turn to the theory of international capital flows we are struck at once by its astonishing formalism. The classical economists adopted as a working hypothesis the entire absence of capital movements between countries (although this did not prevent them from analysing the probable consequences of such movements). Until very recently, foreign investment continued to be discussed with little more than a passing reference to its interrelation with domestic investment and no reference at all to the type of asset that it customarily yields in the recipient country, the flows in the reverse direction that frequently accompany it, or the type of countries between which the movement of capital is likely to be greatest.

There were some economists, of whom Hobson is the best known, who argued that savings might outrun domestic investment opportunities and turn the export of capital into a safety-valve for capitalism. But they did not express their views with any theoretical rigour and the impression made on more orthodox economists was not assisted by the publication of Hobson's ideas in a decade in which the shortage of capital for domestic purposes could hardly have been more apparent. Even Hobson talked in aggregates and abstractions; and in the vulgarized Leninist version in which his theory entered the Marxist canon, the abstractions—'finance-capitalism', 'super-profits' and so on—become largely emotive. All this literature, moreover, centred on the export of capital; until the work of Taussig and his pupils, especially Viner and Williams, practically nothing was written by a professional economist from the point of view of the capital-importing country.

I doubt whether even today we have formulated a theory of investment that does justice to the historical experience and the mass of statistical data that have become available. Existing theory does not even pose, much less answer, the questions material to our present problem. What governs the division of a country's savings between home and foreign investment? What determines which countries will lend and which will borrow? What causes the total volume of international investment to expand or contract? Why is it that, so far from remaining obstinately at home, capital does not move bodily to the countries where labour is abundant so as to create in new locations the kind of industrial complex that already exists in more advanced countries? Or, to put the question the other way round, why do countries that are not inherently incapable of mastering the techniques of modern industry fail to obtain from abroad the resources that might transform them?

I cannot do justice here to questions such as these, although

I shall try to indicate briefly the direction my own thoughts take. Roughly speaking, there have been two different approaches to the relationship between home and foreign investment. There are those who think in marginal terms and concentrate on the functioning of the international capital market, and those who use aggregative concepts and seek to transfer to an international plane theorems originally devised for a closed system. If we follow the first line of thought we make comparisons between the marginal productivity of capital in different countries and relative rates of interest and profit in order to bring out the market forces governing the international flow of capital. If we follow the second line of thought we are led to examine why some countries appear to have a surplus and others a shortage of capital. This latter approach is particularly congenial to those who treat capital requirements as a more or less fixed proportion of output, without much regard to interest rates or variations in capital-output ratios. It used to issue in the conclusion that capitalist countries would eventually develop a surplus of capital and need a convenient 'sink' for it such as foreign investment could provide. It is more commonly used today in order to demonstrate that under-developed countries have a chronic shortage of capital and would develop more rapidly if they could borrow more abroad or find an assortment of fairy godmothers, preferably of international extraction, to bless them with grants and low-interest loans.

I need not emphasize that the view of foreign investment as a 'sink' for surplus capital is by no means dead. It is still part of the accepted dogma of Communist theory, conveniently extinguishing any merit that may seem to attach to a loan or investment by a capitalist country but leaving unsullied a similar act of investment by a socialist country. It was a view to which Keynes was strongly drawn in the thirties. Even today much of the discussion among economists of the duties of creditor countries is coloured by it; there is a common presumption that the need to lend abroad gets built into the structure of an advanced economy as if it were doomed to save more than it could absorb in domestic investment.

It is with the other side of the picture, however, that we are concerned: the shortage of capital in under-developed countries. This shortage can be analysed in various ways. In terms of the first approach the issue is one of the return to be expected from additional investment, the extent to which finance is a bottleneck in development, the availability of domestic savings and their mobilization for specific productive purposes, and the terms on which funds can be obtained from domestic and foreign sources. This is the approach which I shall adopt in the next section. In terms of the second approach it is taken for granted that an acceleration of growth must inflate capital requirements more or less correspondingly and that, as savings are unlikely to change much in relation to income, foreign capital may have to fill the gap. There is, however, an ambiguity in this second approach since it is not clear whether the acceleration of growth can occur in the absence of this foreign borrowing, and merely peters out if the *resulting* capital requirements are not met, or whether growth is itself to be attributed to increased investment so that foreign borrowing is an indispensable condition for acceleration.

It is a matter of some obscurity why, if the second approach is accepted, so many countries have succeeded in industrializing themselves without much foreign borrowing. The historical facts strongly suggest that if more rapid growth operates on capital requirements it also affects the supply of savings and that there are mechanisms in the economic system that help to keep the two in balance without those lurches in the balance of payments that so many models of economic growth would produce. I have dealt elsewhere with some of those mechanisms, amongst which the responsiveness of housebuilding to changes in interest rates and other influences is particularly important. As for savings, the evidence suggests a slow and progressive rise in savings-ratios during the process of acceleration, followed by a plateau when the rate of growth becomes more stable. The narrowness of the capital market and the consequent importance of self-finance also tie savings and capital requirements together more tightly than in an already developed economy.

The adoption of the second (aggregate) approach disposes under-developed countries to treat foreign investment as a residual in their plans. It provides a balancing element in two distinct equations, one relating to the growth of total output and one to the balance of payments. In the first equation it is usual to lay down in advance some planned rate of growth of the economy and then try to devise a set of policies that will enable this rate to be achieved. The rate laid down is taken to imply a corresponding rate of capital formation, on the basis of an assumed capital-output ratio; and this rate of capital formation, taken in conjunction with an assumed marginal rate of savings, leaves a deficit which is interpreted as the resulting shortage of capital. This shortage is then identified with the scale on which it will be necessary to obtain loans and grants from abroad.

At the same time, a second equation is constructed to show the prospective movement in exports and imports over the period of the plan. From this equation emerges a second deficit, this time in the balance of payments, and this deficit, like the first, is assumed to be covered by loans and grants. The two deficits need not exactly coincide, since it may be possible to draw on or add to reserves of foreign exchange. But any substantial divergence between them is likely to lead to a reconsideration of the original targets and to revisions in investment and other programmes designed to reconcile the two sets of calculations.

This procedure, originally applied to individual countries, has come to be used also in relation to the whole group of under-developed countries in order to show on what scale capital must flow to them if their standards of living are to be improved at some predetermined rate. The United Nations experts who reported in 1951 on *Measures for the Economic Development of Under-developed Countries* put the domestic savings of under-developed countries, including mainland China, at a little over $5,000 million in 1949 and went on to calculate that if *per caput* incomes were to be increased by 2 per cent per annum these savings would have to be supplemented by loans and grants of $14,000 million (or, if domestic savings-ratios rose with the growth in income, at least $10,000 million). Of this total no less than 70 per cent was required for countries in Asia.

The same kind of calculation has been attempted by a number of other economists. The most recent attempts are in Paul Hoffman's *One hundred countries one and one quarter billion people*, and in *International Trade* 1959, the annual report issued by GATT. These yield rather more modest totals than the calculations made by the United Nations ten years ago. Paul Hoffman, for example, puts the inflow of additional capital necessary to raise *per caput* incomes by 2 per cent per annum at $3 billion a year and the current net inflow he puts at $4 billion a year.[1] He gives no estimate of domestic savings, but if we take this at 7 per cent of income—the assumption made in the GATT report—we obtain a total for net domestic capital formation of $15·5 billion. Hoffman also estimates the export earnings of the under-developed countries in the sixties at $378 billion over the decade, and their import requirements at $440 billion together with a small deficit of $8 billion on invisibles. This leaves a deficit averaging $7 billion a year, the same figure as the shortage of capital already estimated.

The GATT calculations show how tentative any estimates of this kind must be even if one accepts the logic by which they are obtained. For a group of low-income countries that excludes the main petroleum exporters but includes Australia, New Zealand and South Africa, this study estimates that the average *per caput* income rose from $103 in 1950 to $118·5 in 1958, or by 1·8 per cent per annum.[2] If these figures are accepted it is not very obvious why *any* larger inflow of capital should be required in order to attain the objective of a 2 per cent per annum increase.

It is perhaps as well, before we go on to look at the assumptions behind these calculations, to be a little clearer about the facts. Whereas Hoffman puts the rate of growth of the under-developed countries at 3 per cent per annum, the GATT report adopts the higher rate of 3·8 and thereby comes near to doubling the implied *per caput* rate of growth. All that one can really be sure of is that growth is taking place, that it is much more rapid in some under-developed countries than others, and that it is by no means certain that the *average* (if averages in this context have any meaning) is lower than the *average* for industrial countries. This is not to deny that the gap in living standards is widening: an increase by 2 per cent

[1] Op. cit., p. 46. These figures are for a group of countries which do not include mainland China.

[2] Op. cit., p. 37 *n*. It is not clear what assumption is made as to price changes, but the text of the report implies that the increase is in real terms. Population grew at 2 per cent per annum, so that the annual rate of increase of the national income of the group was 3·8 per cent.

per head is equivalent to only $2 or so in an under-developed country but $20 or more in an advanced country. But if we are talking in terms of proportions it is not possible to say with confidence which group of countries is showing the faster rate of growth.

Again, it is unwise to be dogmatic about rates of saving in the under-developed countries. A few years ago it was common to accept an average of 5 per cent of income, and this may well have been on the high side for countries at a very early stage in development. But for some under-developed countries it is obviously much too low and there is clearly a wide dispersion. The tendency now is to raise the average a little to, say, 7 per cent, without much reflection on the precise significance of such an average. The relevant percentage for most purposes relates to the marginal rate of saving, and here there is a disposition to use much higher estimates: indeed, some countries are prepared to assume that over 25 per cent of any increment in income will be saved, an assumption for which there does not appear to be any firm statistical basis.

Even the current inflow of capital is not known with any precision. For the five years 1954–8 the total for loans and grants (on a bilateral basis only) to low-income countries has been put at $13·4 billion, from which has to be deducted $1·1 billion for capital repayments.[1] This leaves an average of $2·5 billion per annum. Private foreign investment and aid extended through international agencies, including World Bank loans, averaged between $1·5 and $2 billion; and, in addition, short- and medium-term credits amounted to at least £500 million a year. The total inflow of capital may thus have reached $5 billion a year, and as the total was increasing throughout the period it is likely to have been in excess of $5 billion by 1958–9. The GATT report shows a total inflow rising from $1·9 billion in 1954 to $5·9 billion in 1958.[2]

One plain implication of these figures is that the current capital inflow bears a relation to the domestic savings of the

[1] *International Trade* 1959, p. 44.

[2] Ibid., p. 42. These figures include the independent countries of the sterling area, some of which are not low-income countries and have been substantial importers of capital; on the other hand, they exclude the petroleum exporters and most of the French overseas territories which are included in the Hoffman estimates.

under-developed countries that is much higher than was customary in the development of the newly settled countries. If we accept the Hoffman estimates and put savings at 7 per cent of income, net domestic capital formation comes to $12·5 billion, of which about one-third is financed from abroad. If it were possible to increase the inflow at once to $7 billion the ratio would increase to 45 per cent. If, on the other hand, we accepted the extreme position postulated in the UN 1951 Report, domestic savings would furnish only a little over one-quarter of the total supply of capital.

The calculations also suggest that unless foreign capital were supplied by way of grant, external indebtedness would increase very rapidly. The external public debt of twenty-one low-income countries listed by IBRD[1] was increasing at the rate of over $1 billion per annum in the late fifties and there was in addition an increase in private debt on short-term and long-term account. Debt service payments for this group absorbed 7·5 per cent of external earnings in 1958 and the proportion was increasing rapidly. If additional capital was supplied on commercial terms rather than by way of grant, the inflow of an extra $3 billion a year would obviously have very serious implications for the eventual solvency of the recipients and indeed would represent an impossible burden for countries whose entire income does not currently exceed about $125 billion.

The amount of public aid to under-developed countries has in fact grown steadily throughout the fifties. From about $2 billion around 1954 it has increased without a setback by about 15 per cent per annum to around $3½ billion in 1960. As Dr H. W. Singer points out, 'public aid has been a more dependable element in the flow of foreign exchange and resources to the under-developed countries than either export earnings, service payments, flow of private capital or any other balance of payments item'.[2] The problem that calls for thought is no longer the respective contributions of private foreign investment and domestic investment to the development of the less-advanced countries but how best to make use of foreign aid in conjunction with commercial investment.

[1] D. Avramovic and L. Gulhati, *Debt-servicing Problems of Low-Income Countries*, 1956–8 (Johns Hopkins Press, 1960), p. 14.

[2] H. W. Singer, *Recent Trends in Economic Thought in Under-developed Countries* (mimeographed, November 1960). Op. 31.

While an inflow of a further $3 billion would involve great difficulties *within* the low-income countries either from the point of view of immediate absorption or in terms of the burden of eventual repayment it would not impose an overwhelming burden on the advanced countries. If an additional $3 billion a year would allow the under-developed world to take off, it could hardly be regarded as an unduly high price to pay.

In my view, however, it is not possible to buy development so cheaply. The provision of additional capital may yield a more adequate infrastructure but it rarely by itself generates rapid development unless there are already large investment opportunities going a-begging. In the Western world the great dynamic forces have been technical progress and a widening of markets, with all the specialization and economies of scale, internal and external, to which they give rise. Capital accumulation has allowed these forces freer play and conditioned the speed with which individual economies have responded; but it has rarely been the dominant influence. Like many other obstacles to growth, a shortage of finance has yielded to the pressure of opportunity; the existence or creation of outlets for capital has usually been sufficient to encourage a greater effort of self-finance. I believe that other bottlenecks—skill, entrepreneurial talent, administrative experience—yield to the same pressure wherever it is within the power of the individual to respond, and that even social attitudes and institutions unfavourable to growth are slowly modified as the individual perception of opportunities foregone becomes keener. But I do not wish, in saying this, to belittle the importance of capital accumulation or the scope for intervention by public authorities. In all development there is an interplay between individual effort and the social and economic framework within which that effort is exerted; and in the less-advanced countries changes in the framework, which are usually expensive in capital (broadly interpreted), occupy a commanding position.

It is only too obvious, for example, that the widening of the market rests on the creation of a network of communications that in its demands on capital is far beyond the limits of self-finance. Some capital may be raised from the richer members of the community or through varied forms of taxation; but there are occasions when the limits of what can be done in this way fail to reach the minimum scale necessary for a modern transport system. Similarly, if technical progress abroad is to make its influence felt, there has to be a costly outlay on education and other social services that may strain the budget of a poor country. Apart from this, there is likely to be a need to do many things at once, each individually unprofitable, and engage in investment on a large scale so as to reap a collective advantage from mutually supporting projects.

For these and other reasons, which it would be impossible to enter into in detail in this paper, I do not doubt that a higher rate of investment must be a prime object of policy in under-developed countries and that this higher rate is likely to strain the revenues of the central government. The more rapid the rate of development aimed at, the greater will be the need for capital, if only because capital can be used to buy time. Initially at all events savings will have to be supplemented out of foreign capital, whether by way of loan or grant. How long such a state of affairs need continue is difficult to predict. The more-advanced countries may not relish an indefinite unilateral transfer of resources by way of grant and the less-advanced countries may view with equal disfavour a cumulative increase in their external liabilities. At some stage, if the operation is successful, domestic savings should begin to overtake capital requirements, but even if savings-ratios rise relatively quickly, the transfer of capital may have to continue for a long time. This will be all the more true if the pace of development is set by the availability of finance. In my judgment this is likely to be true only if we treat as capital not only the resources that flow into the creation of new fixed assets but also the much larger investment in new forms of social organization, new habits and attitudes, personal experience, knowledge and skills that is a precondition of continuing development. It is this investment, and the effort of modernization that it represents, that some under-developed countries seem to find beyond their powers.

IV

No country likes to depend upon foreign capital when it can mobilize domestic capital for the same purpose. Apart from any political considerations which may tell against foreign borrowing, the assumption of external liabilities mortgages its future earnings of foreign exchange while the assets created may contribute little directly, or even indirectly, to those earnings. An advanced country with the resourcefulness to vary the range of its exports and imports may have little fear of transfer difficulties and be willing to regard new external liabilities as roughly balanced by an equal addition to its domestic assets. But the typical under-developed country, heavily dependent on exports of a single commodity, and with a highly inelastic demand for most of its imports, cannot so freely assume external liabilities. It may not go so far as to limit its foreign borrowing to those cases where it expects an eventual net gain to its balance of payments; but it is likely to treat foreign exchange as a bottleneck limiting economic development and run the risk of further constriction only if this seems the lesser of two evils. Where it is in a position to regulate the inflow of foreign capital, therefore, it will encourage this inflow only where it helps to remove some other important obstacle to the development of the economy, and where this cannot be done by redirecting the flow of domestic investment or by supplementing the flow out of additional savings, private or public.

Foreign borrowing by an under-developed country should be capable of justification, therefore, under one or other of three headings:

(*a*) It may permit of a higher rate of domestic investment than domestic savings alone would support. This is not a necessary consequence of foreign borrowing, especially if one accepts the view that there are latent savings in under-developed economies that could be mobilized at a higher level of activity. With this qualification, the 'topping up' of domestic savings is the main justification for borrowing abroad. Indeed, as we have seen,[1] the world is full of enthusiasts for 'topping-up' who regard a shortage of capital as the principal brake on economic progress in under-developed countries.

(*b*) It may be difficult to mobilize domestic savings for the finance of projects that are badly needed for economic development. This may happen, for example, in the private sector

[1] See above, pp. 52–3.

if, as is often true in the early stages of development, the capital market is itself under-developed. In general, however, it is preferable to set about improving domestic financial arrangements, if this is the only obstacle to the investment desired, rather than make use of foreign capital merely because it is easier to raise it. The improvements necessary usually involve the mobilization of liquid funds through financial intermediaries, the supply of those funds for less liquid purposes to productive borrowers and the creation in long-term securities of all kinds. This is a large subject which I do not propose to discuss further except in relation to agriculture.

(*c*) Foreign capital may bring with it other scarce productive factors, such as technical 'know-how', business experience, and so on, that can make an important and continuing contribution to economic development. To this possibility I return below.[1]

The case for foreign borrowing is generally admitted to be strongest in relation to public-utility investment, and I therefore refrain from developing this case. Instead, I shall confine myself to a discussion of investment in primary activities, beginning with mines and plantations and going on to indigenous agriculture after a short interpolation on manufacturing.

The fear of transfer difficulties that inhibits foreign investment is obviously unlikely to arise when the investment is in enterprises that are themselves the source of foreign exchange, such as mines and plantations. The exports flowing from those enterprises must be more than sufficient to allow the transfer of the profits earned so that from the foreigner's point of view they are relatively attractive. From the country's point of view, however, they have many drawbacks and are often dismissed as enclaves—an extension into the economy of one country of the trading system of another. Not only are they not an integral part of the economy of the host country, it is alleged, but they may disrupt its social structure, disintegrating an established rural economy, creating appetites, habits and standards that cannot subsequently be conjured away, and often laying up trouble by importing alien immigrants who are never entirely assimilated and pre-

[1] See below, p. 63.

vent the local inhabitants from reaping the gains from a higher level of economic activity.[1]

There is obviously a great deal of truth in this view and no one doubts that a country would gain far more if it could conduct the same operations without making use of foreign capital. But this is rarely a genuine alternative. An under-developed country, even if it could raise the capital, is often lacking in the knowledge, skill and experience to manage enterprises of the type run by foreigners, and the management and the capital form a single package such that it is impossible to have one without the other. In some countries where a plantation economy has been created the incentives to economic effort were previously too feeble, and plantations supply a stimulus which in course of time may become unnecessary.[2] In other countries, such as Ceylon and Malaya, it was foreign enterprise which introduced the crops, originally in plantations, that are now the staple exports. It also developed the mineral resources which bring in well over a quarter of the total export earnings of the under-developed countries as a group. These forms of activity furnish resources that remain within the economy and that are strategic to its further development: foreign exchange, which is usually a greater bottleneck than capital, and tax revenue, which can be applied to capital purposes.[3]

It is arguable that all development is likely to take the form of an enclave—though not necessarily a foreign enclave—within an existing social and economic structure. The fact that the enclave is managed by foreigners and employs alien immigrants who are bound to excite antagonisms by their very success intensifies the stress and strain of development and adds to its ultimate social cost. But some stress and strain is inevitable and the better adjusted a society is to primitive conditions the greater is likely to be the disintegration required in order to transform it. The more contact there is

[1] See, for example, S. H. Frankel, *The Economic Impact on Under-developed Societies*, pp. 131 *et seq.*; H. Myint, 'The Classical Theory of International Trade and the Under-developed Countries', *Economic Journal*, June 1958.

[2] J. S. G. Wilson, *Economic Environment and Development Programmes* (University of Hull Publications, 1960). In the New Hebrides, for example, the indigenous population now produces about half the copra exported and this proportion is rising.

[3] Cf. Boris C. Swerling (Stanford University), *Some Interrelationships between Agricultural Trade and Economic Development* (mimeographed, 1960), p. 31: 'The tax machinery can remove much economic remoteness even from mineral enclaves.'

with foreigners the more rapidly the process of transformation can take hold; and however weak the links between an enclave and the rest of the economy it can hardly avoid exercising a powerful influence, by demonstration if in no other way, on the thinking of the population.

The bias, justifiable or not, which is often shown against foreign investment in mining and plantations is rarely extended with the same force to investment in manufacturing. The reasons for this appear to be threefold. First of all, manufacturing is commonly thought of as the spearhead of economic development, not only because a high level of manufacturing is the mark of an advanced country but also because experience in manufacturing opens out a wide field of opportunity. An economy specialized in primary activities can take advantage of improvements in technique that affect those activities; but it cannot move readily between them, except where one crop can be planted in place of another, or between primary activities and manufacturing. On the other hand, there is greater mobility within the various branches of industry and fresh opportunities of development are constantly arising in new directions because of the greater range of technical knowledge that becomes available from year to year. Secondly, the linkages within manufacturing are closer and more powerful than the linkages in agriculture and mining. The growth of one industry is likely to yield external economies by facilitating the development of others which either supply it with materials, components or services, or use its product for further processing, or can take advantage of the facilities which it brings into existence in the shape of better transport and information services, improved banking arrangements, a more extensive range of labour skills and managerial experience and so on. Thirdly, the starting of a new manufacturing enterprise under foreign management may be more compatible with the starting of similar domestic enterprises or a later buying out of the foreign company than in the parallel case of foreign mines and plantations.

It may well be that some of these reasons for welcoming manufacturing investment are not well founded. It is not immediately obvious that a foreign-controlled textile mill must be less of an enclave than a foreign-controlled tin-mine or that the repercussions of a successful export trade in raw cotton or tea must of necessity have a narrower compass than the building of a steel rolling-mill. There are advanced countries like Canada that are just as suspicious of foreign ownership of a large slice of their manufacturing sector as other countries are of foreign plantations; and most under-developed countries are well aware that foreign manufacturing capital usually earns a relatively high return and if employed in supplying goods for the domestic market can be a substantial absorbent of scarce foreign exchange.

In any event the main justification for making use of foreign capital in manufacturing is rarely a domestic shortage of capital. Such a shortage can be relieved at far less cost by borrowing to pay for public utilities since these can usually be financed at the rates charged by international agencies like the World Bank; and these rates, although the subject of constant complaint, are well under half the rates of profit earned on the average by foreign capital in manufacturing. It is not because capital is scarce but because management and technical knowledge are still scarcer that countries encourage foreign enterprises to build local manufacturing plants.

The corollary is obvious: that the less-advanced countries need to find and train men able to run industrial undertakings. This is not just a matter of increasing the supply of risk-capital nor even of encouraging local entrepreneurs. It extends from the top administrative skills to the lowest: from the man with an eye to a worth-while commercial risk and the personality, knowledge and experience to lick a large business into shape to the workman who has to submit to factory discipline and has learned how to take proper care of his tools. The arts of supervision and foremanship are just as important as provision for training in advanced technology. It is not enough to be able to carry on where others have left off. There has to be, throughout the whole industrial system, a power to innovate, a built-in incentive to make further improvements, a linking of personal advantage with those improvements and a readiness to look for opportunities of making them. Without this widespread interest in development and will to develop, coupled with the background of technical knowledge and experience that gives the opportunities of development reality, growth cannot become self-sustaining.

All this, needless to say, is easier to say than to do. It takes time, for in many directions there is no substitute for practice, experience and the confidence that comes from success. Education helps. But education, in the sense of what is learned at the State's expense outside the factory, is only a small part of the complex intellectual and moral endowment that has to be built up.

In the creation of this intangible capital foreign investment has a part to play, especially if local enterprise is allowed to participate and training is given to the local staff. But the physical assets resulting from the investment are of limited value unless the community that uses them makes the simultaneous adjustments that industrialism requires. The scope for foreign investment in manufacturing is also relatively small because manufacturing in a poor country is necessarily a relatively small sector of the economy. In the absence of large export opportunities—which, for reasons already given, very rarely exist—the market for manufactured goods is limited by the low level of income per head, and the narrowness of the market tends to raise costs by restricting the scale of production. Direct investment by advanced countries, therefore, remains small in comparison with their investment in the manufacturing sector of other advanced countries and at the same time tends to be confined to those branches of industry where large-scale investment is possible.[1]

These considerations point to the importance of a general rise in income-levels in the under-developed countries and of ensuring that the expansion of industry is not checked by an inelastic response on the part of agriculture. In all the countries that have succeeded in transforming themselves into advanced industrial economies an increase in agricultural productivity preceded or accompanied the growth of industry and there was no tendency, even in Britain and Japan, to rely more heavily on food imports until a comparatively late stage. On the other hand, there are some grounds for thinking that, in some of the countries that failed to develop under what appeared to be favourable conditions, a sluggishness of agricultural output was a principal obstacle in industrializa-

[1] Of the U.S. direct investments in manufacturing enterprises abroad, over three-quarters are in Canada and Europe and less than 4 per cent in Asia and Africa (*Survey of Current Business*, September 1960).

tion.[1] Agriculture is by far the largest sector, especially from the point of view of employment, in the under-developed countries and it would be surprising if it were left unaffected by rapid growth in other sectors or indeed failed to exercise a powerful influence on their development. The danger that agriculture may act as a brake on the growth of the entire economy has been recognized from the time of the physiocrats and still dominates the plans of many under-developed countries.

Experience suggests that the forces of growth rarely originate in the agricultural sector of the economy and that more commonly it adapts itself to the growth of other sectors.[2] This is noticeable even in localities where the development of an urban market gradually transforms agricultural methods while in more remote areas methods remain unchanged, the degree of adaptation varying with the pressure of demand and diminishing along the radius from the market. Agricultural development usually requires some external stimulus; and it is probable that the stimulus has to be greater the lower the level from which one starts.

If we ask in what ways investment can contribute to agricultural development the answer lies in part in the provision of this external stimulus and in part in the expenditure of capital within agriculture itself.

Historically, the most powerful external stimulus has been an increase in demand arising either abroad or through industrialization at home. This expansion in markets has usually been associated with an improvement in transport, and the first and most obvious use for additional capital to assist agricultural development is in better communications between rural areas and urban markets at home or abroad. The influence of such improvements is not confined to the opportunities for greater specialization and enlarged outputs that they introduce. They also enable new consumer goods to be supplied to the villages and provide fresh incentives to increased production; they make it easier for the natural increase of the countryside to be drained off to other employ-

[1] M. Boserup, *Agrarian Structure and Take-off* (paper delivered at the Conference of the International Economic Association, Konstanz, 1960), pp. 3–4, citing the examples of India in the late nineteenth century and Mexico at the beginning of the twentieth century.

[2] Boserup, op. cit., p. 6.

ment and permit a more rational use of the available land; above all they breach the cake of custom and facilitate that penetration of rural areas with modern ideas from which flows innovation in crops and methods of production.

Investment in transport happens to be an easier and cheaper way of absorbing foreign capital than almost any other. It lends itself to provision under international auspices; for example, through the World Bank, which has already made large loans for transport improvements in under-developed countries. In spite of heavy international investment in the past, however, the transport systems in most of those countries are still relatively primitive and further investment is badly needed if agriculture is to reach its full potential.

The first response of agriculture to a lowering of transport costs is normally towards greater specialization and the growing of cash crops. But this may involve little change in systems of tenure or in methods of production and no continuous improvement in economic levels. Again and again in the past century the opening up of foreign markets has led to an expansion in production and the introduction of new crops but to little change in the institutions and techniques of agriculture in under-developed countries. Much of the increase in production has been offset by a rise in population, and the market for manufactured goods, already far lower than in Western countries at the outset of industrialization, has remained too restricted for rapid growth.

The expansion in trade that results from improved communications is a necessary step towards economic development even if, at first, the trade is usually channelled abroad. It brings into existence a monetary economy without which no economic development is possible. The fact that, typically, there is a high degree of specialization and that most under-developed countries are monocultures in the sense that they are heavily dependent on a single export does not take from the value of this first step. But it does throw into relief the limitations of such a step and the consequences of failure to take the next step and accomplish a general and widespread improvement in agriculture. Although it may raise foreign exchange earnings to a remarkably high level in relation to the national income, it does so at some sacrifice in elasticity and by postponing the really crucial changes in agricultural methods.

When we turn to consider how these methods can be improved and how investment can contribute to this improvement, we at once encounter the thorny question of tenure. In Europe rapid agricultural development was found to be possible under a wide variety of systems of tenure; by far the least favourable system was that of share-cropping. It was only possible to make progress, however, as a result of modifications in the various systems, all of them tending in a single direction: towards the establishment of clear and exclusive rights in land.[1] In many of the under-developed countries not only does the system of tenure that is conspicuously unfavourable to development obtain, but the rights of the cultivator are neither clear nor exclusive. The fact that in others among them, such as Mexico and Japan, economic development accelerated after sweeping agricultural reforms is also significant. While it is no part of the purpose of this paper to argue the case for land reform, it would be utterly unreal to discuss the contribution to agricultural change that can be made by capital investment, domestic or foreign, without stressing the institutional barriers that frustrate such investment.

On the other hand, we know that productivity is far below the levels demonstrably feasible. In Japan, yields were no higher a hundred years ago than they are today in the countries of south-east Asia which present the greatest challenge of all the under-developed countries. Yet they have been raised threefold without any change in the size-distribution of the units of cultivation and with a relatively modest capital outlay.[2] It was this increase in productivity, rather than the expansion in the area under cultivation, that enabled Japan to feed her growing urban population and absorb into industrial employment the natural increase of the rural areas.

If the present low levels of agricultural productivity are to be raised it will not be sufficient to make more capital available. Just as it is true of industrial growth that the supply of

[1] Boserup, op. cit., p. 11.

[2] Cf. Henry Rosovsky and Kazushi Ohkawa, 'The Role of Agriculture in Modern Japanese Economic Development', *Economic Development and Cultural Change*, vol. ix, no. 1, part ii, October 1960, p. 65.

capital is only one element in the situation, so it is true in agriculture. But whereas in industry there is a clearer field since the fixed assets have still to be created, in agriculture the problem is largely one of bringing about a change in the *current* use of the most important fixed asset—land—and persuading the *existing* cultivators to embark on such a change. It is this consideration that makes it so important to couple the provision of capital with policies that extend far beyond finance.

These policies must obviously include changes in taxation and tenure designed to give the cultivator more security and more incentive: consolidation of holdings, fixed rents and the extinction of communal rights (especially of common pasture) are a prerequisite of investment by individual landholders. But if those changes would encourage investment the converse is no doubt also true: if capital were more freely available the changes might be carried out more quickly and smoothly. Similarly, agricultural extension services, improvements in warehousing and marketing, and better credit facilities ought all to be mutually supporting elements in a common programme.

The present situation is generally one in which nearly the whole of the short- and long-term capital made available to agriculture comes from private sources. The All-India Rural Credit Survey showed that in India 70 per cent, of all borrowings were from moneylenders, 23 per cent from relatives, traders and other private agencies, and only 7 per cent from government, co-operatives and commercial banks.[1] Elsewhere in Asia and in Latin America, institutional sources of agricultural credit are equally insignificant. Nor is this situation altogether peculiar to under-developed countries. In Britain, for example, it has been estimated that out of a total indebtedness of £879 million in 1954, £650 million was to private agencies, including merchants. The commercial banks, even in developed countries, are rarely the most important source of capital.

What distinguishes the situation of cultivators in the under-developed countries is not their dependence on private credit

[1] *All India Rural Credit Survey*, 1954, vol. ii, General Report, p. 167. See also H. Belshaw, *Agricultural Credit in Economically Under-developed Countries* (F.A.O. Rome, 1959), pp. 58 *et seq.*

but the high rates of interest paid for it, the restrictive conditions that lenders can impose on their freedom to buy and sell where they choose, and the difficulty of obtaining capital on medium or long term, either for carrying out improvements or for the purchase of land. The cultivator is also in a much weaker position because he has few assets of his own and is more given to borrowing for consumption purposes.

This situation, while difficult to remedy, does at least hold out the prospect of a progressive improvement if the cultivator will refrain from spending any gain in income from additional investment and any economy in interest from less onerous loans. The essential problem is to strengthen those institutional lenders who cater specially for agriculture and to enable them to compete more effectively with private lenders. Sometimes the institutional lenders can mobilize savings by co-operative effort through credit association, savings banks and agricultural co-operatives.[1] But in the poorer countries it is usually necessary for the State to lend a hand by way of guarantee, by participating directly or through the central bank in the capital of mortgage banks and other specialized institutions, or by outright lending.

The need for central government support is the greater where agricultural indebtedness is largely to urban lenders so that agricultural savings are insufficient to effect any substantial net reduction: in India, for example, it has been estimated that only about one-quarter of the total available credit is found within agriculture.[2] The need is heightened by the fluctuations of agricultural markets which oblige co-operatives to strive after liquidity and lend only against good security (usually immovable property), leaving the mass of cultivators who cannot offer this security to borrow from private lenders at usurious rates.[3] A third factor making for active government support is the need to combine credit facil-

[1] For a good account of how this operates in a Western country, see K. Skovgaard, 'Capital Formation and Use in Danish Agriculture', ibid., no. 3, July 1957, pp. 209 *et seq.*; and for a case-study of an under-developed country C. R. C. Donald, *Co-operative Agricultural Credit in Cyprus* (Economic Development Institute, Washington, 1956, mimeographed).

[2] *All India Rural Credit Survey*, vol. ii, p. 169.

[3] In India about four-fifths of the debt owed to moneylenders is unsecured (*All India Rural Credit Survey*, vol. ii, p. 169). For the effects of instability in world markets, see the U.N. paper included in *Selected Readings in Agricultural Credit*, International Conference on Agricultural and Co-operative Credit, 1952, pp. 72–5.

ities with agricultural improvement. Since the education of the peasant in new techniques must form an integral part of agricultural improvement, there is a great deal to be said for trying to combine finance and technical assistance, whether through a system of supervised credit on the Latin American model, or through rural banking facilities under supervision by the central bank and supplemented by a farm extension service, as in the Philippines.[1]

However it is done, more capital has to be fed into agriculture, made available at lower rates of interest and for longer periods of time, and used in ways that will encourage productivity and thrift. If the last of these objects can be achieved the others become progressively easier since agriculture will begin to generate a larger flow of savings and this will either reduce the need for government finance or (more probably) widen the capital market and ease the task of the government and other institutional lenders in raising the necessary funds. But where is the government to get the money in the first place? And in what way can foreign capital help?

It is unlikely that there is any surplus of capital in the urban areas. Indeed, economists tend to assume that agriculture must generate savings in excess of its own requirements if the process of urbanization and industrialization is to be financed. It can be shown that this probably did occur in Japan.[2] It presumably also applied to the USSR since confiscation of the land allowed the State to derive from agricultural revenues what would otherwise have been spent by landlord or peasant. In the USA, and perhaps also in Britain, farmers appear nowadays to save more than they invest in agriculture.[3] But in the days when the frontier was being pushed westwards the normal condition of affairs was surely the other way round. The immigrant either brought capital with

[1] See H. Belshaw, op. cit., pp. 125–6 (for the Philippines), pp. 199 *et seq.* (for Latin America); and D. Brossard, *Manual of Supervised Agricultural Credit in Latin America* (F.A.O., Rome, 1955), for a full account.

[2] H. Rosovsky and K. Ohkawa, op. cit., 60.

[3] The figures given by Ashby for the United Kingdom ('Capital Formation and Use in United Kingdom Agriculture', *International Journal of Agrarian Affairs*, vol. ii, no. 3, July 1957) imply a rate of investment in tenants' capital of perhaps £30 m. per year while farmers' incomes were about £400 m. per annum. It is unlikely that farmers saved much over 7 per cent of their pre-tax incomes.

him or began by taking employment and saving the minimum necessary to stock a farm. In the subsequent improvement and extension of his holding he was usually chronically short of capital and might try to supplement his earnings in the early years by outside employment.[1] Similarly in the early stages of development in Italy there is evidence of the re-investment of trading profits by business men.[2]

Whatever the historical experience, there is not much scope for a large inter-sectoral transfer in under-developed countries. If the State cannot raise sufficient revenue or float large enough loans at home to supply agriculture with capital, it may try to raise money abroad. But this is a decision which, as previously explained, must be governed by the competing claims of other forms of investment, and the willingness of the State to accumulate liabilities in foreign currencies, not by the ease with which capital could be obtained abroad for the specific purpose of agricultural improvement.

Some of the private credit used by agriculturists in under-developed countries, however, is of foreign origin and this credit is highly productive. The movement of cash crops between under-developed countries and metropolitan centres overseas is usually financed by the importing country; and in the import trade of the under-developed countries, credit extended by large expatriate importers may extend down to the petty retail stage.[3] Apart from trade credit, however, there is not much likelihood that private foreign capital will be supplied, as it used to be, through loan companies, bond flotations by agricultural banks, and on deposit with overseas branches of the commercial banks.

On the other hand, now that most foreign capital comes from governments and international agencies and an increas-

[1] For the process in Upper Canada see W. T. Easterbrook and Hugh G. T. Aitken, *Canadian Economic History* (Toronto, 1956), pp. 274 *et seq.* 'The rate at which immigrants became farmers depended . . . primarily on the amount of capital which they could command. The process of assimilating immigrants into the production organization of the colony was essentially . . . a process of investment' (p. 275).

[2] Cf. also V. Ciarocca in 'Capital and Credit in Agriculture', *International Journal of Agrarian Affairs*, vol. ii, no. 4, January 1958, pp. 210–11.

[3] P. T. Bauer, *West African Trade* (Cambridge, 1955), p. 62. For a similar situation in Canadian economic development, see Easterbrook and Aitken, op. cit., p. 281: 'From the markets of Liverpool and London to the millers and merchants of Upper Canada there stretched a chain of debts and credits, paralleling in the sphere of finance the physical transport system of the St Lawrence and the North Atlantic.'

ing proportion of it takes the form of grants, soft loans and contributions towards technical assistance, it is inevitable that agriculture should share in this inflow. There must already be a wide variety of ways in which it is affecting the agriculture of under-developed countries. I shall bring this paper to a close by indicating some of them.

The simplest arrangement is a direct government loan to finance permanent improvements: the most frequent loans of this type are for irrigation and reclamation schemes. A variant is the government loan for a multi-purpose project of which land reclamation and improvement forms part: the most spectacular example is the Assouan High Dam project, one aim of which is to enlarge the cultivated areas of Egypt by 25 per cent. Many of the loans made by the International Bank to the governments of under-developed countries cover the foreign exchange costs of comprehensive schemes of agricultural development. The recent loan to the Sudan, for example, provides about one-third of the total cost of developing 240,000 acres for the cultivation of cotton, grain and other crops through the construction of irrigation canals, a network of dirt roads and branch railway lines, and a large addition to cotton ginning capacity.

A second possibility is to feed in agricultural credit through the central bank or through some financial intermediary enjoying government support. The Central Bank of Costa Rica, for example, has made use of the commercial banks to extend medium- and long-term credits to agriculture and has put itself in possession of the foreign exchange needed for this programme by borrowing from the International Bank. These loans have enabled more farm equipment to be imported and have at the same time helped to demonstrate the effectiveness of modern methods of cultivation. The International Bank has also lent to government credit institutions in Colombia, Peru and elsewhere to finance the importation of tractors and other farm equipment for sale to farmers.

Another possibility is direct participation in the capital of development banks and other financial institutions designed to provide farmers with credit. An example of this appears to be the use in the Philippines of counterpart funds derived from US grants in order to help to finance the Agricultural Credit and Co-operative Financing Administration, set up in

1952 to promote agricultural co-operatives covering production, processing, storage and marketing as well as credit.[1] There is obviously scope for similar participation in other under-developed countries out of grants or counterpart funds.

The provision of agricultural surpluses against local currency is a further example of a capital transfer that has important effects on local agriculture. As it has operated up till now, it has helped to finance a movement of grain from North America to under-developed countries, and while this has a number of undesirable features, even from the point of view of the recipient country,[2] it has probably given the pattern of agriculture in over-populated countries a twist in the right direction. It reduces the pressure on land and cuts out a highly seasonal element in the demand for farm labour. At the same time the supply of food, so long as it can be counted upon, eases two bottlenecks, either of which might slow down industrial development: an agricultural bottleneck threatening inflation and a curtailment of living standards in the towns; and a bottleneck in foreign exchange that would arise if food imports had to be paid for.

But in the main, in agriculture as in the rest of the economy, the burden of finance must rest mainly on domestic savings. It may be possible with foreign capital to speed things up and develop a momentum that allows growth to become self-sustaining: to improve the structure of the economy by borrowing from international agencies for the larger projects, especially in transport and power, and from private investors for the introduction of new manufacturing techniques and products; to channel more foreign capital, borrowed on commercial terms or grant-aided, through financial intermediaries such as development banks, to domestic agriculture, industry and trade.

If our object is not merely to endow the less-advanced countries with the power to develop continuously but so to endow them that they can overtake the more developed countries, a large, continuing transfer seems inevitable; and it seems equally inevitable that it cannot take place on commercial terms. For if we are contemplating higher rates of

[1] Belshaw, op. cit., p. 194.

[2] Swerling, op. cit., p. 34. For example, it stimulates an appetite for wheat, a relatively expensive form of starch, that may prove to be 'premature and unsustainable'.

income growth than have yet been experienced we must almost certainly contemplate higher rates of investment than were necessary in the past; and there is nothing in the historical record to suggest that savings-ratios will rise in countries emerging from a desperate state of poverty, not merely to the level of their most fortunate neighbours, but above them.

CHAPTER 4

The Place of Capital in Economic Progress[1]

CAPITAL occupies a position so dominant in the economic theory of production and distribution that it is natural to assume that it should occupy an equally important place in the theory of economic growth. In most of the recent writings of economists, whether they approach the subject historically (e.g. in an attempt to explain how the industrial revolution started) or analytically (e.g. in models of an expanding economy) or from the side of policy (e.g. in the hope of accelerating the development of backward countries), it is the process of capital accumulation that occupies the front of the stage. There is an unstated assumption that growth hinges on capital accumulation, and that additional capital would either provoke or facilitate a more rapid rate of economic development even in circumstances which no one would describe as involving a shortage of capital.

Yet there seems no reason to suppose that capital accumulation does by itself exercise so predominant an influence on economic development. In most industrialized communities the rate of capital accumulation out of savings is equal to about 10 per cent of income. If one were to assume that innovation came to a standstill and that additional investment could nevertheless yield an average return of 5 per cent, the consequential rate of increase in the national income would normally be no more than ½ per cent per annum. We are told that the national income has in fact been rising in such communities at a rate of 2–3 per cent per annum. On this showing, capital accumulation could account for, at most, one-quarter of the recorded rate of economic 'progress'. Nor were things very different in the nineteenth century. In Britain, savings were a slightly higher proportion of income and the

[1] A paper presented to the International Economic Association's Round Table on Economic Progress in August 1953, and published in *Economic Progress* ed. L. H. Dupriez (Louvain, 1955).

growth of income was rather slower—about 2 per cent per annum—so that capital accumulation made a larger direct contribution to the growth in income. The position was complicated, however, by population growth which cut the rate of increase in income per head to 1 per cent per annum, and diverted about half current savings into maintaining the stock of capital per head.

Even this way of putting things exaggerates the rôle of capital in economic development. For the yield on additional capital would rarely be as high as 5 per cent if there were not a discrepancy between the existing stock of capital and the stock appropriate to the existing state of technique. If innovation in the broadest sense of the term were at a standstill, accumulation would continue until the rate of interest fell to a point at which saving ceased. The sole object of accumulation in those circumstances would be to take advantage of the progressive cheapening of capital in order to introduce more roundabout methods of production, not to keep pace with current developments in technique. Ordinary observation suggests, however, that the scope of investment *in industry* to take advantage merely of lower rates of interest, once the long-term rate is below 5 per cent, is extremely limited, although there may be a good deal more scope in other directions where capital charges form an unusually high proportion of the final cost (e.g. in the erection of dwelling-houses, public buildings and the like).

The contribution of capital to economic progress is not, however, confined to the usufruct of additional capital assets, similar to those already in existence. It embraces three distinct processes. First, a greater abundance of capital permits the introduction of more roundabout methods of production or, to be more precise, of a more roundabout pattern of consumption. This covers the freer use of capital instruments in the production of a given product, the use of more durable instruments, and a change in the pattern of consumption in favour of goods and services with relatively high capital charges per unit cost. Secondly, the accumulation of capital is a normal feature of economic expansion, however originating. This is the process normally referred to as widening, as opposed to deepening, the structure of production. It may accompany industrialization, or any change in the balance between industries that makes additional demands on capital; or it may accompany an extension of the market associated with population growth, more favourable terms of trade, or the discovery of additional natural resources. Thirdly, additional capital may be required to allow technical progress to take place. It may either finance the discovery of what was not known before or more commonly, the adaptation of existing knowledge so as to allow of its commercial exploitation through some innovation in product, process or material.

Now of these three, the first is generally of subordinate importance; it is unusual for capital accumulation, unassisted by other factors, to bring about a rapid increase in income. The second, which also abstracts from any change in technology, accounts for nearly all the capital accumulation that has taken place in the past; forces making for rapid increase in income may be largely nullified unless they are reinforced by a parallel increase in capital. It is to the third, however, that one must usually look—at least in an advanced industrial country—for the main influences governing the rate of growth of real income per head. Whatever may have been true in the past, it is now technical innovation—the introduction of new and cheaper ways of doing things—that dominates economic progress. Whether technical innovation, in the sectors of the economy in which it occurs, makes large demands on capital is, however, very doubtful. Many innovations can be given effect to in the course of capital replacement out of depreciation allowances, which, in an expanding economy, may be fully as large as net savings. Others may actually reduce the stock of capital required. Existing buildings and existing machines can often be modified so as to allow most of the advantages of the new techniques to be gained. It is economic expansion, far more than technological change, that is costly in capital.

The direct, as distinct from the indirect, impact of technical change on capital requirements has been little studied as an empirical process. On the one hand, our knowledge of trends in the stock of industrial capital, whether in relation to employment or output, is extremely scanty; on the other, different types of technical change may have the most diverse effects on capital, from a net economy in the total stock to a very large increase in requirements per unit of output. Thus there seems neither enough statistical material on which to ground conclusions with any claim to validity nor any grounds for presuming that the predominant influence of technical change will lie in one direction rather than another. Most economists have been content to fall back on a study of the flow of gross investment rather than seek to reconcile estimates of the stock at fluctuating prices and rates of capitalization. Even in assembling the statistics relating to the flow of new capital they have preferred to deal in aggregates rather than analyse the broad changes in the pattern within the aggregate. It is practically impossible to trace the growth of capital in any individual industry or the divergence in rates of growth between sectors of the economy subject to rapid technical change and sectors where technical change has been slow or negligible.

The facts, so far as they go, suggest that capital and income do tend to increase at about the same rate. Both in Britain and the United States the ratio between the two has remained comparatively steady over the seventy or eighty years for which data with some claim to reliability exist, although there have been oscillations within that period. This relative constancy is obviously not inevitable and may, indeed, be entirely accidental. But there are also some general grounds for expecting that the ratio will be fairly stable or will change slowly.

In the first place, we are dealing with annual increments that are themselves small. If savings represent about 10 per cent of income and the stock of capital is equal to about four years' income, the rate of increase of capital will be 2½ per cent per annum. The rate of increase of income in industrial countries is normally between 2 and 3 per cent. A marked divergence between the two rates can hardly occur so long as savings maintain some stability in relation to income and so long as productivity rises at what has come to be regarded as a normal pace. Even a divergence of 1 per cent per annum would be a long time in producing an unmistakable shift in the capital-income ratio, given the doubts that must necessarily surround estimates of the stock of capital in conditions of fluctuating price levels and rates of capitalization.

It happens, moreover, that compensatory influences have been at work over the past seventy or eighty years to keep the two rates together. In the early part of the period, population growth was much more rapid than in the later part, while technical progress was more rapid in the second part of the period than in the first. Thus initially the rate of increase of income was boosted by population growth and as this fell off, productivity gained momentum. Together, these influences tended to stabilize the rate of growth of income. On the other hand, there is little evidence, except in the inter-war period, of any really large reduction in the rate of capital accumulation. Savings before 1913 were probably somewhat in excess of 10 per cent of income—perhaps about 12½ per cent in the United Kingdom—and were a good deal lower between the wars; but they appear to have recovered since 1945 to not far short of the proportion that was normal in Victorian times.

Finally there are several important constituents of the stock of capital which one might reasonably expect to increase more or less *pari passu* with income and so help to stabilize the capital-income ratio. In the absence of a change in the rate of turnover of stocks and work in progress, for example, the total value of stocks should preserve a constant ratio to output and income. There is some evidence that this ratio has in fact stayed at about 40 per cent for a quarter, or even half, a century. It is easy to see that, in agriculture, the average should work out at about six months' output because of the importance of the annual crop which dwindles from twelve months' output to nil over the harvest year. In industry and commerce the ratio seems to be rather lower and to undergo little secular change.

A second example of some importance is provided by dwelling-houses. If one could assume that the proportion of income spent in rent and rates remained constant at, say, 10 per cent—and this was once a reasonable assumption—the stock of houses would bear a fixed relationship to the national income unless the number of years' purchase on house-property varied. Taking, say, fifteen years' purchase as a fair average, the stock of houses would work out at one-and-a-half years' income; and this, together with stocks and work in progress, would represent about half the capital stock of the community if the capital-income ratio were of the order of 4:1. Constancy in the rate of turnover of stocks and in the proportion of income spent on rent would thus exercise a strong damping influence on any tendency for the capital-income ratio to diverge from the previous norm.

It cannot, however, be assumed that the proportion of income spent in rent would remain constant in the absence of technical change since houses have themselves been subject to important innovations. The observed tendency towards constancy reflects a progressive improvement both in the number of rooms occupied per person and in the *type* of accommodation in use as income per head increases. Moreover, if rents are restricted, or the rate of interest alters, the argument advanced above is vitiated.

A third example is, or may be, public (non-industrial) property. This has, in some phases of world history, been the largest constituent of capital of all, whether one thinks of pyramids or cathedrals, mediaeval Florence or modern warfare. It is difficult, if not impossible, to reduce any of these to the economics of capital and income; the most important circumstance governing their finance appears to have been the ease with which the capital could be raised by charity, taxation or force. There is at least a presumption that the wealthier a country becomes, the more it will expend on public buildings; not perhaps, in exact proportion to the growth of the national income but at a rate that may not be very far out of accord.

Any force increasing income will almost inevitably, therefore, increase the demand for capital to a more or less corresponding degree in the form of stocks, houses and public buildings, whatever its impact on other sectors of the economy. On the other hand, there may be some types of capital (like the railway system) that need no increase; and if the bias of consumer expenditure is increasingly towards luxury goods and personal services at higher levels of income, this too will operate to lower the capital-income ratio as income per head rises, since luxuries and services normally make greater demands on labour than on capital per unit of expenditure. But it is unwise to lay too much stress on this point, both because the fact of a shift towards services is itself somewhat in doubt and because purchases of consumers' durable goods should, on a strict assessment, be reckoned as adding to the stock of capital.

If the capital-income ratio alters, therefore, it is likely to be because of a change in technique affecting the remainder of the national capital, after deducting houses, stocks and public property. This residue can be grouped under four headings: agriculture, public utilities, the extraction or manufacture of fuel and raw materials, and the processing industries. Of these the last is much the largest in point of employment in a country like Britain, since it includes most of the manufacturing industries of the country, notably the textile, engineering, and food, drink and tobacco trades. But in point of capital employed this group, even in Britain, comes after public utilities and raw materials and in most other countries ranks after agriculture. Thus if the capital-income ratio does alter appreciably it is generally to agriculture, raw materials, and public utilities that one must look for an explanation. Even in those groups there may be a quasi-automatic lift to the employment of capital, not because a larger stock per man is used but because the cost of the assets rises progressively with income per head, the building industry which constructs the bulk of the assets lagging behind in its rate of technical improvement.

If anything, one would expect some slight downward trend in the ratio of capital to income over the past century because the economic progress made in the second half of the nineteenth century made heavier demands on the savings of the period than does economic progress today. There was a rapidly growing population to be housed—and housing has been throughout the largest claim on new capital. There was a revolution in transport to be financed—and transport used more capital per man than any other industry. In 1914, for example, the British railways needed about £2,000 per man employed while cotton textiles, for example, needed only about £200 per man. Finally, there was the opening-up of new countries, largely with borrowed capital—by far the most important 'innovation' increasing real income all over the world. This meant the resettlement of entire communities in undeveloped areas, the building of the railway systems upon which the whole process of resettlement was pivoted and the construction of all the fixed capital needed to house and supply millions of immigrants. By 1913 Western Europe had poured as much capital into foreign countries as the national capital of the United Kingdom and the United

Kingdom herself had about as much capital invested abroad as in the whole of her domestic industry and commerce.

The main impulse to capital accumulation over the years before 1913 came ultimately from the steam engine and the steamship. By 1913 that impulse had largely spent itself. In Britain, for example, perhaps one-fifth of current savings had gone into domestic railway-building in the sixties and seventies, and shipbuilding had taken another large slice. But after 1885 the annual absorption of new capital by the railways was only about a quarter of the amount that they needed in the twenty years before 1885. Elsewhere, and particularly in Canada, railway-building still headed the investment list, and shipping continued to grow with world trade. But by 1914 the major advantages of the revolution in transport had been exhausted and the world's stock of capital had, broadly speaking, been sufficiently enlarged to profit from it.

If now we move to the inter-war and post-war period, it is at once apparent that the requirements of transport have fallen into the background although still far from negligible because of the fresh revolution in road and air transport. A new public utility—electricity—has risen into prominence. But the most striking change has been in manufacturing industry, less in the processing industries (where mechanization has increased capital requirements) than in the group of industries that produces raw materials. Here, capital has been called in to redress the balance of raw material supply. Thus, aluminium, synthetic textiles, cement, chemicals, and even steel—all of which have risen in comparison with other materials like lead and zinc, cast iron, natural fibres, and stone, —make extremely heavy demands on capital. A similar change has been at work in the supply of fuel and power: electricity and oil use more capital per unit of energy than coal and coke. At the same time, throughout manufacturing industry production methods have altered so as to provide the average worker with additional capital and generally also so as to involve the use of more capital per unit of output. This is most evident in agriculture and in factories using mass production techniques. Nevertheless, even now, this last element in the situation is not, in absolute terms, nearly as large in its demands on new capital as some of the others. In the years 1948–50 gross investment by the British engineering industries, excluding vehicles, averaged only £22 per worker, and by the clothing trades only £9 per worker; and some of this was in canteens and the like while a great part was merely in replacement of existing buildings and plant.

In the nineteenth century, therefore, the demand for capital was dominated partly by demographic factors—the growth and resettlement of population—and partly by the major innovation of the steam engine with all its repercussions on transport and on the distribution of population between and within countries. In the twentieth century neither demographic change nor any single outstanding innovation—except perhaps the use of electricity—exercises anything like the same influence. On the other hand, the pace of innovation has quickened and industrial requirements have assumed greater importance.

It is arguable, indeed, that, with the decline in the strain on savings caused by population growth, the absence of any large scale development of new countries and the corresponding shrinkage in foreign investment, technical innovation must come to play in the twentieth century the rôle that was played in the nineteenth by the growth and resettlement of population. If it proves that technical innovation does in fact require only a modest amount of capital then there is an obvious danger of a repetition of the inter-war experience of a prolonged maladjustment between current habits of thrift and the openings for capital accumulation.

This is a possibility which does not affect all countries in the same way. The position has been obscured by the war and its aftermath since one of the effects of the war was to cause a discontinuous change in the capital-income ratio both because of the destruction that took place and the arrears of maintenance and replacement that accumulated. In a country like Britain, the loss of capital was estimated at one-quarter while other assets in natural resources, skill and so forth were left undepleted. So far as the loss fell on overseas assets, the capital-income ratio was unaffected since capital and income disappeared together. But at home the pattern, both of production and of consumption, has been distorted and the efforts of producers and consumers to restore the previous pattern has forced capital to a premium.

Whether a situation of this kind is or is not reflected in

high interest rates, the accumulation of capital acquires a special urgency. There is a pronounced tendency to suck in foreign capital if it is to be had and, because of the pressure on savings, a strong inflationary under-current. With capital accumulating at no more than 2½ per cent per annum it may obviously be a long time before the capital deficiency is overtaken; and if national income recovers quickly and innovation is at work the period may be still more prolonged.

All this is familiar enough in terms of experience post World War II. What may reasonably be asked is why experience post World War I was so different. The answer no doubt differs from country to country. But the two main points of difference are probably the far greater damage and far larger arrears left by World War II, and the higher capital charges that were in operation after World War I. These higher capital charges were probably responsible for more economy in the use of capital goods, notably housing. In Great Britain, for example, efforts to deal with the housing shortage had little effect until some five years after 1918 and this particular deficiency continued right on until 1939. The pushing back of so large a slice of investment made room for other items, many of them relatively small, of greater urgency in the immediate post-war period. A third factor, of special importance in Britain, was the structural change after World War II in favour of the metal and engineering industries and the higher level of industrial activity in general. The rise in the British national income after World War I was largely attributable to an improvement in the terms of trade and did not involve a corresponding investment in home capital assets. But the rise after the World War II took place *in spite of* an adverse movement in the terms of trade, out of additional output, and involved heavy investment to relieve congestion and bottlenecks at various points in the economy.

At present, therefore, the emphasis is on capital as a limiting factor in development. But in the thirties—and even perhaps the twenties—the emphasis was very different. Technical development throughout the inter-war period was extremely rapid and productivity seems to have increased at a rate that is at least comparable with post-war experience. Yet net investment in manufacturing industry both in Britain and America was trifling; capital per man employed seems to have risen slightly but capital per unit of output undoubtedly fell. Capital accumulation was confined to a remarkable degree to housing and public utilities without any apparent inflection of the curve of productivity.

A second consideration, telling in the same direction, is the comparatively narrow base on which to build any large expansion in manufacturing capital. The capital employed in British manufacturing industry probably averages about £1,000 per head and, if so, the total is of the order of one-fifth of the national capital. Current investment measured gross forms a slightly higher proportion of total gross investment. No doubt it bears *indirectly* on all capital requirements and for that reason this consideration may be of limited force. But if technical innovation is to do in the next fifty years what steam and steel did fifty to a hundred years ago, the indirect reactions on capital requirements will have to be pretty vigorous.

To recapitulate the argument so far. Given that the national income is increasing, whether under the influence of technical progress, population growth, or some other factor, there is good reason to expect that additional capital will be required in some important sectors on a comparable scale. Habits of thrift—a phrase that must now be stretched to include not only the practices of corporations in adding to reserves but the propensities of Finance ministers—appear to admit of capital accumulation at a rate of about 2½ per cent per annum, and this has in recent years been close to the rate of growth of income. Provided, therefore, that the capital requirements of industry—the main sector left out of account—are also increasing at this rate, the capital-income ratio will remain constant and the whole of the country's thrift will be effectively mobilized. There can be no guarantee, however, that industry's requirements will in fact mount at this rate, even in the long run. In the short run, for reasons that are familiar, the whole process of capital accumulation may be thrown out of gear.

Now the significant feature of this argument is that it hinges far more on the indirect than on the direct demand for capital. It assumes that technical progress operates largely in independence of capital accumulation and that capital is needed, not in order to allow innovations to be made but in order to consolidate the improvement in income that innovation brings about. Moreover, it implies that if, at any time, the process of innovation creates a bulge in the demand for capital, it should be possible to adapt the pattern of investment so as to accommodate the high-yielding requirements of industry by displacing part of the larger, but less remunerative, requirements of house-building, stock-building, and so forth.

It is hardly necessary to show that this implication may be mistaken. Public policy may maintain the demand for capital in the sectors capable of compression or the capital market may be so organized that industry is unable to draw capital from the sources that finance other forms of accumulation. But unless the bulge is a very large and consistent one it is doubtful whether innovation need suffer greatly.

The effect of technical progress is generally to widen the divergence between the actual stock of capital and the stock consistent with the full exploitation of current worker opportunities. Some part of the additional capital will be needed to finance the innovations in the sectors of the economy in which they arise; some will be linked with the innovations directly, either associated industries are offered a wider market or because social capital has to be provided in an area where it has become insufficient; some will be linked indirectly, in the way already outlined, because the increased expenditure of consumers will give rise to a derived demand for capital. Now it is common to find that, particularly with a major advance in technique, the influence which it exerts on the scope for eventual capital accumulation is far more profound than its immediate impact on the current flow of capital formation. There is generally a chain reaction, strung out through time, one physical asset being wanted only after another has been created. Although the full consequences may be entirely foreseeable, development does not work up to its full momentum until a whole series of changes have occurred: an extension of capacity here, an application of the new technique there; a shift of location in one industry, a building up of new attitudes in another. The introduction of the steam engine, for example, brought into existence a large reservoir of projects that trickled out into capital formation all through the nineteenth century: the stock of capital appropriate to existing technique was far above the existing stock both because the steam engine was capable of wide application and because many industries that themselves made no use of it (such as bridge-building) were transformed in scale or (like agriculture and many pursuits ancillary to it) in location.

Moreover, because the chain reaction takes time and the innovation is, *ex hypothesi*, a profitable one, the process is to a large extent self-financing. If there is a spate of such innovations, interest and profits are likely to show some response and a corresponding shift in the ratio of savings to income will ease the heavier burden of finance. It may happen, however, that the situation is not regulated in this way: interest rates may be sticky upwards as well as downwards. The probable outcome will then be a series of spurts in investment, followed by periods of indigestion. Excessively large bites, inadequate mastication, the selection of appetizing titbits rather than nourishing staples, and all the usual errors of judgment that attend a children's party may give rise to the familiar heavings that were known in the nineteenth century as the trade cycle. The Victorian period can be interpreted largely as a rush to overtake technique.

A variant of this situation is one in which there has been a considerable lag behind the known opportunities for the fruitful use of capital at existing rates of interest. A country may fail to make use of technical knowledge available elsewhere and suddenly become alive to the possibilities of applying that knowledge. At that stage its capital requirements will increase discontinuously and the additional capital which it requires before bumping up against the limits of technical advance may be very large. It appears to be this situation that is in the minds of those who assume that the injection of additional capital into a country's economy will almost automatically speed up its economic progress. Sometimes the argument is framed more specifically in terms of a shift of employment from agriculture to industry, with a large net gain in productivity from the shift, and the large capital investment needed to accomplish it operating as a brake.

This is a complex situation and it may exist in some underdeveloped countries. But it is by no means obvious that additional capital, whether borrowed from abroad or accumulated through the exertions of surplus labour in the countryside, would by itself suffice to start off a cycle of industrialization. The problem is often one of organization quite as much as of capital creation: of training managements and men; of creating new attitudes towards industrial employment; of taking advantage of innovations that need little capital and using the resulting gains to finance investment elsewhere.

On the whole, there is a greater danger that the importance of capital in relation to economic progress will be exaggerated than that it will be underrated. How many successful firms, looking back over their history, would single out difficulty of access to new capital as the major obstacle, not to their growth, but to the adoption of the most up-to-date technique? How many countries in the van of technical progress have found themselves obliged to borrow abroad? It is where there has been a lag, where technical progress has been too slow, that capital is called upon to put matters right. No doubt where capital is plentiful, more risks can be taken and development is speeded up, so that rapid development and rapid capital accumulation go together. But the most powerful influence governing development, even now, is not the rate of interest or the abundance of capital; and the most powerful influence governing capital accumulation, even now, is not technical progress.

CHAPTER 5

Investment and Growth[1]

It is an ancient heresy that you can buy anything for money. It seems to have popped up again since the war in a more subtle form: money makes money. If only you have capital, development is easy; the more capital you invest, the faster you will develop. Conversely, if you are not developing very fast, blame the rate of capital investment. Capital represents purchasing power over all the other factors of production, so that there can be no shortage of any of these factors that does not yield to an adequate supply of capital.

There are a number of reasons why this convenient doctrine is so widely accepted. Is it not obvious that the countries where investment has been highest in recent years have also enjoyed the most rapid advance in production and income? Then there is the fact that capital is something that lends itself to government action. If you haven't enough, you can borrow; if investment is not taking the 'right' direction, you can control it. If poor countries are a political danger and just have to be developed if they are not to become a nuisance, they can be lent or given the necessary capital. If the regional balance within a country is unsatisfactory, measures to supplement investment in the laggard areas will help them to catch up with the rest of the country.

Capital is equally 'manageable' from the point of view of the theoretical economist: he can build it into satisfactory models and watch how the growth of capital and income respond to one another, without stopping to ask whether both may not respond to something else, such as technical progress.

Yet there are some quite simple calculations that suggest that, in a country like the United Kingdom, capital investment cannot account by itself for more than a limited proportion of the growth in productivity from year to year. The

[1] Adapted from 'Reflections on the Growth of Capital and Income', *Scottish Journal of Political Economy*, June 1959.

same line of argument suggests that the acceleration to be expected as a result of additional investment, within reasonable limits, would also be relatively modest.[1]

Net investment in the United Kingdom has in recent years averaged about 10 per cent of national income while the increase in output has averaged about 3 per cent per annum. Given an average social return on the additional capital invested of, say, 10 per cent—and it is unlikely that it would be higher in current conditions—the increase in output attributable to investment comes to 1 per cent, or one-third of the recorded increase; and an increase in the rate of investment by one-half unaccompanied by other changes, would *at most* bring about a change in the rate of growth of output from 3 to 3½ per cent.

Calculations of this kind usually fail to impress economists who are already believers in high investment. They take issue with the suggestion that the average social return on capital is unlikely to be higher than 10 per cent (in real terms, of course) in an advanced industrial country like the United Kingdom; they point out that other changes are bound to occur as investment rises; and they cite other countries, particularly Germany, Russia and the United States, to show that high investment pays handsomely.

The first of these points is difficult to submit to any conclusive test. If one is thinking of manufacturing investment, one may postulate a financial return, after depreciation but gross of tax, of 20 per cent, or even more, as the average outcome of new investment; and one may reasonably argue that the investment will be likely to have some effect on the wages of those who use the capital, or the price of the final product, so that the financial return falls short of the social return. There are difficulties in following this argument too far: the financial return is, after all, uncertain, and if it is possible to *count on* an average as high as 20 per cent, the capital market will have to be highly imperfect to prevent an immediate diversion of capital from other uses where far lower, but more certain, returns are treated as equivalent. In addition, the return is sustained by uninterrupted technical

[1] The same conclusion is reached by a different route in O. Aukrust, 'Industrial and Economic Growth', *Productivity Measurement Review*, February 1959, pp. 48–9.

progress; and if the pace of technical progress remains unchanged, it is to be presumed that the marginal return, giving effect to the less revolutionary changes in technique, will be well below the average return, which embraces the yield on all technical changes to which managements do in fact give priority.

Manufacturing rarely accounts for more than about one-quarter of gross fixed investment and, since it is weighted heavily by comparatively short-lived types of asset, the proportion of net investment is certainly no higher. It is not possible to generalize from this limited proportion to the whole. The social return on total investment depends far more on the return to be expected from the remaining three-quarters, the bulk of which is accounted for by dwelling-houses on the one hand and power and transport on the other. (I leave on one side additions to stocks because, so far as I know, no one is prepared to argue that a faster rate of accumulation of stocks would accelerate economic growth.)

In the years 1953–57 net fixed capital formation in the United Kingdom (if one may accept, without cavil, the official figures) averaged £1,235 m. at 1954 prices. Of this total, no less than £355 m., or nearly 30 per cent, took the form of dwelling-houses. It is anybody's guess what social return should be assumed for this investment, most of which was heavily subsidized, but it would be difficult to enter an average much in excess of the financial return expected on it; for the sake of argument, we may take 7 per cent. Over the same period, net fixed capital formation, by public corporations, almost all in fuel, power and transport, averaged about £200 m. a year on assets other than dwellings, equivalent to a further 14 per cent of the total. Here again it is difficult to know what social return to assume: the financial return, taking depreciation at replacement cost, was negligible. By far the largest item was investment in electricity generation. But, once generating capacity is adequate to meet the peak demand without power cuts, additional investment in electricity generation, while it may make for more efficient operation of the power stations, does very little to add to the efficiency of industry generally: so that, marginally at least, investment in electricity could not offer a particularly high return and would eventually serve only to create surplus capacity. On the other hand, other forms of public investment (e.g. in roads) were obviously starved and the social return in some directions might have been at least comparable with investment in manufacturing. Taking everything all round, I should doubt whether one could claim either an average social return on past public investment, or a marginal return on any future increase, higher than 7 per cent.

If this argument is accepted, it follows that on nearly half the total of fixed capital investment, the social return was almost certainly well under 10 per cent while on half the rest the return may have been as much as 20 per cent. Without going through all the other items, which include schools, waterworks, drainage, etc., on the one hand, and distributive services, agriculture, etc., on the other, I think it not unrealistic to take an average return of 10 per cent as a basis of judgment, *given the conditions ruling in the United Kingdom in recent years.*

It may be objected that conditions could be changed if investment were higher. Would this not introduce a more dynamic atmosphere and force people to re-examine established ideas and techniques so that innovation would proceed more rapidly? We know too little about the forces governing innovation to be dogmatic about an issue of this kind. It seems likely that high investment *expresses* a change in ideas and techniques rather than provokes them; but the sequence may well be of the hen-and-egg type and start with one or the other.

What we can say with more certainty is that it makes a world of difference what sort of country we are talking about. If an industrial country suddenly loses a large proportion of its real assets but still retains its man-power, its skill, its organizing ability, its social institutions and habits, no one need dispute that capital will be a genuine bottleneck to recovery and every act of investment will restore productive power visibly and decisively. If the sparking plugs are removed from an engine and then replaced, the effect is dramatic and not to be compared with the effect achieved by replacing old plugs by new ones of improved design. The case of Germany, therefore, has very little in common with that of, say, India, where the engine has still to be built or, say, the United States, where sparking plugs and engines abound in all possible combinations. Similarly, if a country is in course of industrialization, and can draw an almost unlimited man-power into urban factories from the countryside, as in USSR, capital may be the controlling element in the growth of industrial capacity and output, and additional investment may permit a more rapid mobilization of otherwise idle or under-utilized resources. To conclude from this, however, that *all* economic development is equally dominated by capital accumulation is plainly unjustified. A country at the frontiers of technical progress, already highly industrialized and urbanized and fully employed, has more reason to concentrate on the quite different, but much more difficult, problem of speeding up the commercial and industrial exploitation of new knowledge.

But *is* it a quite different problem? What of the argument that innovation automatically involves investment of capital while investment almost automatically gives effect to innovation? First of all, about half the new (gross) investment undertaken annually in the United Kingdom is in replacement of existing assets. This leaves very considerable room for manoeuvre in taking advantage of technical progress. Obviously, the latest equipment can be installed, instead of the original type of plant, when replacement takes place, and the cost will often be no higher or may even be less. Moreover, industries able to take full advantage of technical progress will, if the capital market is working smoothly, outbid other, less progressive industries, and get the capital they need at the cost of outlay on renewals in the latter. If gross investment in the United Kingdom were to fall by one-half, net investment would become zero, but innovation would not be arrested. A rise in interest rates, for example, might force most of the cut on to house-building and allow industrial innovation to proceed at full speed at the cost of overcrowding or inferior housing.

It is perhaps more in keeping with the facts—in the United Kingdom at least—if we think of the growth in income as the controlling factor in capital investment rather than the other way round. The link between technical progress and investment is then rather indirect: technical progress is one of the principal elements in the growth of income and this in turn is perhaps the principal element in the demand for capital and so in the rate of investment. This idea is easier to grasp if for 'income' we write 'output', and for 'capital' we write 'capacity', since most people recognize that it is usually necessary to expand capacity as sales increase. Technical progress makes it possible to expand output and generate additional income; the expenditure of this additional income creates a shortage of capacity in other directions; and the shortage of capacity leads to additional investment, *not necessarily in the industries where technical progress is fastest.*

If we accept this view, it becomes immediately apparent that it is easy to overdo an increase in investment and merely create surplus capacity instead of giving effect to technical improvements. How real is this danger?

To answer this question we must look at the other sources of demand for capital. If they are showing signs of slackening, there will, of course, be more room left for investment that takes fuller advantage of technical progress. But, on the other hand, there is a far greater danger that the whole post-war process of an interacting expansion in investment and income may lose momentum. It would be little consolation, once surplus capital made its appearance, that there was at last more money to spare for innovation; for those circumstances would be highly unpropitious to the investment of capital in support of new techniques.

Now there are two sets of circumstances in which the demand for capital might slacken: there might be a slackening in the rate of growth of income which would make it unnecessary to add so rapidly to capacity; and there might be a reduction in the capital-output ratio, i.e. the amount of capital required to produce a unit of output under normal operating conditions. It would also check the demand for capital if, after rising steadily, the capital-output ratio levelled off.

It is easy to point to some factors tending to slow down the growth in national income. For example, the post-war growth has been assisted by an unusually rapid expansion in the labour force—an expansion that can hardly continue. The importance of this in the post-war situation has been concealed by the very slow growth in total population. Yet the growth in labour supply and in employment, measured in terms of man-hours worked, was probably faster between 1948 and 1956 than in the nineteenth century when the birth-rate was twice as high as now. An expansion in man-hours worked averaging 1 per cent per annum must have contributed substantially to the 3 per cent per annum increase in national income. No such expansion in employment is to be expected in future.

On the other hand, we cannot predict the contribution that may be made in future by technical progress. Any acceleration of technical progress would help to sustain the demand for capital by raising productivity and output. This would be true even if, in the long run, the tendency of technical progress was capital-saving; and *a fortiori* if it told in the opposite direction. The important fact not to be lost sight of is that, of all the factors that caused income to grow in the nineteenth century—including industrialization, education, free trade, capital accumulation and population growth—the only major one that now operates more powerfully to make income grow is technical progress. The outstanding impression left by a review of those factors is of a progressive narrowing down, leaving the process of growth increasingly dominated by technical progress and innovation.

When we turn to the changes affecting the capital-income ratio a similar conclusion emerges. It has been tending to rise during the post-war period to a more normal level but this movement cannot, unless the 'norm' itself changes, go on indefinitely. There have been heavy arrears of capital construction to be made good because of war-time standstills, wear and tear, neglect, and damage, and because of the big jump in the level of activity over pre-war. These arrears have been tolerable only at the cost of congestion (e.g. roads), breakdowns (e.g. power supply) and capacity operation (e.g. steel); and they have been gradually overhauled by the creation of fresh capacity at a rate somewhat in excess of the expansion in output. Hence the margin between the actual capital-output ratio and the desired or optimum ratio—which is another way of saying the real shortage of capital—has been in course of disappearance. The simultaneous rise in private savings may correspond to a similar overhauling by consumers of their own arrears of durable goods in relation to current income levels. Unfortunately we have no indices by which to keep track of either phenomenon, indispensable though they are to any forecast of the likely tendency of capital requirements.

Against this tendency can be set the impact of technical change which, in some rather conspicuous ways, has made heavy demands on capital in relation to output. It is not easy to be sure that the total effect is in the direction of greater capital intensity. It may well be that while the big inventions —steam power, electricity, nuclear energy, synthetics of all kinds—work in that direction, the host of minor and less familiar inventions operates in the other direction. But when we take account of other circumstances that have affected the pressure to use the bigger inventions, the net effect can hardly be in doubt. The high price of imported materials and foodstuffs, and the high cost of solid fuel, for example, have brought capital-intensive synthetics, capital-intensive agricultural techniques and capital-intensive forms of fuel into more widespread use. There may, therefore, be a real upward movement in the normal capital-output ratio in response to the forces of technical change.

To sum up. In the post-war period, capital requirements have been maintained above the pre-war normal but one of the most important influences maintaining them has been transitory. Either, therefore, investment will now drop (and savings will have to drop, too, or find an outlet in foreign investment or in various forms of social investment) or the forces of innovation will have to operate more powerfully, or there will have to be some acceleration of technical progress in such a way as to make heavy demands on capital.

This brings us back to the argument from which we started. Current discussion fastens too unrelentingly on capital investment, particularly industrial investment, as the prime means of promoting a rise in living standards. An increase in capital-output ratios that does not express an underlying change in technological possibilities is not likely by itself to accomplish much in a fully industrialized economy, and may serve only to create surplus capacity. There is no reason to assume that the really important advances are passed over, either in the private or in the public sector, in favour of less profitable ones. A higher level of investment might, of itself, set up a fresh and perceptible impulse to further technical development; but this is less probable when the level of current investment is already high. The real need is for more rapid technical change and for action to encourage and promote innovation.

CHAPTER 6

The Capital-Output Ratio[1]

I WAS brought up on a theory of capital which took little account, in any explicit way, of the interconnection between investment and innovation. Much of it was directed to explaining the phenomenon of interest and ran in terms of marginal efficiency of capital. The theory was not much concerned with dynamic and cumulative changes in which total output grew, and it either ignored them, in order to concentrate on the length of the period of production, or tended to generalize from the factors governing the behaviour of the individual unit, whether on the side of savings or investment, to the factors governing the aggregates in an entire economy. No consideration was given to the rebound on the demand for capital that follows any increase in income brought about by the use of more capital in a fully employed economy. It was also difficult to be sure, when a writer was discussing an increase in capital, whether he meant an increase in the rate of investment or an increase in the stock of capital.

The current tendency is to start with a macro-economic analysis in terms of capital coefficients, concentrating on the growth of capital and output, and relegating problems of allocation and distribution to a back seat. The supply of other factors of production is largely taken for granted and assumed to accommodate itself to the growth of capital, which, explicitly or implicitly, figures as the controlling element. The idea of marginal efficiency, while not abandoned, is rarely brought into relationship with that of the capital-output ratio; and economists move rather uneasily between the two sets of concepts as the type of problem under discussion alters.

The capital-output ratio is a useful and natural concept for the purposes of national economic planning. This is particularly true where it is necessary to check the consistency of tar-

[1] From 'Reflections on the Growth of Capital and Income', *Scottish Journal of Political Economy*, June 1959.

gets for the growth of national income against the additional capital likely to be available from current savings or foreign investment. But even in calculations of this kind there are important ambiguities.

First of all, there is a tendency to use the ratio as a measure of the productivity of capital, on the assumption that the whole of any increase in output can be attributed to the expansion of capacity resulting from investment. This tendency is conspicuous not only in many of the discussions about under-developed countries, where it may have some slight justification, but even in writings about advanced industrial countries, where the contribution of additional capital to economic growth is obviously far from 100 per cent. In some versions, a looser causal relationship between the growth of capital and of output is assumed, but capital is still treated as the bottleneck and a fixed relationship is taken to do no real violence to the facts.

The capital-output ratio, however, is merely a quotient measuring, in its incremental form, the relative rates of increase of capital and output. If it could be shown that it was fixed in respect of each constituent of total output by technical factors, this would not mean that technical factors alone governed the ratio for total output, since the constituents of output may vary in weight with changes in demand brought about by economic factors. There is, in any event, neither constancy through time in production coefficients, nor constancy at any one time between one firm and another, and the methods of production in use yield, to some extent at least, to the pressure of economic factors such as the relative cost of different productive agents.

If appeal is made to the facts, it appears to be true that for the few countries (all of them industrial) for which adequate data exist, there has been some degree of constancy over long periods in the average capital-output ratio. But this is not true of the *marginal* capital-output ratio. There are, in any event, good *a priori* reasons for expecting any change in the average ratio to be slow (since the yearly increments, both in capital and income, are normally small in relation to the pre-existing totals) and for expecting some of the more important constituents of the capital stock to bear a fairly constant relationship to total income. Fluctuations in the ratio do occur; and it is too early to form any firm conclusion as to the long-term trend and the resistance that would be offered by technical inflexibility to persistent economic forces such as a change in habits of thrift.

If one looks at the practice of countries engaged in national economic planning, there are further grounds for scepticism. In the USSR, for example, it is an article of faith that the capital-output ratio must go on rising; successive plans have provided for a higher rate of growth of producer goods than of consumer goods. On the other hand, in some of the under-developed countries there is a willingness to plan for a falling capital-output ratio; and in some South American countries, where plans are less fashionable, output does appear to have expanded in post-war years a good deal more rapidly than capital.

Apart from these considerations, there is no reason why constancy in the capital-output ratio should be accepted as demonstrating a causal connection in one direction rather than the other. If income is growing, it is almost inevitable that savings will grow, too; the more rapid the growth of income, the higher the proportion of income that is likely to be saved. The accumulation of capital may, in those circumstances, be little more than a symptom of development, rather than its cause. If, for example, all economic activity took the form of agriculture and house-building, and technique stood still in the building industry but progressed rapidly in agriculture, the growth of agricultural output might be accomplished with little or no additional investment of capital, while the increase in income might give rise to a larger demand for house-room and hence for capital. Any constancy of the capital-output ratio in such circumstances would reflect the income-elasticity of demand for housing, not the inflexibility of the technique of producing food or building houses; and the growth of capital would be a function of the growth of income, which in turn would be a function of technical progress.

A somewhat similar situation might occur if technical progress in agriculture (e.g., the use of better seeds) put little demand on capital in that sector of the economy but made it necessary to provide additional storage, transport and port facilities in order to handle the larger crops. The capital-output ratio in agriculture itself might fall; but the fall could be largely or entirely offset by some consequential change in another sector, a change that of itself would do little to promote the growth of output, but might be indispensable in order that the economy should enjoy the full advantage of technical change.

It might be supposed from these examples that this objection to a causal interpretation of constancy in the capital-output ratio rests on the unequal incidence of technical change in different sectors of the economy. That there is such inequality of incidence is apparent enough; but even if it did not exist, the objection still stands. For within each sector also, there is no necessary identity between the areas of rapid change and the areas of heavy investment. The mainspring of economic progress lies in innovation in the widest sense, rather than in capital accumulation; and if innovation leaves the capital-output ratio unchanged, this reflects a particular balance of forces between different elements of technical change and the broader economic factors governing the growth of capital and income, and is in no sense a demonstration of the predominance of capital over the other factors operating on productivity.

Some economists have put this proposition more strongly and argued that all technical change must be capital-saving (in Sir Roy Harrod's sense of the term) since, if there is no change in available resources, including capital, and the productivity of these resources increases, this must imply a fall in the capital-output ratio. In one way this is true: technical progress will raise output without additional *saving*, for example by permitting existing instruments to be replaced by instruments of equal cost but greater productivity. But in another way, the proposition is not true: if technical progress allows more machines to be made at the same cost, capital increases at the same time as output and the capital-output ratio will remain constant if producer goods and consumer goods benefit equally from the advance in techniques. There is, in fact, an ambiguity in the measurement of capital of which too little store is taken in most discussions of capital-output ratios. If one looks at the stock of capital as the cumulative product of past thrift, one necessarily disregards the steady accretion that results from technical improvements in the manufacture of capital goods—improvements that allow depreciation funds to be used to better purpose on reinvestment than when a similar sum was originally invested. Similarly, in any estimation of future capital requirements—in the sense of fresh savings to expand the capital stock—some allowance ought to be made for the continuation of technical change in the producer goods sector before any calculation of incremental capital-output ratios.

This is by no means the only difficulty involved in the operational use of the concept. There are several additional circumstances which make it hazardous to interpret the results of empirical research. For example, in an under-developed country, land is one of the most important forms of capital just as food is one of the most important items of income; land values are unlike other property values and cannot easily be amalgamated with them if the amalgam is to have any theoretical significance. Much the same problems arise when estimates of capital have to be based on current yields rather than on cost of reproduction. Then there are the types of capital, notably consumers' durables, that may gradually replace producers' durables but are commonly excluded from estimates of the capital stock; and on the side of output and income, there are the numerous and important examples of non-monetary transactions and self-supplied consumption that are usually omitted but may form a large proportion of total real income. Further difficulties of interpretation spring from divergent movements in the prices of capital and consumer goods: the process of economic development may bring about a change in the cost of labour relatively to the cost of capital and if there is any difference in capital intensity between the industries producing capital and consumer goods this will cause their prices to diverge and so disturb the ratio of capital to output.

Given the importance that has come to be attached to the capital-output ratio, it is remarkable how little attention has been given to the forces at work on it. In the pre-war literature, much of the discussion abstracts almost entirely from the factors that seem to have been of first importance: technical change, urbanization, geographical discovery, etc. Instead, prominence was given to changes in technical coefficients in response to changes in the cost of capital—a process which now tends to be belittled. In keeping with the emphasis on obtaining the best allocation of resources, it was assumed that the supply of capital would be made to go round by a kind of price rationing which would exclude uses and methods offering an insufficient return. If capital became more abundant, this would increase the competitive advantage of more capital-intensive methods of production, more durable (but more expensive) forms of capital, and products making more lavish use of capital in their manufacture. This 'deepening' of capital was assumed to be governed, with some reservations, by diminishing returns, so that the capital-output ratio, had it featured in the exposition, would have been likely to be represented as tending to increase.

One important reservation concerned the possibility of increasing returns. Most of the discussion on this subject related to manufacturing industry, a sector in which only a relatively small proportion of total capital was employed, and the discussion was directed more to issues of monopoly and competitive equilibrium than to the macro-economics of capital. Nevertheless the same line of argument was obviously as applicable to a railway network as to a steel mill; and in late Victorian times the importance of this reservation must have been apparent. After the middle seventies, railway-building took a much reduced slice of national savings, and this relaxation of the pressure did not prevent the railways from carrying a rapidly expanding traffic.

The possibility of increasing returns rests largely, in the present context, on an expanding population and output. This expansion allows fuller use to be made of capacity created earlier and permits, therefore, of some economy in the use of capital per unit of output. An increase in population does not operate necessarily or exclusively in this direction, however, since it may put pressure on scarce resources and make it necessary to sink increasingly large amounts of capital in order to obtain given additions to the supply. The dominant effect of the increase, leaving these opposite possibilities on one side, and assuming also that employment rises at a parallel rate, is to make capital and output rise together and to preserve constancy in the ratio between the two. The more this process of capital 'widening' enters, the greater the stability imparted to the capital-output ratio. If population is increasing rapidly and unemployment is not resulting, any other factor will have to have a very marked tendency to expand or contract capital requirements per unit of output if the change in the ratio is to be appreciable. In nineteenth-century Britain, the rate of growth of population was about 1 per cent per annum while income and capital grew about twice as fast. Thus fully half of the growth in income and capital was controlled by a factor unlikely to disturb the ratio between the two.

A less obvious factor operating on the ratio is the pattern of demand. This was implicit in the classical formulation, since changes in the rate of interest could affect the demand for the more capital-intensive products such as house-room and bring about a redistribution of demand in favour of those products. There is also an income element to be considered, since the pattern may change through time with the growth of income, its distribution, and all the dynamic elements that change spending habits for reasons unconnected with prices and incomes. The shift towards services and away from food is the most prominent example of a change in the pattern of demand that may have important effects on the demand for capital and the capital-output ratio. The emergence of synthetic materials and products is of comparable importance, but reflects a change in supply conditions at least as much as in demand and is cited below from this point of view.

Industrialization is undoubtedly one of the most important determinants of the ratio. It commonly involves the swallowing by the towns of large numbers of agricultural workers who are largely redundant to the needs of the rural areas from which they come. There are few things that make greater demands on capital than towns and the period of urbanization is inevitably one of high investment; but it is usually also a period in which income seems to grow rapidly, perhaps because of the spurious indices by which it tends to be measured, but no doubt also because of real economies of scale and concentration. Thus the effect of industrialization is to put a strain on available resources of capital, without necessarily deflecting the capital-output ratio a great deal. *A priori*, one might expect the large housing requirements of urban living to push the ratio up; but, as we have seen in Russia, and as we saw earlier in England, overcrowding and slums can provide a buffer if the shortage of capital is acute. Town-building may do no more than meet the bare requirements of industry for the housing of its workers and be carried through at far less capital cost than seems desirable to a later and richer generation.

A rather similar effect, although in the opposite direction, may be produced by the spread of literacy and education. This is generally recognized to be one of the keys to successful development and is likely, therefore, to go with a rapid growth in income. It is sometimes suggested that the outlay involved ought to be regarded as creative of personal capital and that when this adjustment is made, the capital-output ratio may show little change. It is doubtful, however, whether a large change would result even without the adjustment: for with better education there is a tendency to make use of more and better equipment, so that physical capital rises along with human, and the movement in the capital-output ratio is damped.

The influence of foreign trade and investment is also important. Many of the under-developed countries find that development is frequently associated, causally or otherwise, with a more than proportionate growth, especially in the early stages, in foreign trade, and that some at least of their most promising export lines call for heavy capital expenditure. This is particularly true where there are mineral ores and oil to be exploited and a need for extensive transport improvements before trade can be conducted. We know relatively little, however, about the capital-output ratio in the export sector of the economy in comparison with the ratio for the economy as a whole. All we can say is that there may be a divergence between the two and that foreign trade may cause the capital-output ratio to diverge from the capital-income ratio, measured from the side of consumption rather than production.

Foreign investment permits of a similar divergence between the requirements of capital needed to produce a given domestic output and the supply of savings generated by the corresponding income. It is curious, given the historical importance of foreign investment in relation to economic development, how rarely it features in models of economic growth. There is a good deal of evidence that capital requirements at some stage in growth are apt to outstrip domestic savings and at other stages to be outstripped by them. If there is international mobility of capital, therefore, and if different countries are at different stages in the cycle of growth, the explosive interaction of savings, income and capital requirements that many economists put into their theoretical crucibles operates through a safety valve in the balance of payments rather than through wild fluctuations in the level of employment. The saving clause is, however, an important one: for if the major economies are all at the same stage, the safety valve cannot operate.

The importance of this factor was most evident in Britain in the years immediately before 1913 when total capital, including foreign investments, represented about six years' income while domestic capital was only equal to between four and five years' output. Had the current savings of the country all been absorbed domestically, the incremental ratio of capital to output would have had to be very high indeed, especially as, over much of this period, the rate of growth of real income was extremely low. At the *average* rate of growth of 2 per cent per annum the incremental ratio, with savings at 15 per cent of income, would have had to be no less than 7·5, and if the diversion of savings to home investment had had the effect on income growth that one suspects, it might have had to be even higher.

The operations of government can exercise a similar influence. It is obvious that governments can make large drafts on national savings without any visible increase in output. This is so in war-time but it is true also of war preparations that lead to the creation of debt and of many objects of government borrowing even in peace-time. The effect of a long war, moreover, is likely to be to depress the capital-output ratio either through the destruction involved or through neglect of repairs and replacements. Hence an equilibrium that would seem impossible between a high rate of saving and low capital requirements may be maintained through erratic incursions by government into the capital market. Nor is there any reason why the incursions need only be erratic, since the government may systematically regulate the pressure on capital by operating directly on its own requirements, wherever these are capable of postponement, or through the budget surplus so far as this is politically acceptable.

Finally, we can hardly overlook the effects of innovation. It is hardly open to doubt that technical progress has been the most important instrument in raising the standard of living over the past two centuries; nor that, along with population growth and migration, it has dominated the course of investment in time of peace. To discuss the capital-output ratio without regard to the effects of innovation, therefore, is to re-write Hamlet and leave out the Prince.

Nor is it possible to make the heroic simplification that its effects on the ratio are neutral. As has been argued above, the historical stability of the capital-output ratio could be due to quite adventitious circumstances, since the major uses of capital are highly concentrated and need show no necessary identity with the major areas of innovation. Moreover, even if, in the long run, innovation does prove to be neutral, there is no reason why this should imply neutrality in the short run to which most analysis of stability and fluctuations applies. The typical, and by far the most important innovation in the nineteenth century, was the steam engine and its by-product, railway transport. It took half a century at least to build the railway system in this and other countries; and if, at the end of that time, the capital-income ratio was no higher than before, this would prove nothing at all about the pressure of capital requirements in the interval. Current investment in railways in the early phase of railway-building may easily have dwarfed the release of capital for the maintenance and replacement of other forms of transport; while eventually the stock of capital invested in all forms of transport might reach a total no higher in relation to the output of transport services than obtained before the railway age. It is not necessary to hold that this was in fact so; the point of importance is that an *acceleration* of technical progress, or the emergence of a major innovation in a stream of minor ones, is bound to increase capital requirements in advance of output and introduce a disturbance to the existing equilibrium between savings, income and the rate of capital accumulation.

CHAPTER 7

Capital Formation in the Take-off[1]

I

ANY attempt to generalize on capital formation in relation to take-off suffers from five principal handicaps:

(i) First of all, the apparatus of thought and analysis which economists have devised for studying capital accumulation in advanced countries is not necessarily applicable. Many of the models that seek to relate capital formation to economic progress do so in order to show how difficult it is to move steadily along a continuous path of growth. But while it may be interesting to be reminded that there is a certain connection between the amount of alcohol consumed and the unsteadiness of our subsequent movements, this reminder does not help us to learn how to walk. We cannot assume that capital plays the same part at the outset of industrialization as it does once industry is well established or in countries that are already fully industrialized. There is, for example, more discontinuity in the early stages than there is later on and this discontinuity cannot be analysed in purely economic terms. Social change is interwoven with economic change and may dominate both the process of capital accumulation and the process of innovation that lies at the root of economic progress. In any society, growth can never be a purely quantitative affair but is necessarily accompanied by changes in techniques, attitudes and institutions. In the emergence of an industrial society, these changes are of peculiar importance. They are not only the source of the more measurable indications of growth but must find a place in any explanation of how development begins. Thus it is not possible to analyse the 'take-off' in the same terms as sustained industrial growth.

(ii) Next, there is the absence of reliable data. Such indications as exist of the movement of savings and capital forma-

[1] Paper presented to the Conference on the Economics of Take-off into Sustained Growth, at Konstanz, September 1960.

tion in the early stages of growth are usually fragmentary and not such as to permit of confident generalization. In particular, data on investment in agriculture, by far the most important activity in pre-industrial countries, is inevitably defective. In such countries, the problem of measuring capital formation is aggravated by the more limited rôle of the market and the consequent difficulty in imputing values to the assets that are created. Many of these assets are, in any event, intangible and consist in the acquisition of education, skill and experience, the building up of commercial links and familiarity with market opportunities, the establishment of standards of conduct, the improvement of public services, and so on. Expenditure on physical assets may in these circumstances neither reflect the true input of services tending to raise future productivity nor the true contribution of those services to the wealth of the community. Even if the conceptual problems could be overcome, the difficulty remains of assembling continuous statistical series for capital, employment, output, and so on, for countries undergoing industrialization. There is an increasing margin of error in such data the further back in time they are carried; and if use is made of contemporary estimates for countries that have not yet taken-off, there are again large margins of uncertainty attending their use.

(iii) There is also a danger in generalizing from the experience of the countries that have already undergone industrialization to those that have not, unless we have reason to believe that the process of economic growth follows a constant pattern and does not itself develop. The very fact that they are not first in the field conditions the direction that development takes in the latecomers. The investment opportunities open to them are wider in some directions and more restricted in others. They can make use of foreign techniques, foreign technicians, foreign capital, and foreign equipment in ways not open to the pioneers in industrialization. On the other hand, foreign markets confront them with a different range of choices; they are much less likely than European countries were to find outlets abroad for their industrial products. The minimum scale on which investment projects have to be conceived; the degree to which it is necessary to rely on foreign co-operation; the balance between home and foreign markets; the possibilities of State intervention; all of these have changed over the past century and all of them affect the process of capital formation.

(iv) Moreover, there are important differences in the economic conditions of present-day under-developed countries and the conditions ruling in nearly all the countries that industrialized themselves during the nineteenth century. The latter, with the exception of Japan, were all, by the standards of the time, rich countries; the former, by the standards of today, are almost without exception poor countries. Development poses different problems for rich and poor and nowhere so strikingly as in the matter of finance. The problem of generating adequate savings hardly troubled European countries as industrialization proceeded. Although marginal amounts were borrowed abroad, and total intra-European investment reached a substantial level, domestic savings financed all but a relatively small proportion of investment in each country. This was true also in the United States where foreign investment did, however, play a key rôle in the capital market. In other non-European countries, such as Canada and Australia, the magnitude of capital requirements was indeed beyond the resources of local savings; but the circumstances of those newly settled countries, given their investment opportunities and the average income which they already enjoyed, were quite unlike those of all but a very few of the under-developed countries of the present day.

(v) There is a further difficulty in applying a stage analysis based on the circumstances of last century to the wide range of under-developed economies of today. Apart from Japan, nearly all the industrialized countries were industrialized after they had been equipped with the main institutions of capitalist society. The subsistence sector occupied a much smaller place in the economy than it now does throughout Africa and much of Asia. Trade was highly developed; and when industrialization began, the heavy capital requirements of urbanization coincided with those of an expanding industrial structure. But in many countries where the market still plays an almost peripheral rôle, urbanization is well advanced and there are large foreign-controlled and capital-intensive enterprises already established. In such so-called 'dual economies', capital accumulation cannot be expected to trace the same path as it did in Europe and North America.

Moreover, to speak of 'take-off' in relation to underdeveloped countries begs a major question. It appears to imply power to compress within a comparatively short period of years a transition from one type of economy to another. We are invited to contrast the rôle of capital in one phase with its rôle in the succeeding phase of transition. But there may be no such contrast—only a gradual and almost imperceptible quickening of the process of change. If so, there may still be a change in some industry or area, some institution or relationship, that marks a decisive break with the past. But there is then no obvious reason why the change should be one involving the scale of capital formation. On one view of 'take-off', capital occupies a central rôle that it need not occupy on another interpretation.

II

This supposed central rôle of capital formation is one of the principal issues on which the remainder of this paper concentrates. I shall begin by examining the causal interconnection between capital formation and economic growth; pass to the rise in savings that is a pre-requisite of sustained growth; comment briefly on changes in the capital-output ratio in the course of industrialization; and deal finally with the growth of a capital market. In each of these sections I cannot hope to do more than outline a point of view.

I start from the issue of causation. There is general agreement that, in all countries, the processes of economic growth and capital accumulation are closely interconnected. It was in terms of this interconnection that the earliest theories of economic development were formulated; and in the work of modern economists, output is still assumed to be limited by capital, whether there is abundant labour or not. A high rate of capital formation usually accompanies a rapid growth in productivity and income; but the causal relationship between the two is complex and does not permit of any facile assumption that more capital formation will of itself bring about a corresponding acceleration in the growth of production.

In industrial countries this is only too obvious. Capital formation may assume forms, such as house-building or an addition to liquid stocks, that are unlikely to add very perceptibly to productivity although they may yield a sufficient return to make them worth while. If all capital formation were of this character, or represented an enlargement of the capital stock with assets broadly similar to those already in existence, it would be hard to account for the rates of growth actually recorded. A moment's reflection will show that even an average return of 10 per cent to capital in a country saving 10 per cent of its income annually would raise income by no more than 1 per cent per annum.[1] Similarly, efforts to impute the recorded expansion in industrial production to the additional labour and capital contributing to it invariably leave a large unexplained residue.[2] It is necessary, therefore, to take account of other influences, such as technical progress and improvements in social and economic organization, which may operate through investment, or independently of it, so as to raise the level of production. These influences, if they take effect uniformly throughout the economy in competitive conditions, will tend to swell the national income without raising the average return to capital, the extra output slipping through to the consumer, the wage-earner or the government.

How far it is correct to attribute an expansion in output to high investment, when high investment is only one of the factors at work is necessarily debatable. It would certainly be legitimate if capital formation was lagging behind, and finance could be identified as a bottleneck in the process of expansion. It might also happen that the rate of technical advance was itself controlled by the scale of investment, not merely because capital formation was the means by which new techniques were adopted but also because high investment created an atmosphere favourable to experimentation and innovation. There is undoubtedly some tendency for all the symptoms of rapid growth to show themselves simultaneously. But there is no invariable dependence of growth

[1] This point is developed in my 'Reflections on the Growth of Capital and Income' (*Scottish Journal of Political Economy*, June 1959). See also the comments by E. Lundberg, 'The Profitability of Investment' (*Economic Journal*, December 1959).

[2] See, for example, W. B. Reddaway and A. D. Smith, 'Progress in British Manufacturing Industries in the Period 1948–54' (*Economic Journal*, March 1960) and O. Aukrust, 'Investment and Economic Growth', *Productivity Measurement Review*, February 1959.

on a high rate of capital formation and it is easy to imagine circumstances in which efforts to increase capital formation may actually slow down the progress of the economy.[1]

Moreover there is some justification for turning the causal relationship the other way round. If income is growing fast, investment opportunities are likely to be expanding correspondingly fast, so that the growth in income draws capital accumulation along behind it. The biggest single influence on capital formation is market opportunity, and many types of capital accumulation are likely to be embarked upon only when income is booming. If capital formation does not respond, its failure to do so will certainly act as a drag on the expansion in output. But there is no reason why it should bring it to a halt, and, given a re-arrangement of the investment pattern, income might grow a long way before the shortage of capital became acute. In the meantime the rapid growth in income, particularly if it were accompanied by high profits, would be likely to generate additional savings and so mitigate any symptoms of capital shortage that manifested themselves.

All this presupposes that a spurt in income could precede an acceleration of investment, and that capital formation is subordinate to other elements in the process of growth. These suppositions are not altogether extravagant. Technical progress does not always involve high net investment: indeed it may permit of a *reduction* in the stock of capital or an expansion in output without any comparable investment. A change in the pattern of investment could also, by enforcing the continued use or overloading of old types of plant, make possible a far more rapid construction of those newer types which bear the fruits of technical progress in greatest abundance.

Attempts are sometimes made to settle the issue by citing the apparent constancy of the capital-income ratio and deducing from this the 'neutrality' of technical progress. But the capital-income ratio is affected by many things other than technical progress: the distribution of consumers' expenditure between capital-intensive and labour-intensive products; indivisibilities in past investment—for example, in the transport and communication network; changes in the pat-

[1] The ground-nuts scheme in Tanganyika is an extreme example.

tern of trade; investment in social assets such as roads, schools, and hospitals to which no income is imputed; and so on. Even if these influences, too, are neutral and if the capital-income ratio does remain constant—and neither of these assumptions seems well-founded—the fact that capital and income grow at the same rate tells us nothing about the causes of growth in either. There is no reason at all why one should rule out the suggestion that the same circumstances that favour rapid growth of income are also favourable to a rapid growth of investment.

This may seem a rather arid and irrelevant issue: arid, because if capital requirements must keep pace with the growth of income that is all we need to know for practical purposes; irrelevant, because the issue relates to experiences in industrial rather than pre-industrial countries. But when it is so commonly urged that countries will be able to take-off if only they are provided with sufficient capital from outside, the issue seems neither arid nor irrelevant. For this theses assumes the very causal relationship that is in dispute.

My own inclination is to think of this issue in terms of an individual firm and ask myself how often the sudden acquisition of additional finance has enabled a firm to 'take-off'. There are undoubtedly some examples: among small firms particularly, access to finance is limited, and additional funds, without any change in their cost, would accelerate expansion. But the fact that turnover and capacity tend to keep pace with one another provides no clue whatever to the importance of finance as a bottleneck. Observation suggests that expansion goes with market opportunity and efficient management, and that where these are present financial obstacles can usually be overcome.

The parallel between individual firms and entire economies is not likely to be exact and may, indeed, be misleading. Market opportunities can be created and are to some extent dependent on government plans and policies; efficient management is often the fruit of experience and contacts, and may thrive on active encouragement to invest. Above all, the complementaries are different. All investment is a reaction to some real or fancied disequilibrium: it is a step towards restoring balance with complementary forms of capital. But in a firm surrounded by other industrial firms, the most frequent lack of balance to which its investment responds is within the firm itself or within the industry or industries of which it forms part. In an under-developed country, one firm's investment is more closely bound up with the investment of other firms and of the public authorities; their actions overflow more readily so as to affect other investment decisions. Even when each firm regarded itself as in balance, therefore, there might be scope for productive investment involving them all, and the absence of adequate finance might be the decisive factor in preventing investment and growth. This line of argument, which would carry us into a discussion of balanced growth and of 'social overheads' need not be pursued here.

It may also be true, as Albert Hirschmann has argued in *The Strategy of Economic Development*, that the best way of securing a more rapid penetration of the economy with new ideas and values may be heavy investment in some ultra-modern type of plant such as a steel-works. All that one can say about this is that it has not always worked. The railway was, in its day, as modern as the sputnik; but there are many countries that have had a good railway system for nearly a century and are still struggling to 'take-off'.

Whatever one may think of investment as a fast breeder, we need have no reservations about the scale on which investment becomes necessary as development proceeds. The switch from an agricultural, village economy to an industrial, urbanized economy probably involves heavier capital expenditure in relation to income available during the process of transformation than in the subsequent period of growing productivity. But once the switch is in progress, why should it be halted? Is it not self-financing? or if it is not, what is the mechanism by which a financial bottleneck makes itself felt?

This is an issue which is rarely discussed because it is so often taken for granted that output and capital are functionally related so that a shortage of capital can be identified with a shortage of capacity. But there are different types of capacity, and the symptoms of shortage do not make themselves felt uniformly throughout an economy. It is necessary also to show why a physical shortage should persist in the face of a correspondingly remunerative return on additional investment.

The mechanism that most economists seem to have in mind is one involving a two-sector model in which productivity is markedly higher in industry than in agriculture but labour can move out of agriculture into industry only at the rate permitted by the growth in industrial capacity.[1] This in turn is taken to be limited by the rate of profit either because industry is assumed to be completely self-financing or because outside finance is likely to bear a fixed relationship to reinvestment of profit.

This analysis does not strike me as altogether satisfactory. It is difficult to see why *manufacturing industry* should fail to grow rapidly if all that holds it back is lack of capital. Its capital requirements are usually relatively modest, and unless the capital market is highly imperfect, they are likely to take precedence over the requirements of housing, public utilities, roads, etc., in conditions of capital shortage. It is, however, conceivable that industrial expansion may be seriously slowed down by bottlenecks in those complementary types of asset in which a general shortage of capital is likely to manifest itself.

There is some evidence that these bottlenecks do appear and put a brake on industrial development. There is commonly, for example, a physical shortage of housing as evidenced by slums and overcrowding: though it is not altogether clear how far this slows down industrialization nor whether the deterioration in housing standards is in relation to previous rural standards or merely in relation to the standards of later and richer generations. A more direct connection can be traced through congestion of transport and overloading of the power network. Sometimes these effects are put down to failure to raise charges in the face of inflation; but it is more likely that the inflation itself is brought on by the shortage of capital and that inflation, combined with power shortages, railway congestion, and overcrowding, is largely the outcome of an inequality between the rate of growth of income and capital. Savings fail to keep pace with investment requirements.

III

This brings us to the second issue: what is the rôle of saving in the take-off? How are additional savings generated and is

[1] See, for example, H. W. Singer, 'The Mechanics of Economic Development', *Indian Economic Review*, August 1952.

there a discontinuous shift in the ratio of savings to income either before or after take-off? Is it a necessary condition, as Rostow suggests, that 'the proportion of net investment to national income . . . rises from say, 5 per cent to over 10 per cent . . . yielding a distinct rise in real output *per capita*'?[1] Perhaps Arthur Lewis was being a little too dramatic when he suggested that: 'The central problem in the theory of economic growth is to understand the process by which a community is converted from being a 5 per cent to a 12 per cent saver—with all the changes in attitudes, in institutions and in techniques which accompany this conversion.'[2] But it is evident that *some* increase in the savings-ratio must form part of the process of growth.

We can demonstrate this most readily by assuming that the capital-output ratio remains unchanged or that it moves gradually to a lower level below which it cannot fall. This implies that the rate of growth of capital and income must be equal to one another and that if there is an acceleration in the one there must sooner or later be a similar acceleration in the other. But the rate of growth of capital is the savings-ratio divided by the capital-output ratio. Hence the more rapid growth in income can only be sustained if the savings-ratio rises proportionately, or if the capital-output ratio falls proportionately, or if there is some combination of changes in the two ratios that produces a similar result.

It is remarkably difficult to trace either process in the statistical record of industrial countries. As far back as the figures go for the United States and the United Kingdom, for example, the savings-ratio appears to be remarkably constant, and there is also little indication of any consistent decrease in the capital-output ratio. But the record does not cover in any adequate way the period of take-off and so does not relate to any sudden acceleration in the rate of economic growth. For Sweden there are indications of a spurt in the savings ratio (or rather, in the ratio of gross domestic fixed capital formation to gross national product) from about 1900 onwards. But the curious feature of the Swedish figures is that, although industrialization was already in full swing and production rising rapidly long before 1900, gross investment

[1] W. W. Rostow, *The Stages of Economic Growth* (Cambridge, 1960), p. 37.
[2] W. A. Lewis, *The Theory of Economic Growth* (London, 1955), p. 226.

up to the middle nineties fluctuated around 9 or 10 per cent of gross national product so that net investment (including capital imports) remained as low as 5–6 per cent of net national income.[1] For Norway, the figures indicate a progressive fall in the savings-ratio from 7 per cent around 1870 to 1–2 per cent at the turn of the century, followed by a rise to 11 per cent in the thirties and 20 per cent in the post-war period.[2]

These figures do not appear very plausible but serve as a reminder of the difficulty in obtaining empirical verification to which I have already referred. So far as they do, they imply that a rise in the savings-ratio follows rather than precedes the take-off. This is quite conceivable: the first steps in industrialization may not put any great strain on the supply of capital if they are confined to factory production in the less capital-intensive industries. The British cotton textile industry became one of the largest export industries by 1800 on the strength of a total investment of less than £10 m. (roughly equivalent to the national income for a fortnight). Even in the 1870s when the industry employed half a million workers, the capital employed was of the order of £100 m. —about 1 per cent of the national reproducible capital and no more than had been invested abroad in a single year (1872). Yet I should be sceptical of any suggestion that either in Britain or in Scandinavia, it was only manufacturing industry that needed capital or that there was a marked lag in the savings-ratio behind industrial development. It is true that the major capital requirements usually come only with urbanization.[3] But there is plenty of evidence that, even before urbanization, transport was making heavy demands on capital in eighteenth century Britain and in nineteenth century Scandinavia. There are also symptoms of a widening

[1] O. Johannsson, 'Economic Structure and Growth in Sweden, 1861–1953' (paper presented to the Sixth European Conference of the International Association for Research in Income and Wealth, 1959), pp. 23–4.

[2] J. Bjerke, 'Some Aspects of Long-Term Economic Growth of Norway since 1864' (paper presented to the Sixth European Conference of the International Association for Research in Income and Wealth, 1959), p. 64.

[3] In a recent paper on 'The Economics of Housing and Urban Development' (*Journal of the Royal Statistical Society*, 1959) Mr P. A. Stone shows that, of the capital cost of constructing a town for housing 80,000 persons only £11·2 m. out of £85·3 m. would be required for factories (p. 466). This figure, however, is for light industry only and omits the cost of plant and machinery.

and deepening of the channels along which capital flowed before industrialization took hold in Britain. The rate of interest was falling, investment intermediaries were growing and the capital market was better organized.[1] There seems no reason to doubt that there was a genuine rise in thrift.

It is usual to assume that, *before* take-off, the savings-ratio is likely to be about 5 per cent. This assumption is usually supported by doubtful figures for a variety of countries, reinforced by 'partially subjective judgment'.[2] But why 5 per cent rather than nil? If countries save 5 per cent of their income in static conditions, why should it seem difficult for them to save a further 5 per cent when there are genuine reasons for accumulation?

Let us imagine a country in which population and the standard of living, although fluctuating from one generation to another, remain within narrow limits over the centuries. In parallel to the Malthusian checks on the growth of population there would be a set of checks on the growth of capital. War and fire would destroy, and fashion would corrode, any fixed assets, and ceremony would draw on current stocks, so that the need for thrift would never quite die out. The horizon of human life has rarely been so circumscribed, or the passion for self-perpetuation so feeble, that all inclination to build for posterity vanished. There has always been, in pre-industrial societies, some slack in the use of resources and no complete atrophy of the will to accumulate.

If, therefore, we seek to explain the more rapid growth of capital there is no need to present the change in savings habits in semi-miraculous terms. It is reasonable to assume that it has its origin in a new perception of the utility of capital accumulation and a new willingness to accord it priority over other, non-productive, uses of resources. The

[1] See, for example, L. S. Pressnell, 'The Rate of Interest in the Eighteenth Century', in L. S. Pressnell, ed., *Studies in the Industrial Revolution* (London, 1960); G. S. L. Tucker, *Progress and Profits in British Economic Thought* (Cambridge, 1959), and T. S. Ashton, *Economic Fluctuations in England 1700–1800* (Oxford, 1959).

[2] See, for example, Rostow, op. cit., pp. 43–5. The lowest figures, cited from the Office of Intelligence (*sic*) Research of the Department of State appear to show *gross* investment as low as 5 per cent of gross national production in Ceylon and Afghanistan. On the other hand, Burma is credited with a ratio of net capital formation to net domestic product of over 7 per cent in 1938 *plus* net capital exports equal to 11·5 per cent of net domestic product. Mexico, which—unlike Burma—is presumed to have taken-off, had a ratio of net capital formation to net domestic product of only 7·2 per cent in 1950.

pre-conditions of a successful take-off imply a transformation in both respects.

There may, for example, have been heavy expenditure by the government and the richer classes for non-economic purposes—notably defence, religion, monuments and display. Most countries that have staged a successful take-off have enjoyed an antecedent period of domestic peace which prevented the periodic destruction of physical assets and gave greater security to investment. The comparative freedom of the nineteenth century from war must have contributed to ease the financial problems of economic development, particularly in the newer countries, permitted a record rate of expansion of international trade, and encouraged a more rapid change-over from agriculture to industry.

The development of a more secular temper can also, Clavanism and the Quakers notwithstanding, speed up capital accumulation either by diverting expenditure from religious endowments or, still more, by removing inhibitions limiting economic endeavour. No Scotsman, contrasting the atmosphere in which Adam Smith was writing (can it have been *before* take-off?) with the atmosphere of a century earlier, can fail to be conscious that in this lay the biggest transformation of all. Similarly, anyone who looks at the pyramids, cathedrals and pagodas that other civilizations have bequeathed, can hardly regard the construction of railways, dams and power stations as imposing an unprecedented burden on a poor community. If capital assets are the limiting factor and yield the full dividend that development brings, they can be had if they are badly enough wanted—not necessarily without social upheaval and certainly not without tribulation.

Where there is a large outlay on ceremony and display, the scope for greater thrift is correspondingly enlarged: a more puritanical attitude can release resources for investment opportunities that either did not previously exist or were only vaguely realized. Once there is a more widespread awareness of the possibilities of development, moreover, new resources are automatically created in the form of human time and effort. In most countries, as is apparent in war-time, the supply of labour is by no means completely inelastic. It is not even indispensable that most of the fruits of the additional effort should accrue to consumption. In agriculture, particularly where there is scope for capital creation through land clearance and reclamation, and where the occupier enjoys security of tenure, extra effort on the part of the cultivator may result in a higher rate of savings and investment which is rarely adequately reflected in the official statistics. This form of capital creation may well be accelerated when population is rising and when new techniques are being introduced: a more rapid increase in income then becomes almost automatically associated with an increase in the savings-ratio.

Similar and more familiar examples of self-finance on an increasing scale are provided by the individual landlord who sets out to improve his estate instead of spending all his rents and by the entrepreneur who ploughs back his profits into an expanding business. The importance of these tendencies, which have their origin in a high expected rate of return, is discussed below in relation to the supplementary rôle of the capital market in providing capital for purposes that are beyond the scope of self-finance or for which self-finance is insufficient.

We must also take account of the way in which the benefits of a higher income are divided between different social groups. It is possible that the main beneficiaries are more given to saving than the rest of the community, although this is a proposition that is usually supported by assertion rather than by evidence. The usual assumption that wage-incomes form a diminishing fraction of total income is, so far as I am aware, quite unsubstantiated. There are other possible mechanisms that might operate so as to increase the savings-coefficient. For example, an acceleration of growth is likely to increase the revenue of the central government almost automatically, through taxation, so that its power to save is simultaneously improved. The fact that it may apply this revenue to education, health services, and so on, rather than to the creation of physical assets, does not detract from but illustrates this enhanced power to meet capital requirements. Again, if capital is very unevenly distributed—as is usually true in pre-industrial countries—the immediate effect of higher investment may be to aggravate this inequality, and this, too, may give rise to a higher rate of saving. A third possible mechanism lies in the creation of business corporations which set aside some part of their revenue for expansion. These corporations may save less than privately-owned businesses of the same size; but, since they draw on savings that would not normally find their way into industry and commerce, they expand the base on which profits are earned and reinvested, and so are likely to raise the general level of savings.

IV

There is no need to lay all the stress, however, on the need for a higher savings-ratio. The alternative possibility of a falling capital-output ratio must also be considered.

We know very little about the magnitude of capital-output ratios in pre-industrial societies. Estimates varying between 6 and 1·5 have been used, not always on the same basis.[1] We also do not know, with any certainty, whether the capital-output ratio falls or rises or remains constant after the 'take-off'. I propose, therefore, to confine myself to a few rather speculative observations.

First of all, it is natural to ask whether we are any less in the dark about the *incremental* capital-output ratio—which seems to many people the relevant one—than about the ratio of the stock of capital to the flow of current output. Recent data, on the whole, suggests a tendency for the incremental ratio to rise progressively.[2] In the USSR this tendency is not so much an observed fact as an article of religion. Yet one may be pardoned for hesitating to accept any such trend, to which the counterpart is likely to be a consistently rising capital-output ratio, as a universal phenomenon. It is, after all, still a widely accepted view that the capital-output ratio tends to remain constant.

There is, of course, no necessary inconsistency between a rising incremental ratio and a constant average ratio. The price of capital goods tends to rise in relation to the price of consumption goods in any economy where the building industry is the principal source of capital goods. This turns the

[1] See, for example, J. Tinbergen, *Design for Development* (IBRD, 1957), p. 74, and G. M. Meier and R. E. Baldwin, *Economic Development* (New York, 1957), p. 340, for estimates within this wide range.

[2] For example, the estimates of the Economic Commission for Latin America suggest that investment rose faster than consumption in the 'fifties (*Economic Survey of Latin America*, 1957, p. 83). For other countries the evidence for post-war years points in the same direction.

terms of trade, so to speak, against saving and requires the use of a rising proportion of real resources in order to maintain a constant ratio of capital to output. Whether this tendency would be very perceptible at an early date of development, with only a slow rate of improvement of productivity and considerable imports of machinery of progressively better design is, however, very doubtful.

Secondly, we have to distinguish between the capital-output ratio for the entire economy including agriculture and the ratio of capital to output in the sectors in which current investment is likely to be concentrated. When land is included in capital, and agricultural output in total output—as seems proper in an economy where agriculture is the main activity—the average capital-output ratio is bound to be fairly high, particularly if land itself has a scarcity value. On the other hand, there may be a much lower capital-output ratio in the rest of the economy where the main expansion is likely to occur. It would then be possible to have a low but rising incremental capital-output ratio in spite of a high average capital-output ratio. That this is not altogether fanciful may be shown from estimates for the United Kingdom made by Miss Phyllis Deane and Mr W. A. Cole. These estimates have been used by Professor Kuznets to yield ratios of capital to national income that remain at 6·4 between 1800 and 1912 when land is included, but rise from 2·9 to 6·0 when land is excluded, from capital. (See Table 1.)

Thirdly, unless we have data covering a long period of time we must always be on our guard against interpreting the *level* of investment as a measure of capital requirements. The recorded level may be quite compatible with a progressive overhauling of arrears of investment and the restoration of a more normal relationship between capital and output; or it may conceal a growing lag of capital accumulation behind long-term norms. The figures for post-war years may prove to be somewhat inflated just as the figures for the inter-war years indicated a disinclination to maintain previous ratios of capital to output.

Fourthly, apart from the special case of agriculture—and the equally important possibility of foreign lending and borrowing—there are wide variations between the different sectors of an economy in the demands which they make on capital. It is very material, therefore, how these sectors expand in relation to one another, and whether there are possibilities of using capital more economically in the more capital-intensive sectors. For example, the capital-output ratio in manufacturing is usually relatively low while the ratio in transport and public utilities is often extremely high. (See Table III.) If manufacturing is able to make some headway before investment in 'social overheads' becomes heavy, the pressure on capital will be very much less than in the opposite situation.

The usual presumption is that there has to be heavy initial outlay on transport, power and other public utilities but that after a successful 'take-off' manufacturing expands more rapidly than those highly capital-intensive activities which, because of indivisibilities of various kinds, are subject to increasing returns. There may be some tendency of this kind: in Canada, for example, the capital-output ratio is said to have fallen from 3 in the late twenties to 2½ in the mid-fifties.[1] If such a tendency does exist, it would imply a particularly severe pressure on capital at the outset, followed by a gradual relaxation at a later stage. But the evidence is fragmentary and Canada is far from typical.

My own view of the most probable course of events is as follows. The capital-output ratio is normally low at the outset, if the value of land is excluded from capital while agricultural output is included in the denominator. At this stage stocks are a large proportion of total capital and what happens to them when development speeds up may be of very great importance. Industry is, *ex hypothesi*, limited in scope so that the capital-output ratio in industry is, to begin with, largely irrelevant. Investment in residential housing tends to lag or to proceed on a do-it-yourself basis, especially in countries where the climate is not exacting. The most obvious bulge in capital requirements is in public utilities of all kinds, and in government building; but if development gets under way, the bulge becomes less bulge-like and investment in public utilities increases progressively. Some increase in non-agricultural investment per unit of total output is likely to occur in at least the early stages of industrialization.

[1] W. C. Hood and A. Scott, *Output, Labour and Capital in the Canadian Economy*, p. 285.

All this abstracts from foreign investment. But of course it is traditionally foreign investors who supply much of the capital required for public utilities and other capital-intensive activities such as mining, metals, and those branches of agriculture that have long periods of gestation. If the capital-output ratio increases, it is usually in the very directions in which it is possible to seek relief by borrowing abroad on comparatively favourable terms.

V

I turn finally to the emergence of growth of the capital market.

Very little has been written in any organized way on the development of the capital market in the early stages of industrialization. There is a tendency for sweeping generalizations to be put forward embracing the quite different experience of different countries and merging the finance of industry with the financing of other, more capital-intensive, activities. Financial intermediaries other than the banks are largely ignored. But the banks did not play quite the same part in British development as they did on the continent. Bank advances were also of more limited importance than seems to be generally assumed; commercial credit, bills of exchange, annuity bonds, mortgages, etc., were all-important long before the growth of modern industry. The development of the new issue market in the nineteenth century has hardly begun to be studied; and about the local markets in which long-term capital was provided through solicitors and other intermediaries in the early days of industrialization we are also very much in ignorance.

The rôle of the capital market seems to me to be given an inadequate place in some theories of economic development that go near to identifying profits with savings. Professor Lewis, for example, regards the growth of profits as the main pre-requisite of a higher savings-ratio and links the growth of profits with the rise of a class interested in making and accumulating money. The same idea underlies Mr Kaldor's model of economic growth in which the whole of the return to capital is automatically re-invested while the whole of labour's income is spent. In such a model the rate of profit is equal to the rate of growth of the economy so that any spurt in growth finds its explanation in a discontinuous increase in the rate of profit.

It is not clear to me how theories of this kind treat debt and rent. If we take British history as a guide, a large part of the net worth of the wealthier classes in the eighteenth century consisted of bonds and land. Land alone formed over half the national capital until nearly the middle of the nineteenth century and national debt was as large in 1825 as the entire stock of capital assets other than land. I see no reason to doubt that most of the savings of the country came from the landowners and rentiers who owned these assets; and the more anyone insists that they were not interested in undertaking real investment themselves the more he is driven to lay stress on the function of the capital market in transferring the use of those savings to successful entrepreneurs either in industry or in commerce.

The evidence that they undertook little or no real investment is far from convincing. Landowners were at least as conspicuous as any other social class in increasing their outlay on 'improvements'. Profit made from trade was already a substantial element in national income and seems to have been reinvested, almost indifferently, in land or in other undertakings. What is true is that industrial expansion, like agricultural improvement, was largely self-financing. But we should not be misled by this. Most of the savings of the country, as the nineteenth century proceeded, passed through the capital market and were not re-invested automatically. We need only think of the public utilities, of government borrowing, of housing and, most clearly of all, of foreign investment, to appreciate this point. Of the total capital of the country round about 1870 industry and commerce probably accounted for no more than the railways and the tenant-farmers together, or than residential housing by itself. In 1914, Britain had more invested abroad than in the whole of her industry and commerce. Ownership of capital may have been highly concentrated, but it was not concentrated in the hands of industrialists.

There is, of course, no question but that, as industrialization proceeds, profits become an increasing and land rent a diminishing proportion of the national income. This is a natural consequence of the change-over from agriculture to industry that attends a rising standard of living and the greater proportionate expansion in industry. There is no need also to dispute that industrial enterprises are more given to the ploughing back of income than agricultural enterprises. This is a reflection of the greater investment opportunities that confront them. Neither proposition, however, implies that landlords are bound to be slow in moving into industrial investment when they see profitable opportunities of doing so: or that industry will generate sufficient *excess* savings to take care of the large non-industrial requirements of capital in a society in process of industrialization and urbanization. These capital requirements can be met only by government agencies out of taxation or from the mass of investors and investment intermediaries through the capital market or out of foreign borrowing.

Which of the first two sources is used depends upon the extent to which a capital market has already developed, while the use of the third depends upon access to an international capital market and readiness to take advantage of that access. In the comparatively rich countries that were industrialized in the nineteenth century, an active bond market, chiefly in government debt, had been in existence before the take-off, and banks and other financial intermediaries were already lending considerable sums to commerce and industry. Even so, the large investments in transport that were necessary frequently involved government finance or government guarantees. This was less true in Britain than elsewhere—canals and railways were financed privately—but even in Britain the government's contribution was far from negligible.[1] It was perhaps unusual for governments to use revenue surpluses for capital formation but the funds which they raised (for example, for railway-building) had no fixed relationship with the level of private profits, especially if profits are so defined as to exclude land rent.

The development of the capital market on anything more than a purely local basis told, almost inevitably, in favour of the large borrower, and it was the large borrower who,

[1] See, for example, Henry Hamilton, 'Economic Growth in Scotland, 1720–1770', *Scottish Journal of Political Economy*, June 1959, for the part played by the government in road-building.

almost inevitably, had recourse to the capital market. The large borrower of a century ago was generally one seeking to finance some form of public utility and unable to raise funds on the necessary scale through private channels. At the same time, the private investor looking for a readily marketable form of investment was drawn to large issues either by governments or by public utilities. This meant that the international capital market which dealt in such issues was more fully developed than the domestic capital market: all the more because limited liability joint-stock companies were a comparatively late innovation and because the small industrialist had usually little need of outside, long-term finance.[1] It is not surprising, therefore, that in the early stages of industrialization capital overflowed national boundaries and that the capital requirements of the railways and other large borrowers were frequently met from abroad. The pressure of capital requirements in the initial stages tended also to be comparatively severe and made itself felt in the most sensitive area. The combination of these two circumstances accounts for the common phenomenon of foreign borrowing during, or soon after, the take-off: a phenomenon particularly evident in the new countries of the Western Hemisphere and Australasia but visible also in Europe.

VI

I am conscious of having dealt very selectively with the issues that we might discuss. In particular, I have set entirely on one side issues of policy such as dominate most discussions about capital formation in under-developed countries. I have not suggested how the rate of capital formation might be speeded up nor what results might follow. A good deal of what I have had to say has been about the experience of countries that are now industrialized and I have used comparatively little data for countries seeking to 'take-off'. Finally, I have said nothing at all about the social impact of capital accumulation: the tensions, the distress, the erratic fluctuations in employment, that accompanied the emergence

[1] Even an institution like the Crédit Mobilier confined its operations largely to public utilities and to a few of the more capital-intensive large-scale undertakings in industry.

of industrial society. But since my function is to initiate, not exhaust, the discussion, I am well content to leave you to demonstrate how much I have left unsaid.

TABLE I
STRUCTURE OF NATIONAL WEALTH OF UNITED KINGDOM, 1800–1927

	1800	1832	1885	1912	1927
			(*percentages*)		
Land	55·0	51·6	16·6	5·7	4·0
Reproducible capita	45·0	48·4	83·4	94·3	96·0
	100·0	100·0	100·0	100·0	100·0
Reproducible capital:					
Buildings	30·7	27·7	24·2	22·6	23·0
Farm Capital	19·3	18·1	5·7	2·2	2·4
Net foreign assets	—	9·7	19·3	29·1	7·9
Railways	—	—	11·6	8·1	4·8
Industrial & Commercial Capital	46·2	41·1	33·0	29·5	49·1
Public property	3·8	3·3	6·3	8·4	12·8
	100·0	100·0	100·0	100·0	100·0
Reproducible capital as proportion of national income	2·9	3·5	7·7	6·0	4·2
Land and reproducible capital as proportion of national income	6·4	7·2	9·2	6·4	4·4

Source: Estimates by Phyllis Deane and W. A. Cole, amended by S. Kuznets.

TABLE II
REPRODUCIBLE CAPITAL OF THE UNITED STATES, 1805–1948

	Inventories	*Non-farm residential*	*Non-agricultural business*	*Agriculture*	*Govt.*	*Consumers' durables*	*Net foreign assets*
		Structures and equipment only					
			(*percentages of total*)				
1805	27·6	17·3	13·8	41·4	3·4	6·9	−10·4
1850	27·4	19·3	27·5	19·3	2·9	7·2	− 3·6
1900	17·4	27·9	31·9	7·9	5·6	10·5	− 1·2
1948	12·4	26·9	24·5	5·4	11·8	12·8	+ 6·2

Source: **R. W. Goldsmith, *The Growth of Reproducible Wealth of the USA from 1805 to 1950*, p. 306.**

TABLE III

U.S. AND CANADA: INDUSTRIAL DISTRIBUTION OF CAPITAL (EXCLUDING HOUSING)

	United States		*Canada*	
	Fixed capital %	*Capital-output ratio*	*Fixed capital* %	*Capital-output ratio*
Agriculture	12·2	1·35	10·8	1·62
Resource industries	16·5	2·09	15·2	3·94
Primary manufacturing	5·9	·38	8·7	2·53
Secondary manufacturing	27·9	·55	18·1	1·69
Transport, storage and communication	23·7	2·55	32·2	8·15
Trade, services and construction	13·8	·34	15·0	1·04
Total fixed capital	100·0		100·0	

Source: W. C. Hood and A. Scott, *Output, Labour and Capital in the Canadian Economy*, p. 266.

CHAPTER 8

The Stages of Economic Growth[1]

I

THE appearance of Professor Rostow's 'non-Communist Manifesto'[2] has already set off a lively controversy, by no means confined to economic historians.[3] It is intended as 'an alternative to Karl Marx's theory of modern history' (p. 2), dramatizing 'not merely the uniformities in the sequence of modernization but also—and equally—the uniqueness of each nation's experience' (p. 1). This talk of Marx and manifestos is not altogether reassuring and leaves the reader in doubt whether the author's aim is to influence future policy or to reorientate historical research. In evoking Marx does Rostow seek to instil the same sense of destiny in the march of events? To what action is his 'manifesto' intended as a spur? Whatever his intention, there will be many who read into his exposition of the take-off a conviction of predestined affluence for all that is as firm (and perhaps as groundless) as the Marxist's faith in a similar affluence achieved by different means.

In opposing his views to those of Marx, Rostow seems to invite us to return to a deserted battleground. It is surely high time that historians abandoned over-simplified models of social causation in terms of isolated variables like class struggle, technological development, climate, and so on. These occupy a position in relation to modern social science not unlike that of myths in relation to primitive scholarship. Myths are at least a step forward from animism. They are more coherent and vivid; they appeal to the imagination; and they accustom the mind to looking for a recurring causal factor in the variety of human experience. But they do consistently

[1] From *The Economic History Review*, Second Series, Vol. XIII, No. 3, 1961.

[2] W. W. Rostow, *The Stages of Economic Growth* (Cambridge, 1960).

[3] The International Economic Association organized a conference at Konstanz in September 1960, on 'The Economics of Take-off into Sustained Growth'. I profited from the views expressed at the conference in the preparation of this essay.

fit the facts. In history as in science, if we are to fit the facts we cannot content ourselves with striking and colourful first approximations. We have to take as our motto: 'Divide and conquer' and frame more modest hypotheses about limited aspects of human behaviour, even if this means that we are obliged to multiply the variables and qualify the conclusions.

I do not mean to imply that Rostow follows Marx into a world of thought in which class struggle is made to explain history as phlogiston used to explain combustion and ether explained electric waves. It happens that he has relatively little to say about class struggle: in which I think him less mistaken than some of his critics, since he is neither unmindful of what brings classes into existence nor of the diversity of ideologies within each class. But he is perhaps too anxious like Marx to dramatize history; not merely to make it dramatic and give it meaning but to reduce it to a set pattern, to compress the texture of events into too narrow a framework of logic.

This causes him, again like Marx, to adopt a stage approach to history. There is nothing wrong with this provided his stages are no more than a convenient classificatory device, pedagogic in intention, designed to show how the major variables in social and economic development operate in different situations. But it is a mistake to imply that these situations stand in a fixed relationship to one another or that this relationship can be explained in terms of one or two all-embracing variables, whether exclusively economic or not. An approach to history in these terms may make good drama or supply the element of myth required for a popular manifesto; but it does not make good theory, or, for that matter, good history.

In another context, Rostow cites the example of trade cycle theory in which successive cyclical fluctuations can be submitted to analysis in terms of the interaction of a limited number of variables. But this is not a correct analogy. The trade cycle is itself a limited field of study; the hypotheses which economic theory supplies can be tested by a comparison between the predicted behaviour of the variables and their actual behaviour in the full recognition that a large number of other variables, all irrelevant to the cyclical character of economic fluctuations, give rise to important divergences in individual cycles. In explaining the movement of entire economies, no such segregation is possible: the variables are not exclusively economic and although some are more important than others in any particular situation, it is impossible to predict in advance which variables will assume major importance as the situation develops. Moreover, although Rostow draws attention to some of the characteristics of the successive stages of economic growth, he does not put forward any model of the interaction of the variables at each stage such as a trade cycle theorist is driven to devise. There are no definitions of the successive stages that admit of their identification by reference to verifiable criteria. We are not offered an inner logic of the stage-by-stage development comparable with trade cycle theory but rather a series of inductive generalizations that have more in common with the insight by which the *existence* of the trade cycle came to be recognized.

One of the great weaknesses of a stage approach to history is that it provokes but cannot answer the question: what comes next? The engine of growth in the Marxist system is assumed to break down completely when capitalism fulfils its destiny; Marx has nothing to say about the laws of motion of a post-capitalist society. In Rostow's exposition, the last, but presumably not the final, stage is an era of high mass consumption. Although he broods on what lies beyond affluence, he cannot tell us what stages have yet to come and turns quickly away from the unknown problems of the future to dwell on the dilemmas of the present.

His treatment of these dilemmas, and the very fact that they remain dilemmas, demonstrate how uneasily the rôles of historian and prophet are combined. For the dilemmas arise only to a limited extent from the fact that different countries are at different stages of economic development; and they are not necessarily altered by the acceptance or rejection of the notion of five successive stages of growth unless one interprets this notion far more mechanically than Rostow does.

Thus when he comes to present-day problems the interest of what he says is largely independent of the view of history by which it is preceded; the reader may admire his insight without feeling that it derives from the stages-of-growth analysis.

II

The stages of economic growth from which the book takes its title are five in number. There is first 'the traditional society' in which an almost unchanging technology places a ceiling on the level of attainable output per head. In such societies are grouped 'the whole pre-Newtonian world' (p. 5) and those 'post-Newtonian' societies in which modern science and technology are not made use of regularly and systematically.

The second stage is one of transition, in which the pre-conditions for subsequent growth are created. In some countries, settled from Europe and 'born free', this was largely a matter of railway-building and of making it profitable to shift from agriculture and trade into manufacturing. In traditional societies, the most important change required is 'a rise in the rate of investment to a level which regularly, substantially, and perceptibly outstrips population growth' (p. 21). But this is only part of the story. Agriculture has to supply more food for the growing towns; and out of the larger incomes that are yielded by increased agricultural productivity must come an expanding market for manufactures and a larger flow of savings. Social overhead capital has to be accumulated, almost always with substantial help from governments. A new élite must emerge, dedicated to modernization and usually resting on nationalist support.

Then follows the take-off: 'a decisive break-through' in the course of which 'compound interest gets built into the society's structure' (p. 36). By this phrase Rostow means that growth comes to proceed by geometric progression 'much as a savings account if interest is left to compound with principal' (p. 2 *n*). On the basis of suggested dates for nine countries (including Russia) that had taken-off by 1914, the period of take-off is said to last for about twenty years.

The fourth stage—the drive to maturity—occupies a longer period, continuing until 'more or less sixty years after the . . . beginning of take-off' (p. 60). This stage is defined as 'the period when a society has effectively applied the range of (then) modern technology to the bulk of its resources' (p. 59).

After technological maturity, a balance has to be struck between three possible objectives: 'the national pursuit of external power and influence'; the welfare state and a less energetic attempt to maximize output; an expansion of consumption levels, notably through mass consumption of durable goods. Pursuit of the third of these objectives distinguishes the next stage of growth—the era of high mass consumption. This stage does not necessarily follow immediately on the achievement of maturity: the British case is cited to show that 'a certain level of income per head' (p. 68) is also required. On the other hand, the stage of high mass consumption may be reached in advance of technological maturity if income levels are high enough, as in Canada and some other countries.

The second half of the book, which has more plainly the character of a manifesto, purports to apply the stages-of-growth analysis to the twentieth century development of the American and Russian economies, and to the problems of war and peace in the modern world. I say 'purports' because it is very doubtful how far the second half of the book is a logical sequel to the first. This would be more apparent if Rostow limited his analysis to the emergence of industrial society and did not make its subsequent evolution into a spurious fifth stage as if it were of equal significance with the transition from pre-industrial or 'traditional' to modern forms of social organization. It is only his conviction that this further evolution towards an age of high mass consumption will be shared by communist societies that gives continuity to his argument: this and his perception that international economic inequality can be an incitement to foreign aggression.

III

There should be no need to pay tribute to the vigour of Rostow's thinking nor to the skill with which he marshals data from many different countries in support of his generalizations. It is obvious, too, that this is not his last word and that he is setting out his ideas boldly and without all the additional evidence that he might supply in a larger book. The question is, however: does he help us to understand 'the sweep of modern history'?

Let me run over some of the more obvious difficulties. First of all, have we an adequate basis for generalization? The relevant data relate mainly to a dozen countries or so over the past century or two. Even for this dozen countries, the key statistics, until comparatively recently, were highly imperfect: for example, the course of real wages and the movement of savings-ratios are open to serious dispute for all countries before 1913 and so far as I know there is no reliable cost of living index number for any country covering the whole of the nineteenth century.

Next, what precisely is a stage? When we are dealing with biological phenomena, we can mark off stages that are either absolute like birth and death, or follow a recognizable sequence like childhood, adolescence, maturity, etc. Individual experience in any one stage departs from a standard pattern; but the important point is that there *is* a pattern, and that this pattern can be defined in terms of invariable characteristics each capable of identification by prescribed tests. Rostow's stages are not of this kind. We may recognize the difference that exists between what he calls traditional societies and modern industrial societies and we may lay down an analytic basis for the identification of one or other type of society. But what are we to make of the intermediate stages on which Rostow insists or of the stage of high mass consumption into which industrial societies are said to be moving? Can a country fall back into the stage of preconditions after an abortive take-off, or take-off more than once, or keep fluttering as if it were about to take-off without ever doing so? Is the sequence invariable, so that one can tell in advance what lies ahead? And how can one tell whether the transition from one stage to another is complete. When Rostow gives dates for the beginning and end of take-off, by what criteria, open to corroboration by other historians, does he select these dates? Or if the take-off is so plainly decisive and discontinuous, how can one ever need to revise the dates first put forward (as Rostow may yet find it necessary to do)?

Perhaps the most doubtful stage is the last. It is suggestive that Rostow nearly always refers to it as an 'age' or an 'era', rarely explicitly as a stage. If he were to use the phrase 'the age of the automobile' how much of his meaning would be lost? Such a phrase would both convey the tone of a period in which the diffusion of the private automobile has dominated social intercourse and emphasize one of the principal economic factors transforming economic and social life in industrial countries. But it would not imply the kind of revolution in human existence that industrialism has brought. Rostow himself has in mind other consumers' durables as well as automobiles and he refers several times to housing. But it is difficult to see any special significance in the fact that at higher levels of income people show an elastic demand for durable goods. A much more significant fact is the tendency in modern times for rising incomes to go with greater equality—a fact that Rostow does not analyse and that in itself helps to account for the mass consumption of durable goods.

And what is the significance of the threefold choice between national power, social welfare, and high mass consumption in the final stage, when the same choice has had to be made all along the path of growth? If the choice is a free one it need not fall on high mass consumption. Is this then a stage that may never be reached?

The previous stage—the drive to (technological) maturity—gives rise to further queries, particularly if an attempt is made to set precise limits to it: what meaning can one attach, for example, to his contention that Canada reached technological maturity in 1950? It may well be that the manufacturing sector of the Canadian economy was relatively small fifty years ago; but how could it possibly be maintained that the backlog of unabsorbed technology was markedly greater than it is today? Again, the technology appropriate to low levels of income and to the relative factor prices and market conditions that go with low levels of income is by no means the same as the technology that becomes appropriate once incomes have risen. The Indian cotton industry, for example, may be effectively applying 'the range of modern technology' appropriate to local circumstances without making use of the techniques currently in favour in the United States. There is some danger of circularity, therefore, in a definition of maturity in terms of the application of 'modern' technology to the bulk of a country's resources since in one sense this application may be as much a consequence as a cause of development. The real issue is the closeness of the links between the transnational process of technological innovation and the national process of absorbing advances in technique. One ought surely to think of the permeation of a backward society with modern ideas, a process that is necessarily uneven and difficult to measure, often highly localized, and expressing itself only gradually in the application of these ideas.

The stage that has struck the public mind most forcibly is undoubtedly that of the take-off: largely, no doubt, because the aeronautical metaphor—prolonged in the phrase 'into, self-sustained growth'—suggests at once an effortlessness and a finality congenial to modern thought. The reactions of historians and economists have been less favourable. They have grown accustomed to emphasizing the continuity of historical change, to tracing back to a previous age the forces producing a social explosion, and to explaining away the apparent leaps in economic development. They are inclined, therefore, to regard Rostow as a latter-day Toynbee, stressing a discontinuity that is no more than symptomatic of the underlying forces at work and making the symptoms more decisive (if, indeed, symptoms can be said to be decisive) than they really were. Is there a genuine discontinuity rather than a simple acceleration of growth? If so, in what form does the discontinuity show itself? In what sense does the discontinuity herald a decisive break with the past? And is it conceivable that this discontinuity is of such a character that it can be identified with a precise span of time, normally twenty years?

It may well be that Rostow could make a case for a kink in the rising curve of industrial output early in the process of industrialization. But the evidence which he provides in this book is not very convincing and rests largely on the experience of the British cotton industry. This was not a large industry: it has been estimated by Deane and Cole that in the 1760s it accounted for less than one-half of 1 per cent of the English national income and in the early 1800s for between 4 and 5 per cent. This does not rob its growth of significance; but it does suggest that at a time when the national income was growing by between 1 and 2 per cent *per annum*, cotton can have played only a limited rôle.[1]

[1] I do not want to suggest that it was only in the cotton industry that there was a marked acceleration between 1780 and 1800. The volume of exports, for example, grew by over 6 per cent per annum in those two decades, a rate far above any recorded in earlier decades or in those immediately following. But as the annual figures show (see the graph in Schlote's *British Overseas Trade*, p. 44), exports fell very heavily during the American War of Independence and were no higher in 1780 than thirty years previously while in 1800 they were nearing a peak, so that the climb from 1780 to 1800 is quite unrepresentative of the general trend. It is just as true to say that exports doubled between 1730 and 1770 and doubled again between 1770 and 1810.

Even if there was a kink, it seems a little perverse to attribute it to new factors operating within the period 1780–1800 to the exclusion of other factors that had been operating over a much longer period with cumulative force—for example, the improvements in agriculture. If it is necessary to point to new factors that began to operate from 1770 onwards it seems much more sensible to put James Watt's work on the steam engine in the forefront since it was the steam engine that raised the technological ceiling over a wide area of the economy and gave to the ensuing hundred years their truly decisive character. The 'march of compound interest' was far more the march of mechanical power and the engines that supplied it than of any individual industry or 'leading sector'. But Watt did not invent the steam engine nor were his innovations the last in its evolution. Watt's contribution had the discontinuity of a mutation; and the statistics of output in the ensuing period may reflect this and other acts of invention in a discontinuous leap. One may, if he chooses, speak of the 'take-off' of the steam engine and group all earlier improvements to it as pre-conditions. But is this not a little artificial? Even if one limits the argument to Britain, one has to take a long view in order to explain the burst of innovations that set off what may still be thought of as the industrial revolution. No one doubts—least of all Rostow—that innovation is a social process and that its acceleration in the eighteenth century was associated with what he calls for short 'Newtonian science' (it has, in fact, very little to do with Newton and is not simply a matter of science): a new way of looking at the world and a new ambition to change it. The self-sustaining character of development derives from this outlook and ambition, which issue in a continuous effort of technological improvement. But if so, why deflect attention to the *stage* at which this effort bears sudden fruit rather than concentrate on the effort itself: on the change in ideas and the ways in which these ideas took hold of economic activity?

The same point can be expressed differently by asking how one is expected to distinguish between the pre-conditions and the conditions of economic growth. Rostow traces the beginning of take-off in most countries to a 'particular sharp stimulus' (p. 36). One may question some of the examples he gives—the German revolution of 1848, for example. One may also observe that the rest of his examples either involve a sudden change in market opportunities due to events abroad or attribute a special importance to deliberate government policies. But the market opportunities that result from agricultural improvement have earlier been relegated to the stage of pre-conditions; and government policies directed to the creation of social overhead capital are also assigned to the same stage. What distinguishes the stimuli that introduce a take-off and the stimuli that do no more than usher in the stage of pre-conditions?

Pre-conditions are, after all, a logical rather than a chronological concept. Must all of them ante-date the take-off? There is no reason to suppose that agriculture has ever completely fulfilled its required rôle *in advance* of the spurt in growth that Rostow calls take-off or that social overhead capital has to reach some definite stage *before* take-off. On the contrary, the experience of most countries has been that whether agricultural expansion started earlier or not, it continued into the period of industrialization and constituted a large proportion of total growth. Similarly, social overhead capital is needed more than ever as industrialization proceeds. How could one ever suppose otherwise if railways have been one of the most frequent 'leading sectors' in the take-off?

But if the various stages overlap, what then is the meaning of a 'stage'? The less tidy the chronology the more one is driven back to the logic: to the isolation of the decisive factors that initiate growth and give it its 'on-going character'. When we enquire what these factors are we are offered three.

The first is 'a rise in the rate of productive investment from, say, 5 per cent or less to over 10 per cent of national income' (p. 39). This is a view that has been expressed by other economists, notably Arthur Lewis, although no one else, of course, has associated it with the period of take-off. Rostow introduces the idea into his analysis of the stage of pre-conditions as well as of take-off so that one is left a little in doubt whether savings habits are assumed to alter before or during take-off. I suspect that, like many economists who have embraced the idea from first principles rather than after empirical investigation, he has found his initial enthusiasm for it evaporating on further reflection and that he now lays more stress on the other conditions that he gives. However that may be, it is abundantly clear, in spite of the limitations of the statistical data, that the periods during which he supposes economies to have taken-off did not witness a decisive break in savings or investment ratios, that in some countries at least the evidence tells against any antecedent rise, and that the normal experience has been a gradual increase in the ratio of savings and domestic investment to income as development proceeded. There is nothing in the historical record to justify the quite exceptional emphasis laid on a sharp increase in this ratio, however measured, at the outset of rapid growth.

The second condition is the emergence of leading sectors in manufacturing. On the importance of the idea of leading sectors Rostow insists again and again. It is the 'analytic bone-structure' (p. 13) of his stages of growth. 'It is the fact that sectors tend to have a rapid growth-phase, early in their life', he argues, 'that makes it useful to regard economic history as a sequence of stages' (p. 14). Or again, 'growth proceeds by repeating endlessly, in different patterns, with different leading sectors, the experience of the take-off' (p. 53).

Rostow's conception of leading sectors is not unlike what the Scandinavian economists have called 'development blocks'. The growth of any one industry is linked in various ways with the growth of other industries on which its activities impinge: so that if its costs fall sharply or the demand for its products accelerates, the effects ramify over a wide sector. Of these ramifications Rostow provides many interesting examples. They are undoubtedly relevant to a dynamic theory of production; but what is their precise relevance to the take-off? Does it really matter whether one industry leaps ahead and drags others along behind it or whether a large group of industries advance on a broad front under impulses peculiar to each?

To this, if I understand him, Rostow's reply is that the historical experience has been otherwise: that at any one time there has been a particular industry that has provided the real momentum of economic development. It has varied widely in the early stages of growth in different countries; and in any one country there has been a succession of leading sectors after take-off, the power to generate fresh leading sectors being the acid test of self-sustained growth. It would seem, too, that Rostow would admit to the category of leading sectors only an extremely limited group—not more, perhaps, than one in each generation. In Britain this would mean accepting the cotton textile industry at one end of industrialization, the motor-car industry at the other, and not more than three or four between—railways, steel, and electricity, for example.

If this is a correct interpretation, it seems to me highly misleading. The growth of productivity in an economy neither has been nor is governed by the development of leading sectors in this sense. The cotton textile industry was not big enough to dominate the growth of output in Britain in the eighteenth century nor is the motorcar industry today, even when one takes account of all the changes that flow from the use of motor-cars. Of course there are major breakthroughs in each generation and one can single these out and call the group of industries affected a leading sector. But the cumulative effect of unspectacular and unrelated improvements in technique across the whole industrial field may well be of much greater importance.[1]

Even if industrial change does take the form of a series of leading sectors, how does this help us to understand the take-off? We are given no basis on which to recognize a leading sector *ex ante*. What connection is there between the conception and later stages? Merely that there must have been two or more leading sectors before maturity is reached and that a particular leading sector—the motor-car industry—characterized the age of high mass consumption? Or is the significance of leading sectors no more than that this is the *modus operandi* of sustained growth irrespective of the stages through which such growth subsequently moves? And why must the leading sectors be in manufacturing? If railway-building can qualify, why not retail distribution or agriculture? One may sympathize with Rostow's insistence on the need to dig below the aggregate in order to uncover the real forces at work in the

[1] Rostow's aim may be to remind us that all growth is necessarily spasmodic: this is true in biology as well as in economics and accounts for the discontinuities—the bursts, the retardations, and the pauses—that are an inevitable feature of the process. Or if we prefer an analogy from physics, only a quantum theory of development can do justice to the facts. To this extent I agree with him.

economy; one may accept his emphasis on industrial linkages and on the far-reaching consequences of a few major developments; but one may still question whether this provides the analytic bone-structure that he claims.

Rostow's third condition for take-off is 'the existence or quick emergence of a political social and institutional framework which . . . gives to growth an ongoing character' (p. 39). This is the most baffling condition of the three. How it differs from a pre-condition is hard to understand, and understanding is not assisted when two paragraphs later it seems to have been transformed into a pre-condition. The framework indispensable to take-off is defined in terms of its success not of any antecedent properties except perhaps the 'capacity to mobilize capital from domestic sources' (which takes us back to the first condition). But a definition in these terms tells us nothing about the factors at work since we can only deduce their existence from the fact of take-off, never the likelihood of take-off from the ascertained fact of their existence.

In the light of all this, does Rostow's approach help us to understand what went on in any individual case of industrialization or made it easier to see what a country seeking to industrialize itself should do? It would be absurd to answer these questions with a blank negative; a great deal of what Rostow says is undoubtedly helpful. But this is so, in my view, in spite of, rather than because of, the stage approach which he adopts.

If I take, for example, the British case I find it confusing to have the years 1782–1802 given an almost miraculous significance. I want to know what allowed the British economy to 'get up steam' and if it is alleged to have happened in two critical decades I want to know why. I know of no evidence that growth was more self-sustaining in 1802 than it had been in 1782. The issues that seems to me important do not relate to this span of time at all, and they do not all relate to the same span of time. What, for example, was the rôle of foreign trade and expanding markets as compared with technological innovation? Were the two connected and if so, how? What part did population increase play and how was this interconnected with technological change, whether industrial, or medical? Did the standard of living rise throughout or was there a set-back in real wages associated with more rapid capital accumulation? Who were the innovators and from what social classes were they drawn? And so on.

In unravelling these problems economists and historians have much to offer one another and Rostow has made his own contribution to both of them. But in the present volume he seems to me to have made the Muse of History lie on the bed of Procrustes.

CHAPTER 9

The Investment League[1]

IN the International League Tables in which it has become fashionable to pillory the failings of the British economy, special prominence is usually given to the relatively low level of investment, particularly in manufacturing industry. It is not so many years since prominent business men and economists were arguing that British industry was living on its capital and that the current rate of capital formation was less than sufficient to cover depreciation, measured in terms of replacement cost. This is a view which it would be impossible to sustain now, whatever may have been the position in the first year or two after the war. The widely-held idea that the rate of capital formation is lower than before the war is equally unfounded. There is more substance in the comparison, on which pessimists have fallen back, between investment in the United Kingdom and in other countries in Western Europe. An edge is given to this comparison by fears of German competition on the one hand and by the rapid expansion of Soviet industry on the other, for there is no doubt of the high rate of investment in both these countries. This investment must contribute powerfully to economic growth and prompt the supposition that a comparable rate of investment in the United Kingdom would provide an equal stimulus to expansion.

Before any such supposition can be entertained, however, it is necessary to be sure of one's ground. How reliable are the 'league tables' and what exactly do they demonstrate? Is capital formation lower in Britain than in other countries and, if it is, is this necessarily a public misfortune? Is it demonstrable that additional capital would contribute as effectively to an improvement of the British standard of living as it appears to have contributed elsewhere?

First of all, it is scarcely necessary to emphasize how tenta-

[1] From *Progress*, Summer 1957.

tive must be any international comparisons of magnitudes which, however carefully estimated, do not refer to exactly the same thing for each country and are generally subject to considerable margins of error. A comparison of the *level* of investment in different countries is particularly suspect since it is impossible to be sure that repairs and maintenance are treated on a uniform basis. Where figures are published net of depreciation, there may be little or no indication of the way in which depreciation has been estimated: whether, for example, it is based on historical or replacement cost. It is perhaps more satisfactory to base comparisons on the *change* in investment since some fixed date, but this requires the selection of a starting-point that can be regarded as normal for each of the countries, and it is not easy to find such a point of departure.

One commonly quoted comparison which appeared in the *Economic Survey of Europe in* 1955 is shown in Table I. After examining such a table—particularly the first column—the average reader is tempted to conclude that there must be something very wrong with the British economy, that the old habits of thrift and productive investment have been thrown overboard, and that the competitive power of British industry will steadily evaporate for lack of adequate new investment.

TABLE I

CAPITAL ACCUMULATION IN WESTERN EUROPEAN COUNTRIES IN 1954

	Net fixed investment as percentage of net national product	*Net saving as percentage of net national product*
Norway	22	14
Finland	21	23
Austria	15	15
Western Germany	15	20
Switzerland	14	—
Netherlands	13	18
Denmark	13	12
Italy	12	11
Sweden	11	10
Greece	10	2
Turkey	9	6
France	8	10
Belgium	6	8
United Kingdom	6	8

Yet superficially, whatever fears one may have for the future, the British economy does not seem to be doing so very badly; production is increasing, exports are growing, the standard of living is rising quite as fast as in the United States and at the same sort of rate as in most other countries of Western Europe, although not as fast as in Western Germany. Can it really be true that a country like Norway invests over thrice as high a proportion of its national income as the United Kingdom and nearly twice as high a proportion as the Netherlands? Must one believe with the Economic Commission for Europe (ECE) that the United Kingdom is the only country in Western Europe to be setting aside a smaller proportion of its national income than before the war to add to its stock of fixed assets?

It makes some difference whether one takes the first or second column of Table I as the basis of comparison. The first column relates only to investment in fixed capital (i.e. factories, power stations, dwelling houses) and excludes additions to stocks and working capital (which are by no means negligible in an expanding economy and are included in the second column). The first column takes credit for all fixed capital investment, whether financed out of domestic savings or from loans and grants by foreigners; but it excludes loans made to foreigners and current investment abroad, although such investment draws on the national savings just as effectively as capital formation at home and for purposes that may be just as important. The second column counts in all investment, whether at home or abroad, that has been financed out of domestic savings. This column is thus a more adequate index of the investment effort that countries are supporting out of their own means and the order in which countries appear in the second column is more in keeping with general expectations. It is not surprising, for example, to find Finland, Western Germany and the Netherlands heading the list and Greece and Turkey at the bottom; whereas it *is* surprising to find Belgium and the United Kingdom at the bottom in the first column and Norway at the top.

The figures given by ECE also wear a different complexion if taken in conjunction with comparable figures for 1938. Savings formed a much lower proportion of the national income of the United Kingdom in that year—according to ECE the proportion was only half as large as in 1954—while in the Scandinavian countries for which ECE gives estimates the proportion was about the same in 1938 as in 1954. This evidence suggests that the United Kingdom might stand a great deal higher in the 'league tables' if the score were to be registered in terms of relative improvement over pre-war years.

This point is pursued in Table II which is based on data published by another international organization, the Organization for European Economic Co-operation (OEEC). In this table, the figures of investment are given gross of depreciation (i.e. no deduction is made for the replacement and renewal of fixed assets used up during the year); this seems the safer basis of comparison in view of the quite different methods that countries use in calculating depreciation and the unreliability of the available estimates. 'Investment' in Table II also includes additions to stocks and the balance of loans and investments abroad over those of foreigners.

The pattern, both in 1938 and in 1955, is the familiar one, with the United Kingdom as usual at the bottom. But the gap between the United Kingdom and other countries now appears to be rather narrower than before the war. Gross investment shows an increase from 11 to 17 per cent of gross national income and this increase is proportionately larger than for any other country except the Netherlands. No one would inter-

TABLE II

CAPITAL FORMATION AND POPULATION GROWTH IN OEEC COUNTRIES, 1938–55

	Gross Investment as percentage of Gross National Income (at market prices)					*Percentage Increase in population June 1938–Dec. 1955*
	1938	1948	1950	1955	*1955 as Percentage of 1938*	
Norway	27·9	27·4	26·1	27·6	99	17·2
Western Germany	20·6[1]	—	23·7	28·3	138	29·3
Italy	18·1	17·8	17·7	21·2	117	11·9
Sweden	16·4	17·6	20·5	20·0	123	15·8
United States	15·7	20·5	20·2	18·6	119	28·3
Netherlands	14·2	13·7	22·0	27·1	190	24·6
Denmark	13·6	16·7	17·7	18·9	139	17·9
United Kingdom	10·7	13·4	14·7	16·9	158	8·1

[1] 1936 *Source:* OEEC *General Statistical Bulletin*

pret this as a demonstration that the United Kingdom has done as well as most countries in post-war investment or that the Netherlands has outstripped all other countries. But it does suggest that the United Kingdom's position is not worse than it used to be and that the position of the Netherlands is a great deal better.

The order in which countries appear in Table II is very much the same in 1955 as in 1938, with the conspicuous exception of the Netherlands. Such figures as are available for an earlier period, in the twenties, show a similar order. Since investment is simply savings looked at from a different angle, this may mean that decade after decade some countries are consistently more thrifty than others. But it also provokes suspicion. Can it be that some countries have higher ratio of investment to income because they measure investment more generously? Or, to put the point the other way round, may not the upkeep of existing capital in a country so long industrialized as Britain absorb resources which in other countries go towards new assets? This upkeep, which often involves modernization and improvement, normally does not rank as capital expenditure and is excluded from figures of capital formation.

In a period when the cost of replacing fixed assets has risen disproportionately to other costs, this point is of particular importance. There is a natural tendency, especially if no fresh capacity is needed, to prolong the life of existing assets, even at the cost of extra expenditure on maintenance and repair. This reduces the estimate of fixed capital formation and no compensating addition is made for extra repairs, even where these make renewal unnecessary.

It is difficult to judge how far these considerations go to explain the differences shown in Table II. My own view is that they are far from negligible but that they are insufficient to account for the wide gap between the United Kingdom and, say, Western Germany and the Netherlands. This gap must correspond to differences in the pressure to save and invest. The final column of Table II points to one such difference frequently overlooked. Population has grown less in Britain since 1938 than in almost any other country; it has increased enormously in Western Germany, the Netherlands and the United States.

It needs no profound knowledge of economics to grasp the interconnection that must exist between the growth of capital and the growth of population and employment, although the complexities of that inter connection may escape the layman and indeed have received far too little attention from the professional economist. This is most obvious in housing, which normally absorbs about a quarter of gross fixed investment in peace-time. A sharp increase in population, by creating a shortage of dwelling houses, almost inevitably reacts, not only at the rate at which houses are built, but also on the finance available for their construction. However great the shortage in Britain, it was obviously far greater in post-war Germany, flooded with refugees and devastated by war. When one considers the extensive damage that Germany had to make good after the war, the need to expand industrial capacity in step with a swollen population and the overcrowding that had to be overcome, it is obvious that the incentive to accumulate was far more compelling there than in the United Kingdom. The high rate of interest in Germany, where industry has had to pay 10 per cent for debenture capital on first-class security, is perhaps no exact measure of the shortage of capital; but it is significant that industry has been willing to raise capital on those terms and that industrial investment has been greater than in the United Kingdom where capital could be raised more cheaply.

If population is not increasing, every fresh asset brought into existence adds to the stock of capital per head; but if the population is growing fast, even a high rate of saving may fail to keep pace with it. In the days before the First World War, about half the current savings of the United Kingdom went to maintain capital per head and most of the rest was invested abroad. Now that population is growing much more slowly and investment abroad has dwindled to much smaller proportions, there is a larger margin for increasing capital per head, with the advantages of higher productivity and improved amenities that this increase brings.

International comparisons of investment cannot be made really satisfactorily on a 'league table' basis; the rate of investment in one country is no sure guide to the rate appropriate in other countries. How much a country should invest must depend on the opportunities open to it, the arrears from which it is suffering, the growth in the population which it has to house and employ. It is not the volume of investment, nor even the proportion of income saved and invested that matters, but the gains that would flow from *additional* investment. These gains are not the same at different stages of economic development. A country still undergoing industrialization, or with large tracts of territory still to be opened up and fitted out with transport and power facilities and all the other overheads of a modern economy, is far more likely to make large demands on capital than an old country in which the major transformation has already been accomplished. The first may find itself obliged to borrow abroad, as North America did fifty years ago, while the second has capital to spare and lends or invests abroad as Britain did for nearly a century. It is no reflection on the older country, and no measure of its economic prospects, if in these circumstances it accumulates capital less rapidly than the newer country. The real criterion is whether it is being unduly niggardly in the use of capital within its own borders in the sense that it is failing to make capital available for assets that would yield a considerable return.

This is a criterion that is far from easy to apply. One has to rely not on statistics, but on general impressions. It is not enough, for example, to show that new assets might bring a relatively high financial return; part of the return to new investment is taken in tax by the government, part may accrue to the wage-earners who operate the new assets created, and part is likely to be enjoyed by consumers because of a reduction in costs or through increased competition. These additional returns may exceed the direct financial return to the investor; but since investors make their decisions largely on the basis of the direct return expected, the level of private investment is likely to be lower than the social interest would warrant, and the investment undertaken by the state may be inadequate to make up the difference or may distort the pattern.

These are generalities. But they cannot be ignored on that account by someone who claims to have *proof* that investment in Britain is not only less than elsewhere but is less *adequate*. It is doubtful whether, given all the uncertainties of definition and measurement and the incomparability of investment opportunities and yield, it is worth having the judgment of any one person as to the adequacy of British compared with foreign rates of investment. I should myself agree that a rather higher rate of investment in the United Kingdom is desirable; but I should rest this judgment much less on the high rates of investment in other countries than on evidence that Britain's need of capital is likely to increase and that arrears have been accumulating in particular directions, notably roads and commercial building. The figures for foreign countries seem to me chiefly of interest as pointing to a world-wide rise in the productivity of capital and a continuing need for high rates of investment. Just as in the deflationary inter-war years nearly every country had to adapt itself to a reduced pressure for capital formation, so now, in an inflationary world, countries have to struggle against a chronic shortage of capital. No doubt inflation aggravates the shortage just as deflation wiped it out; but there is also a more profound causal connection in the opposite sense. The shortage reflects an effort to bring the current stock of capital into line with long-term requirements: to overtake arrears or take advantage of new opportunities for the more intensive use of capital. The effort strains the resources of the community and especially the willingness to postpone consumption and save; it is out of this effort and strain that inflation is born.

There is one divergence between investment in Britain and abroad that is of special significance in this context. For a number of years from 1948 onwards, public saving, mainly through the Budget of the central government, contributed a large proportion of the savings required to meet the cost of current investment. Later this proportion dwindled, while in many European countries it grew. On the other hand, capital formation by public authorities, including public corporations, has grown and looks like continuing to grow. Thus the government is being brought into more vigorous competition for capital with the private sector of the economy; if the public authorities (again including public corporations) met more of their capital needs without borrowing, investment could be raised without causing inflation, or forcing up interest rates.

At this point we may turn to a second comparison which is

often made. Some types of capital asset have only a rather remote connection with industrial efficiency and the competitive power of industry. Dwelling houses, for example, usually account for a high proportion of fixed capital investment; yet if the number of houses built were cut drastically—as in war-time—industrial production, in the short run at least, would not suffer greatly. If the scale of investment were entirely satisfactory, therefore, the pattern might still be unsatisfactory in the sense that the kind of investment of most importance to productive industry were inadequately represented. If we confine our attention to those kinds of investment, is Britain lagging badly behind her chief competitors?

Most people, when they think of productive investment, have in their mind's eye a factory of some kind—investment in manufacturing industry, not in schools or roads or even power stations. They are surprised to be told that such investment rarely exceeds a quarter of the total and that other kinds of investment—in transport or power, for example—may play a more important rôle in raising productivity and the standard of living. It is by no means obvious that an international comparison of investment in manufacturing industry is more significant than a comparison of total investment. But since many people think it is, it may be worth making.

Fortunately, an elaborate comparison has been made by Dr Barna of the National Institute of Economic and Social Research. In a recent article in *The Banker* he estimates that, before the war, capital per head in manufacturing industry used to average $1,300 in the United Kingdom and $1,800 in Western Germany and that it is now $2,200 in the United Kingdom and $2,300 in Western Germany (all these figures being in dollars of 1950 purchasing power). In other words, he finds evidence of a quite dramatic change in the amount of capital invested per worker in British industry compared with a much smaller change in Western Germany. The figures for the United States, $4,200 in 1937–38 and $5,200 in 1956, while far above the British and German figures, show a more gradual increase than in either of these countries. In all three countries the total stock of manufacturing assets has doubled since 1938.

Dr Barna does not dispute that fixed assets are growing faster in German industry than in British or American industry; but he points out that industrial building was on a huge scale in Britain during the war and that much of this building survived for use in peace-time while in Germany industrial capacity was reduced during and after the war without any corresponding boom in new construction. The expenditure of the Treasury in war-time on manufacturing assets was equivalent at current prices to £2,500 m.—about as much as total expenditure on fixed capital by British industry in 1951–54.

This growth in industrial capacity was not accompanied by so large an expansion in manufacturing employment as was occurring in the United States or has occurred since the war in Germany. There are about 20 per cent more workers employed in British industry today than before the war; but in the United States the increase is over 50 per cent and in Western Germany it is nearly 80 per cent. It has not been necessary, therefore, to expand capacity at the same rate, and more of the new assets have been available for increasing the stock of capital per man employed.

Dr Barna's figures suggest that until 1953 new manufacturing assets were being acquired by British industry on a larger scale than German industry but that the rate of construction of new assets marked time in Britain from about 1950 until 1955, while in Germany it doubled over those five years. In 1955–56 there was a fresh surge in industrial investment in the United Kingdom and last year any difference between British and German investment in manufacturing industry seems to have been quite small. British industry, however, is still rather larger than German industry, in terms of employment or output; thus the rate of investment in new manufacturing assets is probably bigger in Germany.

While the emphasis that has been given to new investment in Britain in the past few years is healthy, it is time that less attention was paid to comparisons with other countries and more to changes in the pattern of investment within the country. It is more important now to debate the volume of public investment, how it is to be controlled and financed, what pressure it may exert on the capital market, and what the rôle of savings by the public authorities and nationalized industries should be, than to concentrate exclusively on investment by private industry. The experience of the past few years suggests that if the government wants more industrial investment, it is relatively easy to encourage it, but that the more important problem is to make sure that some elbow room is left for expansion without throwing the whole economy out of balance.

CHAPTER 10

Banking in Developing Countries[1]

EVERY country is under-developed in at least some sense of that much abused word. Even in North America and Western Europe there is room for an immense amount of further development: new opportunities of growth open out as rapidly as existing opportunities are seized, and the frontier of technological advance is always at a considerable remove from the more settled territory of commercial exploitation. In most other parts of the world, and especially in Asia and Africa, the process of development takes a different shape and involves far more than a struggle to overtake technological arrears: it amounts rather to the replacement of one civilization by another through a transformation in the outlook, institutions and physical apparatus of the entire society. The transformation in outlook may require, for example, the decay of religious beliefs and taboos, the growth of individualism under the play of market forces, and the attachment of increasing social esteem to economic success. The transformation in institutions embraces the rise of corporate forms of organization, and the emergence of large-scale industry, with all that that implies in town-building and the growth of a labour and capital market. Above all, the physical apparatus of an industrial community has to be created out of limited savings.

It is primarily with the countries where this transformation is in progress that this paper deals. But since the process never quite comes to an end, and the problems of the less developed shade imperceptibly into those of the more developed countries, most of what is said is of wider relevance. The peculiar features of under-developed countries are rarely as peculiar as they seem.

This is particularly true of banking. It may be, as I have been told, that no one has ever successfully defined a bank.

[1] Lecture at the Eleventh International Banking Summer School, St Andrews, Sept. 1958.

But it is also true that a bank is recognizably a bank, whereever it is and whoever runs it, if it does the things that banks do, if, for example, it accepts deposits that are repayable on demand or on short-term, and applies those deposits to making loans for sundry purposes. The job of a bank in any country is to mobilize the odds and ends of savings that are made by large numbers of depositors with a strong liquidity-preference and to make use of these savings by lending them, usually in larger amounts and to a comparatively small number of borrowers, for varying periods and on terms that normally allow of easy realization.

For the banking system as a whole, there is also an essential similarity of function: the banks simultaneously provide the means of payment and constitute the most important source of borrowed money. From this dual rôle flow many dilemmas—dilemmas that are nowhere more acute than in the under-developed countries. For whereas the individual bank is always confronted by the ineluctable necessity never to lend more than the resources at its disposal—although it may exert itself to add to those resources—the banking system as a whole suffers from no such limitation and need only lend in order to generate the wherewithal to lend. Every banking system, like the mugs that used to decorate Victorian mantelpieces, has two faces, one gay, one grim, the first marked 'assets' and the second 'liabilities', and the smile on the one can be no wider than the frown on the other. The gay face is an attractive one which it requires great resolution to turn to the wall: for it is by adding to their assets that the banks can increase the flow of funds to new enterprise and promote economic expansion. The grim face, on the other hand, reminds us of the unpleasant truth that every increase in assets is matched by a corresponding increase in liabilities, that bank liabilities generate liquidity and through liquidity may lead on to inflation. Those who have their eyes fixed on the first of the two faces are given to whooping on the banks to increased lending and a freer supply of credit to deserving borrowers. They feel that what is stigmatized as wildcat banking, however productive of bankruptcy, may at times be a duty and a virtue in a developing country where entrepreneurial boldness receives too little support. Those who look at the other side, and see the grim face registering excess liquidity, insist on the ease with which bank liabilities can be multiplied, on the virtues of a stable unit of account, and on the need for safeguards and restrictions.

The business of mobilizing savings, therefore, is linked with much wider issues of social policy. Inflation, which may result from over-lending by the banks, is also the inevitable outcome of over-borrowing by governments and arises far more commonly for that reason. The scale and pattern of investment, which the banks help to determine, is crucial to the control of economic development and, as such, cannot but be of concern to the government. Banking policy and budgetary policy are almost inseparable because of the association of both with the whole process of saving and investment and because of the interconnection between that process and the transformation that we call economic development.

In the transformation of an under-developed country banks can play only a limited part. First of all, there is a limit to the savings that they can mobilize. Under-developed countries are usually poor and save a lower proportion of their income than countries at a more advanced stage of development. Little of what is saved is lent; and although there is some tendency to hoard currency and the banks may succeed in attracting deposits where other borrowers, in need of longer-term finance, are unsuccessful, even the banks are likely to have access to only a comparatively small proportion of total savings. This does not mean that the banks must take a fatalistic view of the scope for their services: there are many ways of encouraging saving, including an extension of the facilities open to the saver, and the banks can do more than any other agency to make habits of thrift seem worth while. But the main determinants of saving lie outside their power to control; any large increase is likely to require a change in attitudes and a rise in incomes that are at once the outcome of economic development and the source of further expansion.

In the second place, the contribution that the banks can make is limited by the demand for financial accommodation. It is by no means inevitable that the shortage of concrete capital in under-developed countries expresses itself in a corresponding incapacity on the part of the banks to provide funds adequate to their customers' requirements. On the contrary, there are some under-developed countries where the deposits accruing locally can find no outlet except abroad. Even in India, a recent World Bank mission reported that 'the amount of capital available for investment is often surprisingly and inexplicably large' in relation to the demand, and that 'very few of the businessmen consulted . . . appeared to regard financing as a serious problem'.[1] Firms may prefer to grow through reinvestment of profits than make extensive use of bank overdrafts; and the more successful they are commercially, the larger the profits available to finance expansion. We know that in the United Kingdom, bank advances form less than 4 per cent of the net assets of companies with a stock exchange quotation. The proportion is likely to be higher in countries where the facilities of the new issue market are far more restricted and where business is more dependent on private finance. But even in under-developed countries it is a mistake to think of bank credit as the principal source of finance or to assume that the banks could everywhere greatly increase their loans for productive purposes if their funds expanded because of some access of public thrift.

Finance is, in fact, only one of the impediments to development and often by no means the most important. This is particularly apparent in industry where there are many obstacles to the successful establishment of new enterprises, and cheap or abundant credit would not by itself transform the situation. Lack of experience with modern techniques, inadequate transport facilities, the high cost of training skilled labour, market limitations, instability of government policies and many other factors, all deter the private businessman and dispose him to look for profits in other directions where he can turn over his capital more quickly. In the same circumstances, the banks have good reason also to take the short view and will generally prefer to maintain their liquidity rather than make long-term investments in industry without guarantee against loss. But it is the circumstances that are unpropitious, not the attitude of the banks, which is no more short-sighted than that of the business community.

If economic development is to get under way, the circumstances must be changed so as to make industrial growth possible. Action can be taken by the government—and very often by the government alone—to transform the environ-

[1] Quoted by W. Diamond, *Development Banks* (IBRD, 1957), pp. 10–11.

ment within which business decisions are made. But if the government is to operate on the broad front that such a transformation involves, it will generally require much enlarged financial resources. The shortage of capital in under-developed countries reveals itself, as a rule, in the form of a shortage of funds at the disposal of the government.

Not that such a shortage is by any means a novelty. From time immemorial governments have been even shorter of money than their subjects and have been full of the most ingenious pretexts and devices for relieving the shortage. Usually, however, it has required a war, and the special urgencies of war, to enable them to break through the resistance of taxpayers and consumers and possess themselves of a large slice of additional real resources. In peace-time a much more powerful resistance movement confronts them. They may try to run a budget surplus and may maintain something in hand on income account. But any finance minister in an under-developed country who aimed at a cash surplus for the purpose of retiring debt, and so putting more savings at the disposal of the private sector, would be unlikely to hold office for long; and he would inevitably regard a heavy investment programme as ample justification for running a deficit and covering it by borrowing in the market. The government is liable, therefore, to absorb a large slice of private savings in order to eke out its own. Indeed, it may come near to monopolizing the resources of the capital market, and in doing so, bring in the banks to take up bonds not sold elsewhere.

This is all the more likely because of the narrowness of the capital market in under-developed countries. The market in government bonds is usually confined to a few large financial institutions. The investment taking place in the private sector, although it may be substantial, is rarely channelled through an organized capital market and is expected to bring in a return well above the modest yields offered on government bonds. Of the private savings that do flow into the larger financial intermediaries, the government can command a substantial proportion at low rates precisely because the resulting debt is marketable. But this flow cannot be quickly increased and the government has great difficulty in attracting fresh savings through larger bond issues. If it is impatient to push ahead with development, therefore, it has to resort to foreign borrowing, higher taxation, or deficit finance (which means, in practice, borrowing from the banks).

Impatience is natural enough in countries anxious to compress their development into a relatively short period and trying to lay the foundations for subsequent industrial expansion. It is easy for them to assume that their first duty is to accelerate the creation of capital assets in the form of public utilities of all kinds—roads, schools, power stations, etc.—and in some at least of the basic industries which the private sector lacks either the capacity or the will to finance. It is easy for them also, in the urgency of their mood, to make light of the danger of inflation and look to the banking system to make good any shortage in the capital available.

If governments take the inflationary tack, it is almost impossible for the banks to steer a different course. Where the government shows the way and runs larger deficits than it can finance by long-term loans, the banks are automatically put in a position to join in the game. The more the government borrows from the central bank the more amply supplied are the banks with liquid reserves on which to erect a larger credit structure; and if prices are rising, there is not likely to be any lack of demand for bank credit. The banks may be expected, therefore, to aggravate rather than alleviate the inflationary forces let loose by government spending.

Moreover, even if the government itself abstains from over-investment, the emergence of conditions favourable to rapid development may bring on inflation through the action of the banks themselves. If, for example, export prices are high and the incomes of exporters are correspondingly swollen, this will raise the level of activity throughout the economy and create a demand for funds to sustain that higher level. The banks with rising reserves will be willing to grant credit more freely, and this additional credit may easily reach a scale larger than is consistent with financial stability and rebound on the price-level with damaging effect.

The susceptibility of under-developed countries to inflation arises not merely out of the political forces making for a high level of investment or the economic forces making for wide fluctuations in export earnings. Inflation tends to be more violent than in an industrialized community because of the inelasticity of the economic system. Additional credit can be expended only on a limited supply of materials and labour, especially skilled labour, and for the purpose of supplying a market that is usually also limited. The industrial sector is a relatively small one, while the much larger sector supplying primary produce can only expand slowly and, as a rule, from year to year. In an industrial community, where the resources are far more varied, the elasticity of supply is very much greater and the response to additional credit is more liable to take the form of an increase in output and less liable to issue in a rise in prices.

Thus the movement of prices tends to be more volatile and inflation to get more quickly out of hand. This is true, equally, of the movement of the balance of payments; the responses that are obvious enough in advanced countries are a great deal more violent in under-developed countries, especially on the side of imports. While exports are usually very limited in range and highly inelastic in supply, the reverse is true of imports, and additional credit gravitates quickly, therefore, towards speculative purchases of imports from which to feed the rising level of demand.

The susceptibility of under-developed countries to inflation makes the task of the monetary authorities in those countries a particularly difficult one. Even where the problem of policy can be easily resolved, there is frequently a further problem of technique. In many under-developed countries, especially in Asia, the central bank is a recent creation and relatively inexperienced in seeking to exercise its control over the banking system. Open market operations may be ineffective because of the absence of an organized money market or because sales of government securities to non-bank holders are out of the question. A rise in the central bank's discount rate may fail to take effect if the commercial banks are out of debt to the central bank, have excess cash balances, or can import banking funds from abroad. Even moral suasion, when the commercial banks are willing to accept the leadership of the central bank, cannot be pushed too far without straining the loyalty of the banks whose commercial interests are most affected.

It would seem, for example, that in the under-developed countries it is unusual for central bank lending to provide over 10 per cent of the funds advanced by the commercial banks to the private sector;[1] there are some countries where the proportion is well above 10 per cent but these seem to be confined to Latin America on the one hand and Western Europe on the other; and of the Latin-American countries the majority appear to have comparatively low proportions. Where there is extensive recourse to borrowing from the central bank, it is common to operate through a specific ceiling on such borrowing, as in Colombia, Costa Rica, Nicaragua and Peru. In the other group, limitations on central bank lending whether by a stiffening of rates, or a tightening of eligibility requirements, or a direct cut in loans to the commercial banks, may not prove sufficient to bring credit restriction into play.

In some under-developed countries whose trade is financed mainly from abroad and which have strong financial links with international money markets, credit conditions are largely governed by the movement of interest rates in those international centres. The large exchange banks which operate in Asia and Africa, for example, can either bring in funds when the demand is particularly pressing and rates are tending to rise or can transfer funds elsewhere if rates are falling in relation to foreign rates of interest. These operations help to stabilize rates and to maintain them below the level in areas with little access to international credit; but at the same time they make it difficult to insulate the banking system from the effects of a restriction of credit in the foreign centres from which funds are drawn.

In the last twenty years there has been a general trend towards the use of variations in cash reserve requirements as a major instrument of credit control. Up to the early thirties, commercial bank reserves were held with the central bank more as a matter of convenience than to meet statutory requirements, and even where minimum ratios of cash assets to deposits were required, the central bank had no power to vary those ratios. Such authority was first obtained by the Federal Reserve System in 1933 and 1935 and by a number of other central banks, including Costa Rica, Ecuador, Mexico, Venezuela and New Zealand before the war. The trend towards variable reserve requirements became increasingly pronounced in banking legislation during and after the war

[1] U Tun Wai, 'Interest Rates in the Organized Money Markets of Underdeveloped Countries' (IMF *Staff Papers*, vol. v, no. 2, August 1955, p. 258).

until, by the end of last year, they were in force in thirty countries either by statute or by formal agreement between the monetary authorities and the commercial banks.[1]

The expedient takes various forms. The most common is a straightforward change in reserve requirements; in Australia a system of special accounts is used, the commercial banks being obliged to hold additional reserves on deposit with the central bank; in Ceylon, the central bank can simultaneously issue its own bills to the commercial banks. The use actually made of the device has also varied and the powers have often been on the statute book for years before they were brought into operation. It has proved easier to reduce reserve requirements, in peace-time at least, than to increase them: an increase may present difficulties either because it shatters the bond market or because of evident unfairness to particular banks. Nevertheless, as a means of giving the central bank effective control over commercial bank lending, especially where there is no developed money market, variable reserve requirements are an extremely powerful instrument.

The use of general instruments of credit limitations has been supplemented in many of the under-developed countries by selective credit controls. These serve a variety of purposes and are often designed to redress some assumed bias towards particular types of investment or to ensure preferential treatment for investments thought to be specially desirable. Credit controls with long-term objectives of this kind cannot be adequately discussed here.[2] Very often, however, selective credit controls are introduced as a short-term anti-inflationary measure or in order to prevent some of the usual side-effects of inflation.

There are several different types of such selective control. First, there are selective exemptions from highly restrictive general credit controls. Such exemptions may make it possible to operate the general controls more strictly, provided the exemptions are sufficiently rare to permit of individual scrutiny. Secondly, the monetary authorities may increase margin requirements on particular forms of collateral such as real estate, inventories, gold, or stock exchange securities.

[1] Peter G. Fousek, *Foreign Central Banking: the Instruments of Monetary Policy* (Federal Reserve Bank of New York, 1957), p. 46.

[2] See, however, I. G. Patel, 'Selective Credit Controls in Under-developed Economies' (IMF *Staff Papers*, vol. iv, no. 1, September 1954, pp. 73–84).

This action operates to make the acquisition or construction of the assets less attractive by reducing their usefulness as collateral; and at the same time it may put some brake on bank lending by increasing the total collateral required against a given total of bank advances. A variant of this, but one less likely to prove effective, is the use of a selective rediscount policy, certain types of paper being either declared ineligible or accepted for rediscount only at higher rates. Finally, importers may be required to make deposits with the central bank when they apply for an import licence and in advance, therefore, of placing an order abroad.

Prior deposit requirements can be regarded as a means of curtailing imports and so keeping the balance of payments under control. It has been argued, however, that this effect is largely illusory.[1] The importer may need additional credit in order to make his deposit but the cost of this extra credit will not be an effective deterrent in conditions of inflation. As for the banks, while they have an incentive to avoid loans to meet import requirements because such loans tie up their reserves with the central bank, they are not, so it is argued, in a position to decide the use to which their loans are put and so cannot effectively discriminate against imports. If they did so, and made less credit available to importers so as to lend more freely in other directions, inflationary pressure would increase and balance of payments difficulties would be aggravated at a later stage.

This argument is not a very convincing one. If importers are put in the position of seeking additional credit at a time when general credit restraint is being enforced, they are faced with a problem of availability of credit and not just one of additional interest charges. In Argentina the banks have been instructed not to grant loans for the purpose of meeting pre-deposit requirements;[2] and in other countries, provided the banks do not operate a system of overdraft limits but make advances of specified amounts, it may be possible for the banks to identify loans to finance imports and to penalize them in order to protect their reserves. There are good grounds, in other words, for regarding import pre-deposit requirements as acting selectively and effectively to reduce the volume of

[1] Patel, op. cit., pp. 81–82.
[2] Fousek, op. cit., p. 72 *n*.

imports. If they did not have this effect, the additional imports that would be made might, in one sense, moderate the inflation by helping to keep prices down; but most under-developed countries would willingly let domestic prices rise a little faster if the drain on their reserves could simultaneously be moderated and a little more time gained for action to bring the inflation under control.

One other strategic area over which it may be necessary to exercise selective credit control is consumer credit. Instalment buying is no longer confined to the more developed countries and exists even in a Communist country like Yugoslavia. At least three under-developed countries—Chile, Peru and the Federation of Rhodesia and Nyasaland—have introduced controls over instalment credit terms; and in many others where consumer credit takes a different shape, it reaches a very considerable total. There is likely also to be a growing use of instalment credit for the purchase of producer goods and the finance for this purpose is usually provided by the same agencies as specialize in consumer credit. The monetary authorities are likely to find themselves obliged, sooner or later, to adopt a positive policy towards instalment credit and decide how to bring it under control if, as usually happens, it fluctuates in the same direction as other forms of credit.

Three general conclusions appear to emerge from the operation of selective credit controls. First, they are particularly difficult to administer in economies where administration, like everything else, is under-developed. As a recent writer has put it:

'. . . it is usually necessary for both the central bank and the commercial banks to distinguish arbitrarily, in precise operational terms that can be followed consistently over a considerable period, between essential and non-essential sectors of the economy, between productive and non-productive investment, and between speculative and non-speculative borrowing. Furthermore, the authorities must continually concern themselves with frequent and at times serious inequities, with possible discrimination as between banks, and with the division of responsibility between the central bank and the commercial banks over the approval of all loan applications.'[1]

[1] Fousek, op. cit., p. 77.

Secondly, as an emergency weapon in well-marked sectors of the economy where credit control can exercise a strategic influence on the progress of inflation, they are of undoubted value. They help, for example, to moderate speculative activity and to put a brake on imports.

But, thirdly, they are no substitute for general measures to limit credit expansion and control inflation and are bound to be ineffective in the absence of such measures. Some of the more important selective controls, such as import pre-deposit requirements, are of a once-for-all character and lose force progressively. Thus they provide powerful reinforcements in a crisis rather than an independent method of controlling inflation or ridding it of its distorting effects on the pattern of investment and output.

If we turn from these problems of the short-run to a view of the longer-term problems of banking in under-developed countries, three problems may be touched on briefly. The first relates to the position of the banks in relation to other financial institutions, the second to the finance of industry, and the third to staff.

In the early stages of development, banks grow relatively fast. When a country is just emerging from a subsistence economy, the banks are not only faced with a growing demand for credit (to meet the needs of trade) but also acquire deposits because of the need to build up cash-balances. Once monetary transactions displace barter, everybody requires to hold money and this money can be obtained by selling current output without spending the proceeds, in other words by saving. If the money so accumulated is held in the form of coins, there is no very apparent advantage to the community since the coins, or their metal equivalent, will have to be imported and paid for. But if the money consists of paper notes the monetary authorities obtain command of equivalent purchasing power free of charge; and if the money is put on deposit with the banks, then it will rest with the banks to make use of the savings so entrusted to them.

It is interesting to see how the stock of currency and bank deposits grow as the national income rises and how the richer countries are, in general, those that maintain the largest stock in relation to their income. In countries like Ecuador and Guatemala, for example, the stock of money represents some

13–14 per cent of the national income and more than half of the stock takes the form of currency. In rich countries like New Zealand and the United Kingdom the ratio is 37 per cent and in the United States nearly 43 per cent. Between these limits come countries like Venezuela with 19 per cent, Ceylon with 20 per cent, India with 21 per cent, Turkey with 27 per cent and Brazil with 32 per cent. In India the currency is more than twice as large as bank deposits and in Thailand nearly three times as large; but in richer countries these proportions are reversed and in the United States bank deposits are nearly four times as large as the currency in circulation.

There is, of course, no strict correlation between a country's wealth and its stock of money.[1] Difficulties of definition would alone prevent this, quite apart from special circumstances governing the monetary habits of different countries. But it is fairly clear that, as national income rises, at least in the earlier stages of economic development, not only is more money held, but the amount held grows faster than income. An underdeveloped country can hope, therefore, to derive an almost automatic addition to its savings as a result of the efforts of the public to constitute adequate cash-balances as their income grows. Moreover, a growing fraction of savings in monetary form will tend to be held with the banks. In other words, the assets of the banks tend to form a rising fraction of the national income. The argument establishing this conclusion relates to the commercial banks; but the conclusion is likely to apply to savings banks as well.

It would seem also that the commercial banks tend to command larger resources relatively to the central bank, the more developed the economy. This must necessarily be a very tentative conclusion, since many central banks are of very recent origin and their assets depend largely on their constitution, not on some law of evolution. Nevertheless, it is perhaps significant that the countries where the assets of the central bank exceed those of the commercial banks include Burma, Egypt, Greece, Guatemala, India, Pakistan, and Thailand, and that in the United Kingdom and the United States the central bank's assets are just over a third and just over a

[1] For a fuller analysis, see John G. Gurley and E. S. Shaw, 'The Growth of Debt and Money in the United States, 1800–1950', *The Review of Economics and Statistics*, Vol. xxxix, No. 3, August 1957.

quarter of those of the commercial banks. There are, however, other advanced countries like France where the ratio is nearly three-quarters; and under-developed countries like Peru where it is not much over a third.

At a later stage in financial development, the commercial banks appear to shrink, not in absolute size nor even in relation to the national income, but in relation to other agencies. Over the past half-century in the United States, for example, the share of the commercial banks in assets owned by all financial intermediaries including insurance companies, pension funds, etc., has declined from slightly over one-half to a little over one-third.[1] On the other hand insurance organizations increased their share between 1929 and 1952 from 12–15 per cent to 27 per cent. A rapid multiplication of intermediaries took place as the capital market became more articulated and these intermediaries have tended to be more successful than the commercial banks in attracting savings from the public. Similar forces are at work in other economies but in the under-developed countries the banks still occupy the leading position among existing financial institutions and are likely to remain in that position for a long time to come.

Banks reared in the Anglo-Saxon tradition are usually chary of taking an active part in industrial development and have sometimes expressed rather doctrinaire views about the wisdom of using their depositors' money to make long-term investments in industry. Continental banks, on the other hand, are represented as having played a dominant rôle in nineteenth-century railway building and in the finance of heavy industry. It is doubtful whether the difference in practice was ever so marked as the difference recorded in the textbooks. But there is no doubt that the continental approach has more to recommend it as a means of promoting industrial development.

The setting up of investment or development banks, often under government auspices or with government participation, has proceeded rapidly in the under-developed countries since the war. It is right to expect a great deal from these banks, but it is as well also to remember their limitations. They offer a method of bringing together the business experience

[1] R. W. Goldsmith, *Financial Intermediaries in the American Economy since 1900* (NBER, New York, 1958), p. 4.

of private industry and the borrowing power of the central government; and they can encourage the long view and the thorough scrutiny of individual projects that are so often lacking. But if they are to turn over their funds, and not act as the continuing proprietors of the enterprises they promote, they will have to unload their investments from time to time on the capital market even if this means creating a capital market. They may wish themselves to retain some part of the equity or to ensure that some other financial institution organized by the government takes over from them a substantial interest in the company once it has been safely launched. They will also be compelled to widen their responsibilities well beyond the provision of finance: the development bank will need to draw on technical and marketing experience both in deciding what projects to endorse and in seeing them through to actual operation. It is not only new projects, moreover, that need finance; and firms seeking additional capital for expansion may and do ask simultaneously for technical assistance from the development bank.

The experience of development banks thus far has been analysed by the World Bank in a volume which deserves careful study.[1] Of the innumerable questions which that experience raises, only a few can be put here.

First of all, many countries have several different institutions all describing themselves as development banks: India has three, apart from the finance corporations organized by the states; Pakistan has two; Japan appears to have four. The functions of these institutions are no doubt quite distinct and clearly set out in their charters; but one wonders whether some of the functions might not be amalgamated. There would seem also to be some possibility of bringing the commercial banks more deliberately into industrial finance, possibly through the use of guarantees along the lines practised by the Mexican Nacional Financiera.

Secondly, what is the best relationship between development banks and government? If there were many competing development banks, the answer would be simple; but in fact development banks are few and rarely if ever intended to compete with one another. Nearly always they are chosen instruments of government policy, the fruit of government

[1] W. Diamond, op. cit.

initiative even when privately owned. Sometimes the government lends most of the capital even when the equity remains in private hands and very often the government looks to the development bank to discharge important public functions in the execution of official industrial policy. The development bank, whether in public ownership or not, is generally conducted much on the lines of a British public corporation. Since the responsibilities of development banks lie in the private sector, this mixed relationship has many advantages.

The major problem of the development banks is, however, the development of a satisfactory capital market on which they can draw for funds and through which they can market their investments. In the absence of such a market, development banks have to start off with ample financial resources and with a large enough equity to absorb the risks of initial loss. In view of the pioneering type of investments that development requires, these risks are considerable and it is usually necessary for the government to make special concessions. The bank may well find itself obliged to turn to the government for additional capital, or for a government guarantee, because its own efforts to go to the capital market bring in funds on highly onerous terms. The Industrial Development Bank of Turkey and the Chilean Fomento, for example, have been unable to float a public bond issue and the Nacional Financiera of Mexico and the Industrial Finance Corporation of India have only succeeded in making issues with full official backing.

Development banks have considerable advantages over other institutions in channelling foreign capital into industry. They can borrow, with appropriate government guarantees, from the World Bank or from other sources, at rates of interest that compare favourably with the rates paid by industrial borrowers even in advanced countries. They can thus provide capital for industrial development in amounts and at rates that individual enterprises in the under-developed countries could not hope to obtain on their own credit. They can also build up a staff familiar with the problems, in finance, organization and engineering, of large industrial ventures and put this staff at the disposition of each new project which they agree to support. Even if they lose some of this staff to the enterprises which they finance, they can comfort themselves in the knowledge that they have added to the sum-total of experience on which industry can draw.

And so we come to the crux of the whole matter. Banking in any country depends on *bankers*. In the under-developed countries the greatest lack is in trained men and this is true in banking as in other activities. But banking occupies a key position. For it lies within the power of the banks, and particularly of the central bank, to train a generation of men in the things that make successful development possible. The rapid development of Mexico, for example, has been attributed in large measure to the foresight of the central bank a generation ago in selecting and training, in Mexico and abroad, a cadre of men skilled in finance and technology and able both to form general policies and prepare industrial projects. Some of the success of Puerto Rico is said to be due to the promotion of bright young men to key posts in banking that they would not normally have held so young. It is said also that in Latin America the central banks are looked upon as strongholds of commercial morality, able to dispense import licences incorruptibly when other government controls are suspect. Perhaps these are fairy tales. They certainly have a moral. As every Scotsman knows, no country is likely to develop that neglects to develop its men.

CHAPTER 11

Migration of Technology[1]

THE process by which technology is transferred from one country to another has received less attention from economists than its importance warrants. Just as, in the nineteenth century, when the international migration of labour and capital was at its zenith, international economics continued to rest on the supposed immobility of the factors of production, so now the international migration of technology finds no place in orthodox theory. The factor of technological transfer is obvious; the fact of major differences in the level of technology is equally apparent. But what controls the transfer and regulates the differences?

It is necessary, first of all, to emphasize that some differences in technology reflect the operation of economic forces. We cannot say that one technique is superior to another in all circumstances, independently of what people feel about it or the use that it makes of relatively scarce factors. Engineers may rank different methods of production by reference to some measure of technical efficiency, but there is no necessary coincidence between their ranking and that of economists or business men, who have to balance cost and benefit before they can judge the merits of a technique. History is full of examples of advances in technology that went without commercial application for long periods because market conditions were not propitious, and of ventures that ended in bankruptcy although, or indeed *because*, they sought to use the very latest technical devices. Even when a firm recognizes that a newly invented machine is technically superior to the machinery it is using, it may hesitate to scrap and replace immediately because of the high capital charges that this would involve. In the countries most alive to the virtues of modern technology, the old and the new often continue side by side for many years before the one supersedes the other.

[1] Published (in French) in the *Bulletin de la Banque Nationale de Belgique*, 1957.

This is a familiar enough point; but it is necessary to remind oneself of it when one asks why countries fail to take advantage of modern technology. Critics of European industry often convey the impression that only ignorance, inertia, lack of enterprise, or some peculiar kink in entrepreneurial psychology and social institutions stands in the way of the adoption of American techniques in Europe. Most people recognize, however, that the market situation confronting the European entrepreneur, or the relative cost of different factor inputs, is sufficiently different to justify some caution, and that more than propaganda or better technical information is necessary in order to produce a closer approximation between European and American techniques. In under-developed countries, the same difficulty exists of deciding how far to attribute differences in the level of technology to the forces of ignorance and inertia and how far to market obstacles and relative factor scarcities and prices. No doubt ignorance and inertia exert a far more powerful influence in those countries and leave correspondingly more room for direct action to raise productivity. But there is also a wider gap in factor prices and the size of the domestic market that might be expected to make American techniques still less appropriate. In America the technological drift is governed largely by the need to save labour, and a superior technology is generally one that reduces labour inputs even at the cost of increasing other inputs; it is a technology appropriate to high real wages and a high standard of living. The under-developed countries cannot achieve that standard of living at a bound, whatever the techniques they employ, and they need a technology that sets more store by economy in other factors, notably capital, organizing ability and technical skill.

These general considerations have not deterred some economists from urging that the under-developed countries should by-pass the methods of production employed in the older industrial countries, particularly those where wage-levels are relatively low, and adopt at once the latest labour-saving techniques. Professor Leontief, for example, foresees the construction of automatic factories on a vast scale:

'The new technology,' he writes, 'will probably have a much more revolutionary effect on the so-called under-developed countries than on the US or other old industrial nations. Shortage of capital and lack of a properly conditioned and educated labour force have been the two major obstacles to rapid industrialization of such backward areas. Now automatic production, with its relatively low capital and labour requirements per unit of output, radically changes their prospects. Instead of trying to lift the whole economy by the slow, painful methods of the past, an industrially backward country may take the dramatic short-cut of building a few large, up-to-date automatic plants. Towering up in the primitive economy like copses of tall trees on a grassy plain, they would propagate a new economic order. The oil refineries of the Near East, the integrated steel plant built after the war in Brazil, the gigantic fertilizer plant recently put into operation in India—these are examples of the new trend in under-developed regions of the world. How formidable the application of modern technology in a backward country may become is demonstrated by the USSR's recent great strides in industrialization.'[1]

There is no necessary conflict between the view expressed by Professor Leontief and the view that there are strong underlying forces in the under-developed countries hostile to the transfer of a technology that is exclusively labour-saving. In the examples cited by Professor Leontief, which cover only a limited sector of industry, it may well be true that the most modern techniques employ not only less labour but also less capital per unit of output. But they also require a scale of output greater than the business men of those countries are accustomed to and often much greater than the local market can absorb. Unless those countries are able to enter export markets in the confident expectation of underselling their competitors, they may be obliged to limit their output to a scale requiring a more capital-intensive technology, even though this raises production costs. They may also have to adopt a less advanced technology because, with a smaller and perhaps technically less efficient plant, the effort of marketing, which is a heavy burden for an inexperienced management to bear, is reduced, and there is greater flexibility and less elaborate planning in the control of operations. In some under-developed countries, such as India, it is also a not un-

[1] W. Leontief, *The Economic Impact* in 'Automatic Control' (*Scientific American*, 1955).

common complaint that the cost of repairs and maintenance is unnecessarily swollen when plants try to copy American techniques because outright renewal takes the place of *ad hoc* repairs and make-do and mend. Even the Russians, as Professor Granick has shown, do not by any means copy American techniques slavishly but go to a good deal of trouble to economize capital and appear, for example, to have installed specialized equipment in place of general purpose equipment only when the scale of output and other circumstances made this possible without raising capital requirements per unit of output.

The problem facing an under-developed country seeking to import the fruits of modern technology is thus not simply one of identifying and adopting the latest practice but of deciding between a number of alternative techniques. The technique that is ultimately borrowed must be adapted to the economic and social environment to which it is transplanted and must in particular take account of the available resources and market possibilities. The scope for such borrowing will depend not only on the technological 'spread'—the gap separating the techniques already in use in the country and those in use abroad—but also on the degree to which this spread has some rational foundation in the economic forces at work and in the attitudes and preferences of the population. It will also depend on the ease with which economic forces can be redirected and social attitudes changed so as to facilitate technological progress.

The transfer of technology is not governed exclusively by the opportunities for borrowing that exist; there has to be some satisfactory mechanism of transfer that guarantees that those opportunities will be seen and grasped. This is true not only of transfer between countries but also of transfer within countries. What then is the mechanism by which a new technique spreads within a country?

The traditional answer is that competition is the most effective weapon for this purpose. Once a new and more efficient method has been introduced by one firm, and that firm escapes the high mortality to which all new-born things are subject, other firms will be forced by competition to follow suit or risk loss and bankruptcy. The social function of competition is, indeed, quite as much to compel imitation as to promote innovation. No one can afford to lag behind and everyone has a strong incentive to get close to the leaders, or, if the rewards to enterprise are great, to become one of the leaders.

Even in an industrialized country, this is far from an adequate account of the matter. Nearly every firm has trade secrets to which its competitors do not have free access; and although the patent system makes it possible for firms to gain access, at a price, to many of the more important industrial inventions, it is increasingly the practice for firms in the newer science-based industries not to patent improvements that grow out of their own special processes or to patent only as a protection against the need to pay fees to other firms that hit on the same idea. Every innovator is for the time being a monopolist; and competition often takes the form of making a quite different innovation rather than of imitating the practice of other firms. Moreover, even imitation generally requires some effort of adaptation, both because the circumstances of the imitator are in some respects peculiar and because he is likely to be imperfectly informed about the original innovation. Cases are not unknown where British firms sought to profit, in the post-war years, from the newly-disclosed trade secrets of their German rivals, and ultimately made no headway until they called in some of the German experts with a working knowledge of the process involved.

The most obvious example of a failure of the competitive process to bring about an automatic diffusion of the latest techniques of production is agriculture. The farmer does not always acquire the knowledge that would enable him to cut his costs or show anxiety to imitate his successful competitors. He may be induced, however, to experiment if the knowledge of new techniques is brought to him in a form that he understands by someone he trusts. Most countries, therefore, make use of agricultural extension services as a means of accomplishing what market forces have failed to do.

For much the same reasons, world competition does not make the farmers of one country adopt the practices of another. The Indian peasant does not copy the Danish farmer if only because he is completely ignorant of Danish methods of cultivation. It is necessary to devise a new method of bringing home to him fresh opportunities of higher output by building up an advisory service and giving him new knowledge, instead of letting competition work blindly in the hope that he will change his ways.

Competition presupposes knowledge and enterprise—even when enterprise goes no further than imitation—and where both are present it works well. If they are absent, they must both be supplied before any transfer of technology can take place. Poor communications, inaccessibility to ideas and information, and limited horizons of experience on the one hand and lack of enterprise on the other are the main obstacles that have to be overcome.

In under-developed countries the supply of enterprise often appears extremely limited. There may be a general disinclination to experiment, particularly where there is only a slender margin to provide against the risk of failure, or where change has not been forced on the community so that there are few examples of successful response. It is common to find, however, that traders all over the world seize opportunities of profit with great promptitude and that they show considerable initiative in searching for such opportunities. Those who trade in markets where long experience or extensive knowledge is unnecessary face incessant competition and are under strong compulsion to be enterprising. If they remain merchants or confine themselves to trade in staple commodities, this reflects not lack of enterprise so much as lack of experience. Their horizons are restricted by the range of their contacts with the outside world and they may hesitate to take up new lines of business or found an industrial undertaking from a diffidence born of ignorance. They have far less difficulty in understanding the art of buying and selling at a profit than in grasping the art of running a factory or in mastering the essentials of modern technology. Moreover, it is possible to vary the scale of commercial operations, and to conduct them on a very small scale, far more easily than it is with industrial operations. The financial commitment involved can also more readily be faced; it is one thing to tie up a limited amount of capital in stocks for a limited time and quite a different thing to put the same capital into fixed equipment that may be several years in paying for itself.

Thus although there is usually no lack of enterprise among those who are already in business, the early stages of industrial growth may be prolonged because the enterprise of merchants finds only a narrow outlet. One group of merchants often play a part out of all proportion to their numbers, namely those whose business involves them in foreign travel or brings them into frequent contact with foreigners. A striking example of this is the prominence among those who have pioneered in the establishment of large-scale industry in India of industrial leaders drawn from a few narrowly defined business groups, notably the Parsis and Gujeratis, and more recently the Marwaris. Mr Henry Aubrey, in commenting on this and on the similar predominance of a few specific communities in the industry of Pakistan, points out that all these communities are drawn from the oldest and most important trading region of India: the Bombay-Gujerat-Kutch area.[1] The Parsis and the Gujeratis have a long-standing connection with the processing and exporting of cotton and the import of textiles; and the Parsis are alleged to have been assisted in establishing business connections by their close association with the British as their agents in foreign trade. Men from these trading communities enter upon industrial undertakings with the double advantage that they not only know the market opportunities but are also well placed to obtain information about techniques of production. On the one hand, they have been trained in the calculation of costs, the anticipation of prices, the assessment of chances of gain and loss; they have had to plan further ahead than those who are engaged solely in domestic trade; they have already acquired, or have access to, substantial capital; they often have wide experience in dealing in the commodities which they now propose to manufacture. On the other hand, they know where to go to order equipment, to obtain technical advice, and to recruit experts from abroad. For reasons of this kind, and not because of some tie of race or religion or some inherited bent, it is hardly surprising to find groups from a single community in the forefront of industrialization and the transfer of technical knowledge. Members of these groups are industrial entrepreneurs because they are already internationally-minded and alive to business opportunities.

For the same reasons, one often finds that new industries are founded by immigrant traders: Lebanese and Syrians in

[1] Henry G. Aubrey, 'Industrial Investment Decisions: a Comparative Analysis', *Journal of Economic History*, December 1955, pp. 345–6.

Latin America and various parts of Africa; Italians in Brazil; Chinese in South-East Asia, and so on. Throughout history, the trader from abroad and the immigrant artisans have been the main channel for the importation of foreign techniques. At the beginning of the Industrial Revolution in the eighteenth century, there can have been scarcely an industry in England that did not owe its origin to immigrants from abroad, many of them refugees. In many under-developed countries the same phenomenon is visible today: new industries are built up by foreigners who are both driven to look for business opportunities and enabled to discern them by the special circumstances of their migration. Often their very success makes the immigrants unpopular and immigration is restricted in consequence, as in West Africa. Where the immigrants are likely to merge themselves in the community which they have entered, these restrictions are bound to retard industrial growth without much social justification.

Foreigners may also introduce new techniques without actual immigration. The branch factory and the foreign subsidiary company are increasingly important in the diffusion of technology and provide both a direct injection of foreign experience and a channel for the transmission of the latest improvements from the parent concern to the branch or subsidiary. Remarkably little has been written about the branch factory as an instrument of technological transfer, and there is no general appreciation either of the impact that foreign branches can exercise on the industry of a country or of how recent that impact is. Before the first world war very few industrial concerns ever set up branches in other countries except to supply themselves with raw materials. The often-quoted failure of British industry to build textile mills in India in the nineteenth century is only one of the more striking examples of this proposition. On the other hand, to take an equally striking example, half of the investment in manufacturing industry in Canada since the second world war has been in American-controlled firms.

There is no question that the branch factory is a highly effective way of importing technology. It usually provides, along with the technical expertise, the capital that is not easily mobilized in under-developed countries for new industrial ventures and the managerial experience that can so rarely be supplied by them. Their very power to break all the bottlenecks at once, however, can be, from the point of view of the host country, their most damning feature. For if they do so, it can only be by supplying *from outside* each of the scarce factors and charging a price corresponding to the scarcity. If they are parasitic on technological progress elsewhere, and carry on little or no local research or attempt no new development, they offer no guarantee of starting off an independent chain reaction within the economy that will reduce the need for further imports of foreign technology. So far as they make use of foreign managements, they do little to train local entrepreneurs and give them experience of large-scale organization. The more successful the venture, the more highly the capital is rewarded (the return on it representing payment for technical and managerial experience quite as much as local rates of profit) and the larger is the cost of eventually bringing the company under local ownership and control. There is at least a risk, therefore, that branch plants may be an expensive and ineffectual way of injecting new technology into the economy. As a rule, however, foreign plants go to some pains to encourage local development and seek to make themselves less vulnerable to criticism by offering training facilities, inviting local participation in management and so on.

New techniques may also be transferred in other ways. Apart from the internationally-minded merchants to whom reference has already been made, there are internationally-minded scientists whose training enables them to follow the course of technological change and who are likely to be in touch with foreign scientists or technologists. The manufacture of weapons of war, and of a very wide range of military supplies, is also likely to respond quickly to the influence of foreign ideas and to provide a point of entry for new production methods into other industries catering for civilian or export needs. Then there are the artisans who may graduate from a small workshop to a large industrial plant, particularly if they have themselves some inventive gift. It is doubtful, however, whether artisans as a group play an important part in introducing techniques from abroad since they have generally less contact with foreigners and foreign ideas than other groups in the community unless they happen to have travelled abroad or to have received a long technical training. They are more likely to imitate what has already been introduced into the country than themselves to introduce it. Other groups that have been of importance in the past are government officials and landlords.

The latter are obviously in a particularly favourable position to become pioneers of new agricultural techniques but they have also, on occasion, developed a keen interest in the industrial and other sectors of the economy and established new ventures employing an imported technology. The history of the agricultural and industrial revolutions in Europe affords many illustrations of innovating landlords. The agricultural development of Scotland, for instance, dates unmistakably from the founding, by the landed gentry, of the Honourable Society of Improvers in 1723. In Japan, the deliberate importation of technology by the landed interests in the last quarter of the nineteenth century provided the principal impetus to industrialization. Many of the key figures in the early industrial growth of Germany were wealthy landlords. Once their interest was aroused, the landlords had little difficulty in possessing themselves of the necessary knowledge and were also in a strong position to recruit technical staff and advance the capital for the enterprise.

A study of historical experience in the transfer of technology suggests, therefore, that many different groups supply the enterprise necessary to effect the transfer and that no one group has a monopoly.[1] It suggests also that the volume of enterprise that takes this form depends largely on the range of experience of likely entrepreneurs, their contacts with foreigners and foreign ideas, and the ease with which they can extend their experience. It depends also on the prevailing interest in technology, particularly in those classes that are in a position to find an outlet for their enthusiasm. The readiness of the community to admit foreigners either as immigrants or as employees of foreign-controlled business is a third factor of importance. All of these depend, in some measure, on government policy and can be influenced by government action and example.

[1] For a highly stimulating discussion of historical experience, especially in Germany, see Fritz Redlich: 'Entrepreneurship in the Initial Stages of Industrialization', *Weltwirtschaftliches Archiv*, 1955.

Governments can also operate on the knowledge without which enterprise runs to waste. They can do much to improve the supply of technical information through research institutions and extension services. They can send students abroad for training or bring foreign technicians to provide training locally. They can also send missions to report on interesting technological developments abroad or invite missions to come and advise on the lines along which development should be pushed. Of particular importance are the technical press, the style and availability of technical publications, and the space devoted to matters of techniques in the daily press. These are not all within the power or influence of governments except in so far as governments are themselves often the largest publishers. Nevertheless, more might be done in most underdeveloped countries to give not only greater publicity but also greater concreteness to technological problems.

One of the limiting factors in the spread of new techniques is the cost of acquiring experience of them. The importance of this at the level of management has already been emphasized. The training of skilled workers raises similar problems. It is possible to import workers from abroad but this is expensive just as bringing in foreign management is expensive. The workers may quit their jobs and go back home or may be tempted by other offers after they arrive. On the other hand, if local workers are sent abroad for training, they may find life abroad very attractive, and foreign employment very well paid, and be under strong temptation to stay abroad instead of returning to their own country. Even if foreigners are recruited to impart their skill on the spot in the new factories and workshops, they may do no more than raise local skills and local ambitions to the point at which migration to some more prosperous area becomes possible. This is one of the difficulties encountered in Southern Italy, for example. The whole process of training, with the high costs that it involves of moving people about, and the high wastage rates that individual entrepreneurs, or even the whole economy, may have to face, is enormously expensive and adds greatly to the capital investment necessary for new industrial ventures.

It is common to regard finance as one of the principal, if not the principal, impediment to technological transfer. There is no doubt that new techniques usually do involve capital investment and that the very fact that they are new tends to make them speculative. The capital that is required can be obtained only on comparatively onerous terms, both because capital is generally scarce in under-developed countries and because it is not readily forthcoming if the return is uncertain. If the new techniques do represent a great advance over the existing ones, however, these circumstances will not effectively prevent the investment from being undertaken so long as the absolute amount of capital required is fairly small. There are always some low-yielding investments that can be deferred, particularly in construction work, to make room for new investments that offer a high return. Where the capital required is large, it is often possible to borrow from abroad at comparatively low rates of interest, since the international capital market (like the domestic capital market in many industrialized countries) is much better organized to handle loan applications for, say, large public utilities than for small industrial projects.

This is far from dismissing the financial obstacle as unimportant; but it often exerts its influence in roundabout ways. The capital market in under-developed countries is highly imperfect and the terms on which capital can be raised vary enormously. The peasant may undertake heavy investment through his own unpaid exertions but be unable to employ this time in ways that will bring him in additional cash so that he cannot make much use of new techniques involving a cash outlay. A small business may also have very limited access to capital except out of profits because the proprietor is unwilling to share control or because his contacts with potential lenders are few.

One of the main ways in which shortage of capital limits technological transfer is through its impact on the various services that are the normal concomitant of industrial growth. The technology appropriate to one firm depends upon the services on which it can count from other firms; and the more it has to provide those services for itself, the higher is the initial investment required and the greater the strain put on its financial resources. The need to provide repair facilities, for example, may tip the scale against the use of modern methods because of the additional capital outlay involved. Another, more obvious, example is the transport and communications system which represents an enormous outlay, far beyond the resources of a single firm. If transport facilities are poor, the market is automatically restricted, and the scope for the use of mechanical power and mechanical appliances suffers correspondingly. It is hardly too much to say that good transport is the most powerful single weapon for accelerating the importation of modern techniques.

It may happen also that innovations in techniques cannot be made one at a time but require simultaneous action by a number of industries. One of the best examples of this is the introduction of the mechanical cotton-picker and the mechanical cotton-weeder in the United States. The economy of the Southern States bore a considerable resemblance to that of many under-developed countries until a generation ago. There was the same dependence on a limited variety of crops, over-employment in agriculture, comparative isolation from outside influences, absence of mechanical techniques. The introduction of the cotton-picker and cotton-weeder had to wait until the atmosphere was more favourable to labour-saving and was delayed by the difficulty of spinning yarn on existing machines from cotton picked mechanically. Once it became clear that mechanical picking was bound to spread, this difficulty was rapidly surmounted and adaptation took place all along the line through spinning, weaving and marketing.[1]

A similar example can be quoted from the experience in India a century ago with a kind of technical assistance programme for the cultivation of cotton. Efforts then made to persuade the peasants to grow American cotton were a total failure, partly at least because the existing channels for the marketing of cotton were not adapted to the change in the product handled and no higher price was received by the peasant for his higher quality American cotton than for the Indian cotton which he was accustomed to growing.

The fact that techniques can rarely be borrowed without adaptation also adds to the capital cost, since the effort of acclimatization may last for a considerable period and involve

[1] J. H. Street, 'Cotton Mechanization and Economic Development', *American Economic Review*, September 1955.

much disappointment and loss. A landowner travelling abroad may be impressed by the livestock and import some animals to graze on pastures that are by no means so rich. He cannot tell in advance whether they will do better than the local breed and he may have to experiment with several different breeds and run up a large bill before he can be sure that he is on the right track. How quickly this happens depends on his competence as an entrepreneur, and the more competent he is, the less heavy is likely to be his capital outlay.

This is a truth of general application that is commonly overlooked. The shortage of capital and of managerial ability in under-developed countries are to some extent interconnected. A good manager can economize capital and make a success of an innovation with a smaller initial investment than a less competent one. The capital installed in the plants of under-developed countries often shows a remarkably low intensity of use, one reason for which is certainly poor management. On the other hand, the countries in which capital is relatively abundant often have a similar abundance of managerial talent, both because the managers are trained to use their capital intensively and because this very training helps to make good managers.

One of the most important influences on technological transfer is the market to be supplied; both its size and the rate at which it is expanding. Modern techniques may have done little over the past generation to increase the size of the average industrial establishment, measured by numbers employed but, taking a longer view, the average post-industrial establishment is obviously larger, by any test, than the average pre-industrial establishment. In order to take advantage of modern techniques, notably the assembly of workers in factories to operate machines, it is necessary to produce on a certain minimum scale that is often beyond the limited requirements of the domestic market. One of the industries to which this limitation does not usually apply is the textile industry, where the technical optimum is low and the size of the market comparatively large; and it is no accident that textile mills are among the first industrial establishments to gain a footing in under-developed countries.

The size of the market is a much more nebulous concept

than it appears, since part of the time of most managements is spent in *creating* a market, and this may be even more necessary where communications are poor and consumers are set in their ways than in a country like the United States. The need to create a market can be just as severe a limitation on technological transfer as a narrow market since it presses on two bottlenecks simultaneously: finance and management. Creating a market involves a capital outlay and it involves diversion of managerial time when this is the critical shortage in many young concerns.

A rapidly expanding market creates an environment highly congenial to rapid technological advance and to all forms of innovation, including the importation and adaptation of foreign techniques. It makes it easier to plan for a larger output, using more advanced techniques than would be justified at the current level of demand. It allows managements to concentrate on production, and rewards those that are on the side of expansion, both by making room for plants erected through miscalculation of demand and by providing easy profits out of which to finance further construction. On the other hand, in a contracting market it rarely pays to be enterprising or to introduce new techniques. A new plant has to engage in a long contest with prevailing techniques that may last as long as the equipment they use or even longer. In a decade such as the world has just lived through, the atmosphere is obviously far more favourable to the rapid spread of new techniques than it was in the decade before the war.

Little consideration has been given above to 'atmosphere', in the sense of social attitudes, customs and beliefs, as a factor in the transfer of technology. Yet no one doubts that this can be one of the most important factors governing technological progress. Fear of unemployment, indifference to efficiency, suspicion of the interests that new techniques are expected to serve, may all thwart endeavours to introduce machinery or forms of organizations that have contributed in other countries to economic advancement. If to innovate is to court having your house burned down and to install new machinery is to provoke a riot or at least a strike, there are not likely to be many innovators. In most under-developed countries, the atmosphere is by no means so uncongenial; but it is true nonetheless that a gradual change in the temper, horizon and calculus of action may be necessary before rapid technological advance can take place. The social overheads that have to be created extend far beyond the physical assets that generally occupy the attention of economists.

It is obvious from all this that the wide gap in technology between the industrialized and the under-developed countries no more gives rise to a swift transfer of technology from the one to the other than does the wide gap in wages give rise to a swift movement of industry. Yet industrial growth does take place at a rate that is probably much more rapid in the under-developed areas of the world than was ever reached elsewhere in the early days of industrialization last century. Technology does cross frontiers and the attention of the world is concentrated increasingly on methods of accelerating the movement. Thousands of experts have gone from the United States and other industrial countries under programmes of technical assistance; and thousands of students and business and professional men have moved in the opposite direction for education and training. The long-term effects of these movements are bound to be great and a powerful impulse has already been given to economic development. This impulse has probably been greatest in agriculture where there is already a long history of attempts to combat a technological lag by advisory services, where simple expedients can yield startling results, and where the men who might listen to the advice and use the expedients are already in a position to do so.

In industry the situation is different. There are few industries to work on and the problem is one of creating business units, not of making existing ones more efficient. There is simply not enough enterprise, public or private, to exploit all the opportunities that exist and no easy way of determining where those opportunities lie. It is here, perhaps, more than in any other way, that technical assistance might help. The under-developed countries need guidance from economists, engineers and administrators in deciding which industries could both find a market, given the prevailing poverty, and supply it at reasonable cost, given the scarcity of nearly every kind of resource except unskilled labour. They need guidance on the techniques that they might borrow without making too heavy demands on capital, skill and managerial ability.

They also need guidance on methods of organizing industrial research and of bringing the results to the attention of those who might apply them. Such guidance is not easy to give. But if there is a strategy in technological transfer, it is on issues of this kind that it should concentrate.

PART III: TRADE

CHAPTER 12

Patterns of Trade and Development[1]

PROFESSOR NURKSE'S Wicksell Lectures,[2] delivered only a few weeks before his death, must be ranked with his best work. The ideas are expressed with all the force and clarity that are characteristic of his writing, the stream of argument flows steadily and persuasively, the historical perspective is wide and revealing, the statistical data support without interrupting the exposition, and the theory is put in the context of earlier doctrine, more as a natural sequel to it than with any object of throwing its defects into relief. Although they are presumably to be regarded as an interim report, in the same way as his earlier Cairo Lectures were a sketch for his 'Problems of Capital Formation in Under-developed Countries', the two Wicksell Lectures contain the gist of Nurkse's latest views on international trade and growth and show in what directions he would have wished to modify current theory on those matters.

The argument of the lectures is that the nineteenth century 'engine of growth' through foreign trade does not nowadays operate sufficiently powerfully to allow primary producing countries to make full use of their expanding resources without a special effort to develop their domestic markets. Trade cannot be analysed exclusively in terms of international specialization, but is also the means by which growth is transmitted from the centres of economic expansion through a steadily rising demand for imports of primary commodities.

[1] Originally published in *Kyklos*, Vol. xiii, Fasc. 4, 1960, as 'International Trade and Economic Development'.

[2] R. Nurkse, *Patterns of Trade and Development* (Stockholm, 1959).

This rising demand not only provides an expanding source of employment in the primary producing countries but also attracts capital and labour to them and accelerates the process of growth-transmission. The process is most easily discernible in the interaction of British development in the nineteenth century with that of the new countries in the world's temperate latitudes: it was from these countries that the increment in British imports was greatest and to these countries that the flow of British capital was largely confined. In the twentieth century the process has been muffled by a variety of forces, of which Nurkse lists half a dozen. These forces have given rise to a lag between the growth of output in the industrial countries and their intake of raw materials, and this lag has been communicated to their imports of primary products, especially if petroleum is left out of account. Thus the primary producers are faced with sluggish export markets while their resources in capital and labour have continued to expand comparatively rapidly. The disparity between these two rates of growth puts them in a dilemma. In seeking employment for their additional resources they cannot be guided merely by their comparative advantage in the existing export sector, since their 'incremental' comparative advantage in these exports may be low, but must find other activities for which the demand is, or can be made, less sluggish. They may try to develop export markets for the more simple types of manufactures; but this is not likely, in the modern world, to be a very easy or successful policy. This leaves only one recourse: to develop the home market by simultaneously industrializing to meet domestic requirements and improving the output of agriculture. So we come round to the familiar remedy of balanced growth, now re-stated to mean the promotion of 'increases in output that are *diversified in accordance with domestic income elasticities of demand* so as to provide markets for each other locally' (p. 44. Author's italics.) Nurkse emphasizes that the various patterns of advance are not simple alternatives and that they can easily be combined; the weight given to each will naturally vary with the circumstances of the country and will change over time.

There is a great deal in this argument with which it would be impossible to differ, especially as it is stated with great moderation and freedom from controversial asides. But there are also some points which the reader may hesitate to accept without further demonstration.

I

Let us start from the contention that the 'mechanism of growth transmission is now in comparatively low gear (p. 27). Transmission from where to where? The nineteenth century 'engine', as Nurkse emphasizes, operated on a limited group of recently settled and predominantly rich countries, many of which are now industrialized or well on the way to industrialization. Are these included in the generalization or are we to think exclusively of those poor and less developed countries—'the exotic countries, the "outsiders" '—that were relatively neglected by the expansion of export demand as well as the flow of capital (p. 18)? If the latter, where is the evidence that the mechanism operates less powerfully on them now than in the nineteenth century or any other period? Could anyone hope to sustain this view of, say, African development? If the former, where is the evidence that it is demand rather than supply factors that have limited the growth of their exports of primary produce?

Is Nurkse's thesis intended to apply to, say, the Argentine? Or should we regard a country like India as more typical of the group he has in mind? Both countries felt the workings of the 'engine of growth' in the nineteenth century and the exports of both have shown little change in scale since 1913. Their exports (taking the two countries together and counting in Pakistan and Burma) were once one-third of total exports from the three poorer continents (excluding Japan); now they are about one-seventh. But is this due to a failure of external demand? What of the industrialization that has completely changed the composition of Indian exports so that half the total now consists of manufactures—a higher proportion than applies to Canada.[1] The 'lag' in Indian exports surely reflects domestic as well as external circumstances—industrialization, population growth, changes in domestic levels of consumption have all played a part. How else can one account for the divergence in trend between Indian exports and world exports of primary produce over so long a

[1] P. Lamartine Yates, *Forty Years of Foreign Trade* (London, 1959), p. 182.

period? The 'lag' in Argentine exports appears to have a similar origin.

These are not trivial examples. India and the Argentine together are important enough to exert a strong damping influence on the total. If we leave them out for one reason and Africa for another and the petroleum producers for a third we are bound to ask ourselves what significance can be attached to the rump. Are we talking about Indonesia or Australia, Guatemala or Venezuela, Ethiopia or the Belgian Congo? Does an aggregate for these countries have any real importance and do conclusions based on such aggregates form a satisfactory guide to policy in any one of them? To which, if any, of the parts are we to apply the generalizations which are said to be valid for the aggregates?

In many under-developed countries one of the most important tasks of economic development is to unite the subsistence and the market sectors of the economy and in so doing provide fresh opportunities of development. This task is facilitated by the pressure of export demand (but not always carried a great deal further, or we should hear less of 'dual' economies) provided the fruits of high prices abroad are passed on to native producers. In post-war years this condition has not always been fulfilled: governments and marketing boards have been more concerned to skim off finance for other forms of development than to let high prices do the job of extending the market sector at the expense of the subsistence sector. At the same time they have not been disposed to put much faith in an elastic supply from existing producers. Export levies and export taxes have reduced the pressure of foreign demand on the output of primary produce; they provide one further reason for hesitation in attributing any lag in exports to factors on the side of demand.[1]

Again, what periods are we comparing? The years before 1914 and the years since 1950? Or some longer intervals of time such as the thirty years 1928–57 covered by the tables in the GATT report on *Trends in International Trade* from which Nurkse quotes? So far as the earliest of these periods is concerned, it is just not true that 'in the years before 1914 exports of primary produce were expanding more rapidly than

[1] Changes in capital flows, including various forms of aid, may also have contributed by reducing the pressure behind exports.

exports of manufactured goods' (p. 20). In terms of relative values there was very little change between the late seventies and 1914 and in terms of relative volumes there is evidence that primary products were growing less rapidly than manufactures after 1896. It was between 1914 and 1937—and particularly between 1929 and 1937—that the volume of primary products gained relatively to the volume of manufactured goods entering into international trade. Since 1937 this 'lag' has been more than made up.

If we look back over the past thirty years, therefore, as Nurkse does, our view embraces two very different periods, one between 1929 and 1937 in which trade in manufactured goods slumped while trade in primary produce held up, and one since the war in which trade in manufactures has expanded with extraordinary speed while trade in primary produce has tended to lag behind. In 1950, for example, the volume of trade in primary produce was still below pre-war (and indeed below the level of 1929); and this was true of exports both from non-industrial and from industrial countries. On the other hand, world trade in manufactures far exceeded the pre-war level by 1950. Since 1950 both kinds of trade have grown rapidly but the growth in manufactures has continued to be the more vigorous.

What conclusion one reaches about comparative trends hinges, therefore, on the precise span of time used for the comparison, since pre-war and post-war trends are in strong opposition. It also hinges on whether we make the comparison in terms of volume or value since there have been large changes in relative prices. The comparison which Nurkse makes is on the basis of figures from *Trends in International Trade* showing that the share of non-industrial countries in world trade (by value) fell between 1928 and 1957 from 33·8 per cent to 31·3 per cent; or, if oil-exporting countries are omitted, from 32·2 per cent to 24·4 per cent. This comparison does not lend much weight to his argument (as indeed he recognizes) unless there are good reasons for omitting the oil-exporting countries. But are there? Is it right to exclude the most striking example of the nineteenth century mechanism of development that 'survives' and then deduce that the mechanism has lost some of its former power? Can we include exports from the industrial countries to the countries producing petroleum on the one side and then omit the exports that go back in payment on the other? The fact that oil exporters are few in number and have been particularly lucky is not sufficient reason for segregating them, since on similar grounds we might omit the exporters of coffee, cocoa and tea, or of mineral ores and base metals. On the other hand, it is fair to lay emphasis on the very large share of petroleum and petroleum products in the growth of exports from non-industrial areas: half the increase, by volume, between 1928 and 1955 and two-thirds of the increase between 1937–38 and 1955.[1]

Mr Lamartine Yates's 'Forty Years of Foreign Trade'—which appeared too late for Nurkse to use—indicates rather different long-term trends. If we take the three poor continents, Africa, Asia (excluding Japan) and Latin America, we find that each enjoyed a rising share of world exports between 1913 and 1953.

This favourable trend might be due to the emergence of the oil exporting countries over the last half century and mask a quite different trend in other under-developed countries. Closer inspection of Mr Yates's data, however, shows an increase in the share of the three continents in world exports of each separate SITC category of primary produce. Undoubtedly the exporters of petroleum enjoyed a particularly favourable market: but the omission of all exports of fuel (SITC Category 3) still leaves a total which increases faster for the three poorer continents than for the richer continents between 1913 and 1953.[2]

Let us suppose, for a moment, that the lag in exports from the poorer countries is real. How could we account for it? Nurkse lists six factors:

(i) the change in industrial structure in favour of 'heavy' industries with a low content of imported raw materials;
(ii) the rising share of services in the total output of advanced countries;
(iii) the low income-elasticity of consumer demand for many agricultural products;
(iv) agricultural protectionism;

[1] *Trends in International Trade* (GATT, Geneva, 1959), p. 22.
[2] P. Lamartine Yates, op. cit., Table A.23.

(v) economies in the use of raw materials, e.g. through reprocessing of scrap;
(vi) the introduction of synthetic materials.

TABLE I

Share of three poorest continents in world exports (at current prices and excluding Soviet bloc)

Continent	*Total exports*		*Primary produce*[1]		*Manufactures*[2]	
	1913 %	1953 %	1913 %	1953 %	1913 %	1953 %
Africa	4·0	6·5	7·1	10·9	0·3	2·2
Asia (excl. Japan)	9·5	10·2	13·6	17·5	4·3	2·8
Latin America	9·1	11·3	15·6	21·1	0·9	1·4
Total	22·6	28·0	36·3	49·5	5·5	6·4

[1] SITC categories 0–4. [2] SITC categories 5–8.

Source: P. Lamartine Yates, *Forty Years of Foreign Trade*, Table A.23.

This is not a very convincing list. The second and third did not suddenly begin to operate in the twentieth century; and if the fifth has operated more powerfully in recent years it may have been for purely economic reasons such as the high price of non-ferrous metals. The fourth factor Nurkse himself discounts as more likely to affect non-tropical than tropical agriculture; and, as he points out, manufactures also are protected. This leaves us with the first and sixth factors. As to the first, the expansion of the heavy industries in advanced countries has been partly in replacement of lighter industries, such as textiles, which have not disappeared but have migrated to the less advanced countries. This expansion is also to some extent a symptom of the high level of world investment that goes with full employment. It is difficult, therefore, to discuss the effects of the first factor in isolation from other elements in the situation which exercise a complex influence on the volume and structure of world trade. The introduction of synthetic materials has undoubtedly been a major factor limiting trade in primary produce. But is it quite fortuitous that it has operated to produce economy in the use of materials that are not only expensive but often relatively more expensive than before the war? In both of the last factors in Nurkse's list an element of economic incentive may have reinforced technological influences; this element cannot be dismissed at random, given the movement in relative prices.

What Nurkse seems to leave out of account is the price factor. But the growth in world trade in primary produce in the nineteenth century did not spring simply from an overflow of demand in the industrial countries. It originated also in the power of overseas primary producers to capture a larger *share* of the market in Western Europe and particularly in the United Kingdom. They were the low-cost producers of the world and could offer large savings to their customers provided the latter would withdraw from primary activities, for which they were ill-suited, in favour of secondary activities in which they had a cumulative advantage. The specialization that grew up was not, as Nurkse rightly insists, a static one; nor was it merely dynamic in the sense that additional resources flowed from the centre to reinforce it; it was also progressive in the quite different sense that it took time for the structural adaptations to cost differences to be brought about, for the exporters of primary producers to capitalize their advantages, and for the importers to make room in their industrial structure for the larger volume of imports. It was this *progressive* element in international specialization that multiplied world trade threefold between 1850 and 1880; and it is the disappearance—or dwindling—of this element that accounts for the subsequent decline in the rate of growth; for whatever may be true of *comparative* rates of growth, the total volume of international trade did not grow after 1880 as rapidly as in the earlier period.

That specialization in the form of an interchange between primary produce and manufactures could not increase indefinitely is obvious enough. The extinction of primary activities in the industrial countries would represent the limit to which it could be carried. But long before that stage the competitive position of surviving elements in the industrial countries would be strengthened, if only by the operation of diminishing returns in reverse, and the competitive position of the expanding elements in the non-industrial countries would be weakened, if only by population growth. Government policy in both groups of countries was also bound to pull against so extreme a form of specialization and, as is emphasized below.

the war provided strong reasons to both groups for reversing earlier trends.

The fact that the specialization that grew up was, in the main, between rich countries also helped to make it self-limiting. The richer the domestic market in the developing primary producing countries, the easier it was for industry to take root. Industrialization did not at once reduce the scope for foreign trade since total resources were growing. But as it proceeded, it necessarily came into conflict with the expansion of the primary sector based on foreign markets, until eventually that sector began to shrink in relation to the rest of the economy. Of the newer countries in which this process is most easily observed, the United States is by far the most important; and the fact that she has now replaced the United Kingdom as the dominant economy should not blind us to her simultaneous rôle as an exporter of primary produce. The United States has industrialized herself more quickly and more completely than the other countries on which the nineteenth century mechanism operated. In doing so, she has changed the structure of world trade and the form which progressive specialization now takes. The growing markets for primary produce are to a lesser extent in the old industrial countries—in 1913 Europe (including the United Kingdom) took 74 per cent of world exports of such produce and in 1953 only 54 per cent[1]—and lie increasingly in the continents developed in the nineteenth century. The specialist exporters of primary produce have to look for markets, therefore, in countries that are also large exporters and by no means in the weak competitive position of the United Kingdom a century ago.[2] It is more difficult to compress the primary sector in those countries and carry specialization a stage further than it was to gain a footing at the expense of high-cost European producers.

The dominance of a highly competitive primary producer —the United States—contrasts with the dominance in the nineteenth century of the major importer of primary produce —the United Kingdom. It would be curious, however, if we made use of this contrast—itself a proof of the effectiveness

[1] F. Lamartine Yates, op. cit., Table A.24.

[2] North America supplied as high a proportion of world exports of primary produce in 1953 as in 1913.

of the 'engine of growth'—to cast doubt on the continued functioning of the 'engine'. It would be more reasonable to deduce that we are unlikely in the twentieth century to find low-cost sources of supply so much more competitive than the low-cost sources opened up in the nineteenth century that they can now capture a larger share of the domestic market in primary produce in those very countries. The development of the poorer primary producers cannot but be an immensely more difficult task than was the development of the richer. They tend to be limited to a range of produce in which they will not have to compete with the industrial countries, although they cannot avoid competition with one another; and they have the utmost difficulty in supplementing development in primary activities by industrialization either for home or foreign markets.

The fact that progressive specialization is now less evident in primary activities does not mean that it cannot assume other forms. It is possible for countries that are unwilling to allow their agriculture to contract further, or at a more rapid rate, and are in a position to adopt a more liberal import policy, to admit larger imports of manufactures instead. It is arguable that this is what has happened in the United States and Germany, and that to some extent it accounts for the remarkable expansion in trade between industrial countries in manufactured goods. The fact that the United Kingdom has not imported a much larger volume of manufactures testifies more to the compulsions on her to limit her total imports than to any exceptional tenderness towards manufacturers. In conditions of full employment the industrial countries appear to be willing to allow considerable international specialization within the industrial sector and to trade more freely in manufactures than in agricultural products.

One test of the trend in international specialization is to compare exports of primary produce from the non-industrial countries with exports from the industrial countries. The latter do, after all, account for a large proportion of the total trade as sellers as well as buyers; if we include all OEEC Europe in the industrial group, as in Table II, no less than half the world's exports of primary produce come from industrial countries so defined, although the proportion is very much less on other definitions.

As our earlier argument implies, there has been a long and steady rise in the share of the non-industrial countries in world trade in primary produce. Between 1913 and 1953 the three poorer continents raised their share from 36·3 to 49·5 per cent (see Table I). Unpublished calculations by Mr Maizels of the National Institute of Economic and Social Research show a continuous rise, using a wider group of non-industrial countries, from 44·4 per cent in 1899 to 68·0 per cent in 1950, followed by a fall to 66·0 per cent in 1957. Although the turning-point by value came in 1950, by volume it came in 1937 and the continued improvement in the relative value of exports from the poorer countries up to 1950 was entirely due to the extraordinary rise in their price. Here, first, are the figures by volume:

TABLE II

Volume of exports of primary produce, 1899–1957
1913=100

	1899	1913	1929	1937	1959	1955	1957
Industrial countries	71	100	113	96	108	141	163
Rest of world (residual)	62	100	144	157	132	183	198
World total	65	100	132	134	123	167	185

1. These figures are taken from an unpublished study by Mr A. Maizels.

In 1937 the volume of exports of primary produce from the industrial countries was slightly lower than in 1913 while exports from non-industrial countries were over 50 per cent higher. Unit export values had climbed about 10 per cent for the industrial countries and fallen slightly for the others. By 1950 there had been a spectacular change. Exports from the industrial countries had increased while exports from other countries had fallen sharply. At the same time, while unit export values doubled for the first group they more than trebled for the second. In 1957 both groups had added 50 per cent to the volume of their exports of primary produce and the divergence in unit export values had narrowed only slightly.[1]

[1] For the industrial countries they rose from 200 to 225 (1913=100) and for the rest of the world 326 to 335.

There are two points of the greatest significance here. The first is that the non-industrial countries have made less headway than the industrial countries since 1937 and no greater headway even since 1950. No doubt they took longer to recover from the war; and no doubt, too, an expansion by 50 per cent in seven years is not bad going by any standard, whatever the mechanism that produced it. The fact remains that, in contrast to the period before 1937, the non-industrial countries show no sign of taking a larger share of world trade in primary produce. Indeed, other figures suggest an even less promising competitive position. If we take imports into the industrial countries alone, the non-industrial countries seem to have been falling behind between 1953 and 1957, particularly in agricultural products.

It is difficult to resist associating this change of trend with the second of the points emerging from Mr Maizels' calculations; the wide and continuing divergence since 1937 in unit export values for the two groups of countries. If, after twenty years, the non-industrial countries are getting prices that have risen half as much again as the prices obtained by industrial countries for primary produce, it is hardly surprising if the demand for their exports shows some signs of 'sluggishness'. Here, surely, is a powerful reason for industrialized countries to develop domestic supplies of primary produce, to economize in the use of imported materials, and to accelerate the introduction of substitutes.

It is in fact difficult to make sense of the post-war decade if we leave this price factor out of account. It reflected the acute pressure on supplies of primary produce in a fully-employed economy—a pressure that continued because of the low elasticity of supply of this produce. This low elasticity was aggravated by the concentration of effort in many underdeveloped countries on industrialization rather than agricultural development. They had many reasons, some good, some bad, for trying to broaden the base of their economy but in doing so they could hardly fail to make agriculture less responsive to external demand. The industrial countries had equal cause for action to economize imports in the abrupt swing of prices against them and in their inability to obtain even the pre-war volume of supplies five years after the end of the war. That they turned to one another, quite as much as to non-industrial countries, for supplies suggests some movement of demand from the dearer to the cheaper products, although the special rôle of North America as an elastic source of supply must also have contributed.

Undeniably, however, a great deal must have depended on the luck of the draw. It would be foolish to assume any broad identity between the categories of primary produce exported by the industrial and the non-industrial countries, and the expansion in world demand may have been concentrated on the former for reasons largely unconnected with price. As Mr Maizels has reminded me, different primary-producing countries specialize on different exports which have been far from uniformly affected by the growth of the world economy and few of them can do much to shift from the less fortunate to the more fortunate commodities, as the pattern of demand alters. It may be that, for some at least among them, the engine of growth has worked in the way Nurkse suggests.

TABLE III

Imports of primary produce into industrial countries, 1953–1957 (billions of dollars)

	Imports from			
	Non-industrial countries		*Industrial countries*	
	1953	1957	1953	1957
Food and tobacco	7·28	7·79	4·84	5·94
Raw materials	6·07	6·17	3·61	5·19
Ores	0·94	1·43	0·74	1·52
Fuels	2·42	4·09	1·87	3·32
Total	16·71	19·48	11·06	15·97

Source: International Trade 1957–1958, Table 7 (GATT, Geneva, 1959).

II

Let us turn next to a second main query suggested by the very different treatment of growth transmission by Professor Haberler in his Cairo Lectures on 'International Trade and Economic Development'. Was the nineteenth century mechanism as limited as Nurkse's argument seems to imply? His propositions run in terms of (i) a declining propensity to import in the advanced countries, (ii) a corresponding decline in the rate of growth of the export market for the products of the less advanced countries, and (iii) a consequential falling behind in their general rate of growth unless they take steps to develop their home market by a process of industrialization. There are good reasons for doubting the applicability of the first of these propositions to the post-war period, and the second, as we have seen, by no means follows from the first, especially if it is applied to the poorer countries that were developing relatively slowly in the nineteenth century. What are we to make of the third?

Economic growth can be transmitted from one country to another both directly and indirectly. Trade does much more than provide a market and encourage the growth or reallocation of the resources necessary in order to supply it. It also transmits experience and ideas, changes attitudes and institutions, and blows up obstacles to further development. Haberler lists four such indirect benefits, all of which are likely to vary (although not in any rigid, functional way) with the scale on which trade is carried on. They include the provision of capital through international investment (a benefit of which Nurkse takes full account); access to the means of development in the form of raw materials, semi-finished goods and machinery; access to knowledge, skill, managerial abilitv, and so on; and the galvanizing influence of competition.[1] These indirect benefits are likely to be much greater in the less advanced than in the more highly industrial countries; and they might well be such as to exceed (or even dwarf) the gains flowing from specialization as such. The larger the indirect gains the less reliable is the growth of exports as a measure of economic development. Even if exports remain quite modest, there is no obvious reason why the same forces that have permitted the American economy to expand without a corresponding growth in exports should not permit other less developed economies to expand in the same way. Market forces may be adequate to multiply a small growth in exports into a much larger (and more than proportionate) growth in national income. The chances that this will happen will be greatest if the indirect benefits of trade are manifesting themselves in a general rise in productivity.

[1] G. Haberler, *International Trade and Economic Development* (National Bank of Egypt, Cairo, 1959), pp. 10 *et seq.*

Now it may be that Nurkse has no quarrel with this rather rosy view of the matter.[1] Unfortunately his argument, when it turns to policy, becomes ambiguous: it is not clear how far he regards his patterns of growth as alternatives between which market forces will decide and how far he has in mind the setting of a pattern or combination of patterns by government. His preoccupation is with the need to make full use of available resources; and the sense of his argument, with its emphasis on the limitations of export markets, requires him to take a stand in favour of an active policy of industrialization.

Again, however, there is an obscurity: it is not clear what action he would like governments to take. The 'balanced growth' which he recommends would be consistent with a policy of import restriction without further interference with market forces or it might require government investment in new factories. Whichever course was adopted, it would be necessary to *create* a market for industrial products and this would mean initially the exclusion of some imports from the domestic market. But would that be enough? Would the building of factories in a poor country add so significantly to employment and income as to give them an adequate market at prices that covered their costs? We are, after all, thinking of countries where the market is too small for a single factory in most industries and where this would continue to be true at levels of income perceptibly higher. Why should the simultaneous construction of several factories alter the situation decisively? The additional employment and demand that would result could not be large in relation to the national income unless the process were continued for many years and would be likely to have early repercussions on the output of the agricultural sector. If the output of the largest industry in the country—agriculture—were improved, the additional income would itself enlarge the market for industrial products and provide a firmer basis for the launching of new industries. This Nurkse frequently emphasized. But he rarely laid similar stress on the way in which industrialization normally starts: with a few of the most promising industries, often quite unrelated to one another, displacing imports on the one hand

[1] He agrees that 'economic growth in aggregate terms, if not *per capita*, is probably more widespread and, in the world as a whole, perhaps more rapid today, in the 1950's, than ever before' (p. 49). But he doubts whether, outside industrial countries, this growth can be classed as growth through trade.

and handicrafts on the other. These industries may refrain, when they start, from exporting; but they have very often reached that stage by the time the next crop is on the way. The process which the Americans call 'spearheading' seems much more typical than advance on a broad front.

III

Haberler approaches his subject much more belligerently. He starts off, forthrightly enough, by asserting his belief that 'substantially free trade with marginal, insubstantial corrections and deviations, is the best policy from the point of view of economic development' (p. 5), and adds, a few pages later, 'especially of the under-developed countries' (p. 15). He dismisses the idea that governments can improve on comparative costs as an allocative mechanism; they may be static but changes in production functions take place slowly and usually cannot be foreseen (p. 10). There is no systematic tendency for the terms of trade to move against or in favour of primary producing countries (p. 23). The assumption that 'there are large masses of unused resources free for the asking and ready to be put to work' is 'entirely unrealistic' (p. 27); disguised unemployment is 'wishful thinking' and the reality is low productivity (pp. 26–7). The relationship between developed and under-developed countries is one from which the latter gain much and lose little, if anything, and talk of backsetting effects is vague and usually without real substance (pp. 28–33).

This is good knock-about economics calculated to make some readers bristle and others purr. The case put does not rest on mere assertion but is supported by forceful arguments that are not easy to rebut. It is true, to take the last point first, that one can overdo the first principle of development, 'to him that hath shall be given': an early start can be an advantage but it can also be a handicap. It is also true that poor countries gain from having rich neighbours and would lose if they ceased to prosper. But the fact remains that making a beginning is peculiarly difficult in economic development and that the leap forward has to be all the bigger the more advanced technique becomes. In some ways, therefore, continuous development in the industrial countries may make it *more* difficult to 'take off'. From the point of view of a foreign industrialist, able to choose freely where he will put a factory, an under-developed country becomes a progressively less attractive alternative unless some form of governmental support is offered. From the point of view of an indigenous factory-owner, it becomes steadily more difficult to compete with imports unless the process of industrialization is already well under way. Until then he is, in almost every sense of the term, isolated; and isolation imposes a larger handicap as technique advances. This is so because, as a rule, the range of industrial facilities required tends to grow, the variety of product to which the latest technique is suited tends to narrow, and the minimum scale of production worth considering tends to expand. An industrialist trying to establish himself in an under-developed country finds his market too limited for specialized production, the variety of his output too wide to allow him to use the most advanced technique, and the investment necessary in order to train labour and provide ancillary services too large to make it possible to raise the capital on reasonable terms. These handicaps, unless redressed by government action or by good luck (e.g. in war-time), may well become greater with the passage of time.

This argument applies with much less force once the initial stages of industrialization have been completed. It is true that, within an industrial country, the progress of one area may do harm to the development of another. The growth of the more successful areas seems to become cumulative and the movement of productive resources of those areas takes on the character of a snowball. But, as Haberler points out, this proves nothing about the *international* distribution of industry. So far as there is any movement of resources between industrial and pre-industrial countries, it mainly takes the form of investment by the industrial in the pre-industrial countries and this is calculated to narrow any divergence in rates of growth, not to widen it. Even if the divergence remains, the chances that more rapid development in the industrial countries will actually slow down development in countries already well advanced towards industrialization seems relatively slight.

On this point Haberler and Nurkse are in general agreement. Where they differ is in the historical perspective in which they see the interaction of development in the one group of countries on the development of the other. For Nurkse the interaction is becoming feebler but for Haberler the harmony of interests is as strong as ever.

The main differences between them arise over unused resources and the value of comparative costs as an allocative mechanism. Both are agreed on the low level of labour productivity and the large social investment that is necessary before labour in under-developed countries becomes cheap to employ.[1] But for Haberler there are no unused resources and for Nurkse the major problem of policy is to find a use for the steady addition to resources in under-developed countries. Perhaps the truth is different in different countries. But the general experience of most countries is, surely, that if the demand for labour and other resources drops, there is some genuine unemployment, some short-time working and some shift to less productive occupations. In the under-developed countries there is evidence of all three phenomena: it does not matter very much whether we call the third 'disguised unemployment', so long as we recognize that an increase in the demand for labour and in the productivity of labour are likely to go together. The supply of labour is usually unbalanced, and there are bottlenecks at various levels of skill (foremen, supervisors, etc.), so that mere pressure of demand is not enough to get rid of all the slack. But, given sufficient investment in training to get rid of the bottlenecks, the level of employment (and productivity) can be greatly increased. Thus the dispute is really between those who think, with Haberler, that output is held back by the low productivity of the entire labour force and those who think employment capable of responding elastically to demand provided key workers can be trained fast enough to overcome the problem of labour organization.

Coupled with this difference is another. Nurkse thinks that additional resources should be employed in accordance with 'incremental' comparative advantage rather than absorbed in production for traditional exports that are in inelastic demand. Haberler makes no such distinction and trusts to comparative costs to allocate total resources, increments and all. He is, however, prepared to accept a uniform import tariff.

[1] Nurkse, op. cit., pp. 37–8; Haberler, op. cit., p. 34.

on manufactured goods and seems ready to accept a level of protection up to 20–30 per cent (p. 36). As to primary produce he would no doubt dismiss Nurkse's fears by pointing out that exports of such produce have in fact commanded terms of trade showing no strong secular trend. Where then is the difficulty in marketing the output of additional resources on terms as favourable as those obtained by existing resources?

On this crucial point it is not clear what Nurkse's reply is. He does not argue for a persistent trend in the terms of trade against the under-developed countries and yet, if lack of demand rather than of supply accounts for the lag in their exports, some fall in their relative price would be natural. Although markets are not free, and the output of many primary commodities has been deliberately limited in order to maintain prices, there are surely enough other commodities with free markets to let the terms of trade register any failure of demand.

At the end of it all, the reader may still feel that neither Nurkse nor Haberler has settled the primary issue: how far a shortage of foreign exchange (as contrasted with capital, skilled labour, land, etc.) is a limiting factor in economic development. The majority of the under-developed countries are monocultures, dependent for their earnings of foreign exchange on a single commodity (or at most two or three).[1] These earnings are highly inelastic except when exports of the principal commodity form a small fraction of the world's consumption. At the same time, nearly all the plant and machinery that they require has to be imported, so that the scale of industrial investment is limited by the foreign exchange available to pay for it. In those circumstances, what should be the policy of a country seeking to accelerate its development? We know what most countries have done; it would be interesting if we could be told, by an economist of the standing of Nurkse or Haberler, what the results have been and what they should have done.

[1] In 1953 there were thirty countries that depended on a single product for at least half their export earnings and between them these countries accounted for 40 per cent of all exports from the three poorer continents (Yates, op. cit. p. 180).

CHAPTER 13

International Trade and Economic Development[1]

ECONOMISTS have singled out, at one time or another, a great variety of causes of the wealth of nations. Among them are three that have been accorded particular emphasis: the growth of markets, the accumulation of capital and the progress of technology. All three, like everything else that economists write about, interact with one another, so that the influence of any one of them makes itself felt as much through its repercussions on the other two as by its direct impact. A high level of capital investment, for example, allows new techniques to be exploited more quickly and at the same time helps to speed up the improvement of these techniques and the discovery of still newer ones by providing opportunities of experimentation on a commercial scale. Investment widens markets by enlarging the community's productive powers and contributes to the progress of technology by ensuring an outlet for innovations in technique. Nor is this the end of the matter: the resulting widening of markets and progress in technology react on one another and both create scope for yet more investment. Interactions so complex and far-reaching make it difficult to isolate the consequences of any single element in economic growth and development. They permit economists, indulging an individualism that is at once the charm and the reproach of our science, to pick their own thread to guide them through the maze, and set up their own signposts to prosperity.

The fashionable route today is by way of higher investment—except perhaps on the Continent where investment is already relatively high and the appeal of a larger market is correspondingly greater. In Britain it has also become fashionable to look in the direction of technological education and heavier expenditure on research and development for a

[1] A public lecture delivered at the London School of Economics and Political Science on 13 February 1961, and published in *Economica*, August 1961

short-cut to higher productivity. I have no quarrel with putting up these signposts provided they are not represented as the only ones to follow. No one can fail to be conscious in the modern world of the enormous dependence of economic progress on advances in technology and on the investment that is necessary in order to give them effect. But there is a danger, particularly in the under-developed countries, that the third major influence on development, the widening of markets, may be allowed less than its due. This influence is now regarded with scepticism and distrust. I propose to consider how far this attitude is justified in under-developed countries and how international markets affect their economies.

Everyone knows what an electric effect a change in market opportunities can have on a firm or an industry. A sustained pressure of demand can overcome, in course of time, all kinds of obstacles to an increase in output. Whatever the qualifications necessary in mining or in agriculture, the normal experience in industry is, surely, that if market obstacles to expansion are removed the other obstacles are rarely insurmountable. The production problem is relatively simple if the marketing problem can be disregarded. The same often applies to a whole community. There are rural areas in under-developed countries that for centuries have followed an almost unchanging routine and seem quite unresponsive to economic forces. Yet when the international market offers new and tempting opportunities, it often happens that old attitudes yield, the social framework adapts itself, unsuspected energies are released, and output responds on a scale that far surpasses initial expectations.

Equally, no one doubts the propulsive rôle of foreign trade in the development of the countries that we now think of as advanced. Whether one thinks of Britain at the outset of the industrial revolution or of the United States in the nineteenth century or of Japan in the twentieth, the expansion of exports gave a conspicuous momentum to the economy and helped it on its way to industrialization. Over the past century and a half the growth of international trade has continued to open up new opportunities of specialization and development for all the countries engaging in it. These opportunities were particularly apparent in the primary-producing countries overseas that were still in process of settlement, since trade enabled them to bring into use their great unexploited natural resources and freed them from the limitations of their own domestic markets. The international division of labour that resulted simultaneously helped the importing countries to meet their expanding requirements of materials and foodstuffs from low-cost sources of supply and afforded their export industries the double advantage of a larger scale of operations at lower real cost and the further economies that normally accompany a rapid rate of industrial growth.

In spite of the contribution that it has made to world economic development, international trade is not a popular engine of growth. The reasons for this are well known.

First of all it carries with it dependence on external forces. This means that the pace of development cannot be set by domestic policy but is set by forces that are not within the control of the indigenous authorities nor indeed of any authority, indigenous or foreign. The further exports rise, the higher this dependence mounts. More resources become tied to export requirements and less are left to meet the needs of the domestic market, so that there is less room for manoeuvre in organizing an economic structure adapted to those needs. In the under-developed countries dependence on external forces is particularly resented since it is associated with colonialism and loss of status and with the sense of inequality that always accompanies the dependence of the poor on the rich. Whether these attitudes are justifiable in terms of history or not, and whether they are harmful or otherwise to the countries where they prevail, their very existence itself limits the scope for foreign trade and the use that can be made in the future of patterns of development that were important in the past.[1]

A second source of objection is that foreign demand impinges only on a limited sector of the economy. The under-developed countries include a large number of what have misleadingly been christened monocultures. Whatever the variety of their agriculture many of them—thirty, to be exact—depend upon a single product for at least half their export earnings. Between them these thirty countries accounted in 1953 for 40 per cent of total exports from the under-developed

[1] Cf. B. C. Swerling, *Some Inter-relationships between Agricultural Trade and Economic Development* (mimeographed, November 1960), p. 30.

countries; and the number of countries showing this degree of dependence on one export shows no long-term tendency to fall.[1]

It is a further source of disquiet that the export sector in such economies is rarely the vehicle of rapid innovation in other sectors. If the exports are agricultural, agriculture is damned as hidebound and incapable of imparting momentum to the rest of the economy; while if they are mineral, any gains are alleged to accrue to foreigners or to be confined within an enclave that is only loosely tacked on to the rest of the economy. Worst of all, to ship out oil is to part with the nation's patrimony. Mines and plantations supplying foreign markets are only too likely to be run by foreign managers and immigrant workers on behalf of foreign shareholders and with the help of imported equipment and materials, so that they form an intrusion from some other economy rather than an integral part of the economy of the under-developed country. The gains may flow abroad while the long-term costs, in the shape of a colony of unskilled and unassimilable alien workers, remain behind indefinitely.

Not only does foreign demand bear on a limited sector of the economy but it tends also to be highly variable. Most of the demand assumes the character of an overspill from the industrial countries of the world and fluctuates accordingly with the level of industrial activity. These fluctuations are not easily offset by parallel changes on the side of supply, for supply is highly inelastic over the short period of a cyclical swing and the result is a violent fluctuation in prices whenever demand and supply diverge.

The average prices received for exports are also thought to be unfair. In some versions they are so attractive that they encourage a kind of Gadarene specialization, resources rushing down the line of least resistance to the lowest possible level of utilization from which there is later found to be no way back. In the more usual version, prices are thought to be unfair for the opposite reason—that they sink lower and lower, the impoverished producer having no option but to submit to greater and greater exploitation by the lucky countries that have chosen to specialize in industry. The two versions may even be combined—as I have heard them combined—in a single woeful account of betrayal by higher prices

[1] F. Lamartine Yates, *Forty Years of Foreign Trade*, 1959, p. 180.

followed by repentance throughout a secular slide in the terms of trade.

There is a more recent and more sophisticated argument against putting one's faith in foreign trade. While that may have worked in the past, we are told, it is not working now and will not work in the future. Foreign trade no longer operates as in the nineteenth century so as to allow the primary producing countries to make full use of their expanding resources. The growth that takes place in the centres of industrial development is still transmitted to less advanced countries through a steadily rising demand for imports of primary commodities. But the process works more and more feebly because the intake of materials is not keeping pace with industrial output and more of the materials are obtained without importation from under-developed countries. The export markets of these countries are consequently sluggish. On the other hand, they have a growing population to employ and may be losing an opportunity of developing other assets through sheer stagnation of demand. In such circumstances, it is urged, they have no option but to adopt a new pattern of advance and make deliberate efforts to develop their home market. The transmission of growth from foreign markets through foreign trade has ceased to be a sufficiently powerful engine of development.

I shall not attempt to discuss all these arguments. There are some with which I find myself in sympathy: for example, the prices of primary products are notoriously volatile and the damaging effects of this volatility on the economies of the exporting countries are beyond question. With other arguments I find myself almost entirely out of sympathy: the world economy is not so constructed that primary-producing countries are doomed to a *dégringolade* in their terms of trade with industrial countries. In any event the terms of trade of a group of countries are of very little interest to individual members of the group unless they are all affected in roughly the same way—an assumption far removed from everyday experience. These are not matters on which I have anything to contribute that is not already well known. I shall refer to them only in so far as they help to explain the current pessimism about long-term trends in world trade and its impact on the development of the less advanced countries.

Let me begin, in considering the pessimistic attitude that I have outlined, by emphasizing the importance—indeed, the uniqueness—of the contribution that foreign trade can make to economic development. There is nothing necessarily regrettable about dependence on foreign trade. It is true that in engaging in trade a country puts itself at the mercy of external events: this is the price that any international division of labour exacts. But a country that seeks development must invite foreign influences if it is to succeed. It needs foreign equipment, foreign capital and foreign ideas. How can it pay for this equipment without earning foreign currency by exporting? Or arrange a transfer of capital, in or out, without those other transactions in goods and services that give effect to the transfer? Or allow the economy to be permeated with the ideas that are the seed of true development without the kind of contacts with foreigners that trade automatically produces? Trade is no mere exchange of goods, least of all when it takes place between economies at different stages of development. As often as not, it is trade that gives birth to the urge to develop, the knowledge and experience that make development possible, and the means to accomplish it.

The importance of foreign trade is particularly great in countries that lack an engineering industry and are obliged to import almost all their machinery. In such countries exports may easily become the limiting factor on productive investment and on the successful development of the economy. The common experience in under-developed countries is not that exports are already a dangerously large element but that they are not large enough to give adequate elbow room in the financing of new investment. A high level of exports enlarges the volume of imports of equipment that can be financed without endangering the balance of payments, and this greater degree of freedom makes it easier to take a long view and plan domestic investment without the constant interruption that destroys half its value.

There is nothing particularly surprising when external demand bears on a narrow sector of the economy. This presumably reflects the much higher productivity of resources, especially land, in some specialized use, such as the growing of coffee, than in any less specialized alternative use. Foreign trade opens up large possibilities of immediate gain by concentrating on a product that foreigners will buy and for which they will pay a relatively attractive price. It helps to transform subsistence into monetary economies by providing a market for cash crops, and raises the standard of living of monetary economies by bringing a higher return for the same effort. But it does not and cannot by itself do more than this. It does not, for example, result in an automatic modernization of agricultural methods; nor does it guarantee that the domestic market which it creates or widens will nurse local industry to factory-scale volume. The attitudes, practices and tenures of peasant cultivators may be little altered and they may buy their manufactures not from the towns but from abroad. Development may be blocked by a social structure that keeps the response to economic forces within narrow channels and itself withstands transformation by those forces. An expanding foreign demand will not be translated into a self-sustaining process of development in every sector of the economy unless many other conditions are fulfilled simultaneously. But the chances are that if these conditions are not fulfilled the same obstacles will stultify development so long as the forces of change are purely economic.

I confess to some scepticism about the supposed ineffectiveness of foreign trade in producing innovation and development. It does not strike me as entirely plausible to speak as if foreign trade could be contained within an enclave without transmitting its dynamic influences to the rest of the economy. How can one contain the so-called demonstration effects? By what magic is a steel mill supposed to revolutionize an economy while a railway or a copper smelter leaves it essentially unchanged? Every new departure is initially an enclave and it takes time for all innovations to work through and be absorbed. The influence of foreign trade may also make itself felt slowly. Sometimes the influence is bound to be indirect; there is not much in an oil refinery that will transform the agriculture of an Arab country. But indirect influences are not to be discounted: they may embrace half the profits of the oil companies and a good deal of free technical education for the local staff. As Professor Swerling has pointed out, 'the tax machinery can remove much economic remoteness even from mineral enclaves'.[1]

[1] B. C. Swerling, op. cit., p. 31.

Most of the countries that we now think of as advanced have been at one time or another dependent on just as narrow a range of exports. Japan in the early stages of industrialization was heavily dependent on exports of silk, the United States and Canada on exports of grain, Britain on exports of wool, or, at a later stage, on textile manufactures which once supplied over 70 per cent of her export earnings. If you want to make a start you must use what you have, not lament that the other fellow who is ahead of you is less highly specialized. The more foreign exchange is felt to be a bottleneck, the more important it is to foster in every possible way the limited range of activities from which foreign exchange can be derived.

Yet the risks of specializing on a narrow front are very real. In the long run there is the danger of a substitute produced at lower cost by factory methods; in the short run there is the danger of wide fluctuations in price. Of these two the long-run danger is the more alarming even if, so far, it has been rare for a natural product to be superseded by a synthetic one. The world's consumption of cotton, rubber, jute, butter and other products threatened by substitutes is higher than ever before in spite of the rise of synthetics. The function of the synthetic product has generally been to supplement an inelastic natural supply and meet rapidly expanding industrial requirements rather than to displace the natural products altogether.

Far too much emphasis is put in current literature on the forces operating to limit or diminish the demand for primary produce and far too little on the constant opening up of new requirements throughout the world as the standard of living rises. It is a useful exercise to list the major raw materials in use today and consider how many of them were available, even a hundred years ago. Steel and petroleum are barely a hundred years old. In 1860 aluminium was a precious metal used like platinum in royal gifts. Rubber, newsprint, synthetic fibres are for all practical purposes twentieth century creations. Nor is it only the advanced countries that benefit when new materials emerge. The less advanced countries, with luck, can shift from one crop to another or find within their borders the mineral products that technological change brings to the front. If there are losers through the obsolescence of materials, there are gainers as well.

There are, it is true, limitations on the range of produce that the under-developed countries can supply. It is perhaps significant that most of them—particularly those in Asia and Africa—lie in the tropical latitudes and are highly dependent on the world market for tropical produce. This means that they are partly screened from competition with the advanced countries except when science produces a substitute or when high prices make the development of substitutes commercially attractive. They are not screened, however, from competition with one another. They have between them an enormous population—Asia alone has half the world's population—and the competition is correspondingly intense. Any one country may have advantages of climate or soil that give it some shelter in its chosen field; but among all the tropical countries there are sure to be some that are almost equally well placed. Thus, so long as they keep within the usual round, they are not likely to do much better than their neighbours. They may, for a time, enjoy a run of luck as producers of bananas or coffee or rubber; but if they do, other tropical countries will soon join in and put an end to any exceptional gains. Indeed, if they export tree crops (which form about one-quarter of total exports from this group of countries) the gains are only too likely to be followed by exceptional losses once new plantings have had time to come into production either at home or in competing countries. In minerals, on the other hand, the competition of other tropical countries is without special significance, the success of individual countries being governed largely by geological factors peculiar to each.

The situation confronting agriculture in an under-developed tropical country is thus essentially different from the situation faced in the countries settled from Europe during the nineteenth century. The latter were all or nearly all in temperate latitudes and could supply the industrial centres of Europe with foodstuffs in *replacement* of the higher-cost foodstuffs produced there. The specialization between the old world and the new was on a basis that brought low-cost farmers overseas into competition with high-cost farmers in Europe and gave to the development of the newer countries all the leverage of a large cost-differential. The new countries were in a very real sense the frontiers of an older economy.

But the under-developed countries of today are selling in a more inelastic market.

This is so for two reasons. In the first place such elasticity as there is derives from competition with other products, not from substitution for a similar, home-produced commodity. The Canadian wheat-farmer found it easier to sell his wheat in the British market because British farmers were able to switch from grain to grass, but the only kind of substitution that Brazilian coffee-producers can profit from is substitution on the part of consumers. Secondly, exports of tropical produce bear a much higher relation to world output than exports of primary produce from temperate latitudes. The principal consumers of coffee, rubber, sugar, and so on, lie outside the producing countries so that domestic demand is largely unaffected by changes in output and price. Canadian wheat is a very small fraction of the world crop but Brazil produces nearly half the world's coffee. A given increase in the Canadian wheat crop or in Canada's exports of wheat involves, therefore, far less disruption in the world market than an equal proportionate increase in the cultivation or exportation of Brazilian coffee.

This brings me to what seems to be the central issue. Is the market for the exports of the under-developed countries so inelastic that it no longer provides a satisfactory engine of growth? Is their development being cramped by stagnation of world demand for their traditional exports?

That the nineteenth century process of growth-transmission works rather differently nowadays is not in dispute. The under-developed countries are no longer the frontiers of an expanding world economy and the division of labour between them and the individual countries of North America and Western Europe does not involve those vast territorial shifts in primary production that lie behind the rapid growth of world trade in the nineteenth century. In the middle of the nineteenth century that growth averaged about 13 per cent annually, the total volume trebling within thirty years largely as a result of the inflow into Europe of primary produce from countries overseas.[1] Since the scope for similar displacements is now far more limited and the industrial countries are less willing to see their agriculture contract further, it is unlikely

[1] A. H. Imlah, *Economic Elements in the Pax Britannica*, pp. 96–97, 190.

that trade will ever grow so fast again over so long a period. To the extent that the under-developed countries have to rely on exports of tropical produce, there can be very little displacement of production and the rate of expansion is bound to be limited by the growth of world demand. For other products, however, notably base metals and petroleum, this limitation does not apply.

It is an illusion to suppose that, even in the nineteenth century, mere pressure of demand was sufficient to transmit development from one country to another. It certainly did not by itself ensure the *industrial* development of primary-producing regions. The fact that the United States ultimately became the leading industrial nation should not blind us to the failure of the Southern States, from which came a high proportion of American exports of primary produce, to undergo industrialization or to enjoy the rapid growth experienced in the north. Latin America remained comparatively under-developed. Australia and New Zealand, although enjoying a high standard of living and far from negligible as producers of manufactured goods remain, as exporters, almost exclusively dependent on primary produce.

Again, the countries to which European growth was most successfully transmitted were already comparatively rich countries. Although their development was geared to the supply of export markets, they already had a sufficiently high standard of living to provide an opening for domestic manufacturers. The countries that remain under-developed started from a much lower level so that their domestic market is narrower and far less favourable to the building up of local industries. The example of Japan, however, shows that there is no insuperable difficulty in starting from a low level provided the industries that take root are not confined within the limits of the domestic market.

It was possible in nineteenth century development for a growing foreign trade to accompany a still more rapidly growing domestic market. This was certainly true, for example, of the United States after the Civil War. There was nothing inconsistent between reliance on exports of primary produce to open up new investment opportunities and a shift in the sources of consumer goods in favour of indigenous producers. This shift might come about through the unassisted operation of market forces or it might be induced or accelerated by protective policies. The important point is that foreign trade could remain the driving force behind an economy even when exports were a diminishing fraction of total production. A demonstration that exports are being outpaced by production does not prove that the motor force which exports provide is running down. On the contrary, it is more likely to mean that the process of growth transmission is really working, that the domestic market is being transformed, and that an industrial structure is taking shape within a hitherto non-industrial economy.

It is true that in the nineteenth century the dominant pattern was a different one. Trade grew faster than production, both in the industrial and the non-industrial countries. World trade in the early years of the century grew at 7 per cent per annum in the mid-century at 13 per cent, and at the end of the century at 7 per cent. World industrial production may latterly have reached 7 per cent and equalled the rate of expansion of trade, but *total* world production never equalled it. It is legitimate to argue, therefore, that in the nineteenth century foreign markets were growing faster than domestic markets and that the external impulse to growth not only took causal priority over the domestic impulse, but was operating more powerfully.

In this sense, twentieth century experience has not followed the nineteenth century pattern. There was a long period when trade showed no net growth at all while world production registered a large expansion. Between 1926–30 and 1948–50, for example, the volume of trade both in primary produce and manufactures contracted slightly while world output of primary produce grew by over one-quarter and of manufactures by over two-thirds.[1] Since the war the growth in trade has returned to the normal pre-1914 rate of 7 per cent and is again roughly in line with the growth in world industrial production. But this has not restored the nineteenth century pattern. For in recent years it has been the trade of industrial countries with one another that has grown fastest, not their trade with non-industrial countries. In the nineteenth century, the latter were dominated by the

[1] These estimates are derived from unpublished calculations of Mr A. Maizels of the National Institute of Economic and Social Research.

newly settled countries, including the United States, which were then the growing points of the world economy. These countries are no longer non-industrial, and those that remain under-developed are a much smaller element in the world economy. They cannot complain that world trade is not expanding rapidly: it is expanding as fast as it ever has done at any time except in the thirty years following the repeal of the Corn Laws. The countries that were drawn along by world markets in the nineteenth century enjoyed no better fortune if rate of growth of trade is the test to be applied. If the engine of development has lost power, it is not because the demands of industrial countries have ceased to overflow national boundaries. It must be because those demands have changed in character or because the under-developed countries are less well placed to meet them. For one reason or the other, their share of world trade has begun to diminish.

Now in some ways it is odd that this should have happened in the 1950s. In that decade the world was in one of those recurring situations in which a high level of industrial activity presses on the supply of primary produce and makes it necessary to develop fresh supplies. Such a situation arose, for example, in the 1850s, and again in the twenty years before the First World War. It is a situation that is normally accompanied by inflation because raw material costs are pushed up; and it is also a situation that generates inflation because capacity to produce raw materials (including fuel and power) tends to make far heavier demands on capital than capacity at later stages of manufacture. In the nineteenth century, when marginal supplies of primary produce could most readily be drawn from overseas, the rise in investment tended to be concentrated abroad and to be financed to a large extent through foreign loans. Hence the coincidence, on which economists have frequently commented, of rising costs and profits, higher foreign investments, and relatively favourable prices for foodstuffs and materials.

Something of all this we can recognize in the 1950s; for example, the rapid development of petroleum in many parts of the under-developed world with the aid of foreign capital and in relief of a shortage of fuel in the industrial countries of Western Europe. But in general the industrial countries have not met an increasing proportion of their requirements from supplies from under-developed countries, and with some exceptions have not sought to open up new sources of supply there through heavy investment. Since the early 1950s, moreover, there has been a drift downwards in the price of many important materials, the United Nations index for primary products (excluding petroleum) showing a fall in the six years 1953–9 of 7 per cent. The past decade has been exceptional, therefore, in that a rapid growth in production and trade has been accompanied by a marked change in the terms of trade *against* primary produce.

It is possible to put a pessimistic construction on these facts and conclude that the under-developed countries can neither count on an expanding market nor on reasonably stable terms of trade for their exports. Economies in the use of materials, the development of synthetics, agricultural protectionism, and other forces damping down the demand for imports of primary produce can be cited as evidence that the trend against the under-developed countries will continue. This evidence, however, is not conclusive and a quite different interpretation of the facts is possible.

In the first place the trend in the past decade has to be seen in the light of what went before. The war disorganized the normal sources of supply for many primary products and at the same time raised the level of demand discontinuously. This lack of balance continued into the post-war period, especially after the change-over to production against peace-time requirements, and it was aggravated by the stock-building rush in 1950–1 at the outset of the Korean war. By 1951 there had been a very pronounced swing in the price of primary products and in the terms on which they were exchanged against manufactures. What took place after 1951 was a return towards more normal price-relationships as the supply of the scarcer materials was expanded. If one takes the early 1950s as a starting point, therefore, we are accepting as normal prices which, in the light of history, were anything but normal, and interpreting as a trend what was to some extent no more than a return to more durable price relationships.

There seems to me a particularly strong case for this view in relation to tropical produce. As I have already suggested, the products exported by the under-developed countries are heavily concentrated in a limited group, of which tropical produce forms a large part. A general price index for primary products may, therefore, convey a misleading impression of what is happening to the export prices of the under-developed countries. Mr Maizels has estimated that while primary products exported by industrial countries doubled in unit value between 1937 and 1950, primary products exported from other (mainly under-developed) countries more than trebled. Similarly, it has been calculated that over the same period tropical foods rose by 235 per cent in unit value while non-tropical foods rose by only 135 per cent.[1] There is plenty of evidence that in the post-war years many of the under-developed countries started out with unusually favourable export prices.

If we abstract from the trend in prices and consider only the change in the volume of exports, it would seem that the under-developed countries found a quite rapidly expanding market for their exports of primary produce. Between 1950 and 1957, for example, these exports rose by 50 per cent or 6 per cent per annum. This was certainly below the rate at which trade in manufactures was growing, but not by very much. It would seem, therefore, that the *main* cause of the divergence in trend between manufactures and primary produce lay in a divergent movement in prices.

Moreover, if we take a longer view and, rather than accept the past decade as the touchstone of future prospects, look back as far as 1913, we do not find any conspicuous lag in exports from the under-developed countries. Each of the poorest continents in the world—Africa, Asia and Latin America—had a larger share of world exports in 1953 than in 1913. In both years they had a quite negligible share of world exports of manufactures, but their exports of primary produce had by 1953 overhauled those from the three richest continents—North America, Europe and Australasia. Forty years earlier they had differed in the ratio of 1:2, by 1953 the difference had almost disappeared.

Whether one takes a long view or a short, these aggregates are of limited value in interpreting what is going on in the under-developed countries. Every under-developed country is unique and is affected by the market conditions and prices for its own products and not by the movement of index numbers.

[1] Based on *International Trade* 1957–58, GATT, 1959, Table 4, p. 15.

To aggregate or average the experience of the group of countries that we think of as under-developed is to presume common elements that may have no real existence.

Nevertheless, it may help to give some concreteness to my argument if I turn at this point to consider just what the under-developed countries as a group do export and what part trade plays in their economy. For simplicity I shall divide the world into the three poorest and the three richest continents, the first group being made up of Africa, Asia and Latin America and the second of Europe, North America and Oceania. This means that one or two advanced countries such as South Africa and Japan will be included in the group of poor countries but their exclusion would make little difference to the results. At times I have been obliged to use a grouping prepared by GATT which adds Australasia to the three poorer continents and labels the mixture 'non-industrial areas'. The Communist bloc of countries is excluded throughout, unless otherwise indicated.

The so-called non-industrial areas, on examination, turn out to be very far from non-industrial. According to GATT they import only about one-third of their consumption of manufactures, and this proportion is falling.[1] The remaining two-thirds of their consumption of manufactures is produced at home. Many of them already have a flourishing textile industry and some of them are net exporters of textiles. Of the manufactured goods which they import, a high proportion consists of capital goods, base metals, and so on, while manufactured consumption goods are relatively small, constituting not much more than 10 per cent of total imports. Nor are they by any means entirely dependent on foreign markets for the sale of their primary produce. This is particularly true of food and feeding stuffs; nine-tenths of the output is consumed at home while only the remaining tenth is exported. Many of the foodstuffs that form their staple diet are quite unimportant in foreign trade. Exports of fuel and raw materials (including materials of agricultural origin) take a higher proportion of total production—on the average, about two-fifths,[2] and sometimes, as in the oil countries, nearly 100 per cent.

[1] *International Trade* 1959, GATT, 1960, p. 14.
[2] Ibid., p. 13.

Just as it is a mistake to think that under-developed countries have no industries, so it is a mistake to think of them as the major sources of primary produce. Every country is a primary producer, and the more advanced it is, the larger, broadly speaking, is its output of primary produce. There can be few countries that fail to grow at least half their food supply or to produce a wide range of raw materials. It is true that some advanced countries employ very little of their manpower in agriculture and that their raw materials are often manufactured rather than mined or grown. But the fact remains that the advanced countries produce more food and more raw materials than the less advanced countries. What they import from the less advanced countries meets only one-tenth of their requirements of food and one-quarter of their requirements of raw materials.[1] Nor are they all net importers. Some of them are large exporters, and the three richer continents account for roughly half of world exports of primary produce. They are in fact larger exporters, just as they are larger producers, of primary products than the so-called primary-producing countries.[2]

The less advanced countries, in the same way, are importers as well as exporters of primary produce: indeed, their imports are half as large as their exports. Thus it is quite wrong to think of the world as if it could be divided into two sets of countries, the advanced and the less advanced, with primary produce flowing exclusively in one direction. On the contrary, international trade brings the primary producers of every country into competition with one another, and the margin of advantage does not necessarily shift steadily in one direction.

Seven items or groups make up nearly three-quarters of the total exports of primary produce from the under-developed countries. Listed in order of size they are; petroleum, beverages, textile fibres, base metals, sugar, oilseeds and fats, and rubber. The same group of items make up less than 40 per cent of the exports of primary produce from the developed countries. But what is perhaps of more significance is the change that has taken place over the past century. For the

[1] Ibid., p. 14.

[2] This is true only if we exclude Australasia from the primary-producing countries. See my 'International Trade and Economic Development', *Kyklos*, vol. xiii (1960), p. 549.

seven items selected the share of the under-developed countries in world trade has risen from 43 per cent to 64 per cent. For all other items, representing nearly half the total volume of world trade in primary products, the share of the under-developed countries has remained a little below 30 per cent. It has been where their share was already high that it expanded most.[1]

On the other hand there has been an unmistakable tendency towards a contraction in their exports of cereals and livestock produce. Exports from the developed countries, especially those in North America and Australasia, have shown a corresponding expansion. The three under-developed continents supplied 31 per cent of world exports in 1913 and only 21 per cent in 1953. No doubt this trend is partly associated with American aid. But by itself this is far from adequate to account for it, and it seems to have a deeper origin in the pressure on available land in some under-developed countries and the efforts at industrialization in others.

Exports of cereals and livestock products are a comparatively small proportion (about 7 per cent) of total exports from the under-developed countries. Exports of other foodstuffs are much larger—over one-third of the total. Of these exports, tea, cocoa and coffee, in which they come near to having a monopoly of foreign trade, form nearly half, and other tropical produce, such as sugar, oilseeds and fats and tobacco make up most of the other half. Thus within the food group there is a large tract over which competition is limited. In food that can be grown in temperate latitudes the under-developed countries have either contracted or show little expansion. But in tropical foodstuffs they have enjoyed a rapid growth. For example, they were supplying 73 per cent of world exports of sugar in 1953 compared with 64 per cent in 1913. For the group of foodstuffs other than cereals and livestock products (in which their share contracted) and beverages (in which their share was virtually 100 per cent) they improved their share of the world market quite perceptibly.

Foodstuffs, however, account for less than half the total exports of primary produce from the three poorer continents. Petroleum, crude and refined, accounts for about one-quarter

[1] The estimates in this and the succeeding page are drawn from Lamartine Yates, op. cit.

(depending upon how the exports are valued) and raw materials, including those of agricultural as well as of mineral origin, unwrought metals and crude fertilizers, for nearly one-third. For materials as for foodstuffs there is some tendency for the exports of the developed and under-developed continents to be in non-competing groups. Nearly all the world's output of rubber and jute, over 40 per cent of its petroleum and a high proportion of its hides and skins, mineral ores and crude fertilizers, come from the under-developed areas. But in other textile fibres and in base metals they are in direct competition over a wide area.

From this analysis of the trade of the under-developed countries I draw four conclusions.

First of all they are highly dependent on a very narrow range of exports. A large proportion of these exports consists of gifts of nature: petroleum, mineral ores, crude fertilizers. How much a country can earn from exports of this kind is largely a matter of luck and of willingness to make use of foreign capital. Other exports suffer from great variability in supply and low elasticity of supply. The source of these exports tends to be either foreign-owned plantations or peasants who may lack the means, the knowledge or the incentives to adopt modern methods of production. On top of all this nearly all capital equipment has to be imported, and a shortage of foreign exchange frequently sets a sharp limit to the scale and firmness of any forward planning of investment. These facts point strongly to the desirability of widening the range of exports wherever possible and developing domestic sources of the simpler types of imported manufactures.

Secondly, it would seem that exports from the under-developed countries are governed less closely by the level of world demand than is usually supposed. Where they are in direct competition with the more advanced countries, their share of the market depends also on the terms on which they are able to compete: on the movement of their costs and in the alternatives which they can choose. If their exports have lagged behind the exports of the other advanced countries, this is partly because they have been running a large external deficit (now of the order of $5,000–$6,000 m. a year) and this necessarily implies some downward drag on their exports compared with the exports of the countries from which they buy. Other, but not unrelated, factors tending to hold back their exports have been inflation, relatively high prices, and the encouragement of other sectors of their economies.

Thirdly, since agriculture is by far the most important activity and is usually directed more towards domestic than export markets, there is everything to be gained by trying to expand agricultural production. Without a general improvement in agricultural production and incomes, the mass of the population will remain hungry and poor and domestic industry will be stifled for lack of markets. Such an improvement is not dependent on some precise rate of growth of exports. An expanding foreign market can, however, contribute, both by putting more cash in the hands of the cultivators and by introducing a competitive element that may make technical change in agriculture more acceptable.

But what, fourthly, if agriculture proves unresponsive and the government has to think of industrialization without any expansion in foodstuffs? The fact that under-developed countries produce about two-thirds of the manufactured goods which they consume shows that some progress towards industrialization has already been made. Industrial development *is* occurring, assisted by higher export earnings and foreign investment and loans. But the industries that have grown up are not, as a rule, very efficient. It is curious, for example, that Latin American countries meet nearly all their own textile requirements but have a negligible share in each others markets or, indeed, in any foreign market.

One of the principal obstacles to more rapid industrialization is the limited scale of operations in a manufacturing plant supplying only the domestic market of an under-developed country. It is precisely this limitation which international trade can remove. If, therefore, we are anxious to encourage development in the poorer countries and doubt whether agricultural expansion will clear the way for industry, might we not turn to a new model of the traditional engine of development and see what could be done through freer trade in manufactured goods?

I see no reason, looking at the experience of Hong Kong, Puerto Rico and similar countries, why the engine should not be a powerful one. There are countries where costs would still be too high even if new market possibilities were opened. But in general my expectation would be that if there were complete confidence that the markets of the industrial countries would remain open, the supply of the simpler manufactured goods from under-developed countries would increase by leaps and bounds. No doubt sufficient people share this view to make it certain that the markets will not be opened and that no one will ever be quite sure that, if opened, they will remain opened.

My object is not to argue the matter. But I think it right in a country that used to plead for 'Trade not Aid' to recall that slogan and to suggest that one of our chief economic obligations to the under-developed countries is to offer them a market. We should be asking ourselves not whether market forces work but whether we are allowing them to work so as to reinforce such aid as we can offer. We should also remember that the industrial countries have learned in the 1950s to conduct a much greater volume of trade in manufactures with one another without conspicuous injury and indeed with great mutual advantage.

I have no wish to exaggerate the contribution that trade can make to economic development. Development is not governed in any country by economic forces alone, and the more backward the country the more this is true. The key to development lies in men's minds, in the institutions in which their thinking finds expression and in the play of opportunity on ideas and institutions. It happens that the opportunities trade opens up in under-developed economies are in a sector where outlook and institutions are alike highly conservative and in which external impulses tend to be dampened rather than amplified before they are transmitted to the rest of the economy. It is true also that the effort of grasping these opportunities may prove too great for a poor and backward country. But this does not justify us in minimizing the opportunities that trade affords or in pretending that they are losing an effectiveness that they once possessed.

CHAPTER 14

World Trade in Manufactures since 1900[1]

I

THIS paper has a modest objective. It is neither an analysis of the forces governing international trade in manufactures nor an assessment of the main trends over the past fifty years. It is directed instead towards bringing to the attention of economists the wealth of statistical data now available that bear on the *structure* of trade in manufactures, towards indicating how the statistics can be utilized, and towards emphasizing (what is so often neglected) that the ease with which adjustments are made in international trade is in part a function of the structure that is in course of adjustment.

The growth of world trade in manufactured goods was first analysed by the League of Nations, the pioneer work being that of Mr Folke Hilgerdt.[2] In the past few years there has been an increasing literature[3] and two important studies of changes in the commodity composition of world trade in manufactures over the past fifty years have appeared, one by Mr Tyszynski[4] and the other by Professor Svennilson.[5] Unfortunately, each of these economists uses a slightly different system of classification: Hilgerdt, who confines himself to

[1] From *Economia Internazionale*, vol. viii, no. 4, 1955. I am indebted to the late Mr B. Weber for help in the preparation of this paper.

[2] See especially his *Industrialization and Foreign Trade*, 1945, pp. 154 *et seq.*

[3] These include an unpublished study undertaken in 1945–46 by E. A. G. Robinson and Miss M. E. Hill; E. A. G. Robinson, 'The Future of British Imports', *Three Banks Review*, March 1953; M. Fg. Scott, 'The Problem of Living within our Foreign Earnings', *Three Banks Review*, June 1955; W. A. Lewis, 'World Production, Prices and Trade', 1870–1960, *The Manchester School*, May 1952; A. K. Cairncross and J. Faaland, 'Long-term Trends in Europe's Trade', *Economic Journal*, March 1952; A. K. Cairncross, 'Britain's Export Prospects', *Times Review of Industry*, June 1954; 'The Trend of UK Exports', *Board of Trade Journal*, March 27, 1954; 'The Network of World Trade in 1952', *Board of Trade Journal*, May 29, 1954; 'International Trade 1952 and later years' (GATT); and the *Quarterly Bulletins* and *Economic Surveys* of the Economic Commission for Europe.

[4] H. Tyszynski, 'World Trade in Manufactured Commodities, 1899–1950,' *The Manchester School*, September 1951, pp. 272 *et seq.*

[5] Professor I. Svennilson, *Growth and Stagnation in the European Economy*, Geneva, 1954.

movements in the total trade in manufactured articles of a score of countries from 1871 onwards, uses Group IV of the Brussels Classification of 1913; Tyszynski evolves a classification of his own under 16 headings and analyses the figures for each of 11 countries in the years 1899, 1913, 1929, 1937 and 1950: Svennilson, basing himself, like Tyszynski, on Class III (Articles Wholly or Mainly Manufactured) of the classification in use in Britain up to 1953, gives figures for the United States and seven European countries (all of them included in Tyszynski's calculations), selecting for this purpose the years 1913, 1928, 1938 and 1950. Svennilson also analyses long-term changes in the exports of manufactures from some of those countries to selected markets outside Europe.

In the meantime, all the countries which are the subject of study by Tyszynski and Svennilson now prepare statistics in accordance with the Standard International Trade Classification, so that trade figures are readily available under headings that are comparable for each country but different from the headings used by Tyszynski and Svennilson. The task which they set themselves should from now on be a relatively easy one; a study of the changes currently in progress in the structure of world trade in manufactures no longer calls for elaborate calculations. Nevertheless, remarkably little has been done to put such a study on any regular footing: there are no indices of the changes in world trade under the main commodity headings, and even the United Nations index for *total* world trade in manufactures is based on a limited group of countries and left uncorrected for 'special category' exports from the United States.[1] It is also surprising that no attempt has been made to link current figures under SITC headings with the series already prepared for the past half century under the headings used by Tyszynski and Svennilson.

In this paper an attempt will be made to show how the work of Hilgerdt, Tyszynski and Svennilson can be used in conjunction with the new SITC data in order to establish the

[1] The countries included in the index issued by the United Nations in their *Monthly Bulletin of Statistics* were until lately: Belgium-Luxembourg, Canada, France, Western Germany, India, Italy, Switzerland, United Kingdom and United States. To these have now been added Japan, Netherlands and Sweden, so that the index covers about 90 per cent of total exports of manufactured goods.

main trends in world trade in manufactures. Tyszynski's data provide a particularly useful link, both because he has used a large number of groups and because there is no marked divergence between his groups and similar groups in the SITC. Hilgerdt gives totals only but, unlike Tyszynski, he gives total imports by country as well as total exports so that it is possible to use his data in order to establish how the different markets for manufactures have grown. Svennilson's classification is much broader than Tyszynski's and although it is adequate to bring out the more important trends, it is more difficult to link with the SITC.

II

The commodity classification used by Tyszynski and Svennilson is compared in Table I with the SITC on the basis of British exports of manufactures in 1950[1]:

Table I

Exports of manufactures from the UK in 1950 on alternative classifications

Group of Manufactures	*SITC £m.*	*Tyszynski £m.*	*Svennilson £m.*
Machinery	434·1 (71,72)	444·1 (6, 7, 8)	402·1 (III F, G)
Vehicles	342·7 (73)	385·4 (9, 10)	358·2 (III S)
Textiles	360·7 (65)	349·9 (12)	415·8 (III I-M)
Metals	155·0 (68)	156·1 (1, 2)	232·6 (111 C, D)
Chemicals	144·3 (5)	119·1 (3)	107·7 (III O)
All other items	385·3 (Rest of 6, 8)	338·3 (4, 5, 13–16)	295·6 (III B, E, H, N, Q, R, T, U)
Total	1822·1	1793·0	1842·0

(a) The figures in brackets relate to the number of the class or group in the classification referred to.
(b) Omitting Group 11 and the unclassified group in Tyszynski's classification and the unspecified group in Svennilson's.

[1] The main differences in the groupings may be briefly summarized:
(a) *Machinery.*
Svennilson excludes tractors which he puts under 'vehicles'; Tyszynski includes tools; the SITC includes aero-engines.
(b) *Vehicles*
Svennilson and the SITC exclude rubber tyres and tubes.

There is close agreement between Tyszynski's classification and the SITC in the totals for textiles, metals and machinery and in the aggregate for all manufactures but rather a large difference in the total for chemicals and a smaller difference for vehicles and miscellaneous manufactures. If the largest item, machinery, is further subdivided and electrical equipment and agricultural machinery shown separately, the sub-totals remain in close agreement; if the total for vehicles is sub-divided into new means of transport and old there is also fair agreement in the sub-totals.

Equally close agreement is shown when the two classifications are compared on the basis of other countries' exports of manufactures in 1950. In Table II the groups remain the same as in Table I except that vehicles and machinery are amalgamated under the heading 'Engineering products'.

The main divergence arises in the figures for the United States and results from the exclusion of special category exports (chiefly engineering products) in the one set of figures and their inclusion in the other. There are also substantial differences in nearly all the totals for the miscellaneous group of manufactures. In the aggregates for all manufactures, the differences are less than 2 per cent in four of the seven countries shown (Canada, France, Germany and the United Kingdom), and between 5 and 7 per cent in the three others (Belgium, Sweden and the United States). Since the differences are frequently in opposite directions, there is obviously less danger of error in moving from one classification to the other when aggregates, either by country or commodity group, are being used than when the figures relate to a single commodity group and to a single country.

(c) *Textiles*
Svennilson includes, and the other classifications exclude, apparel.

(d) *Metals*
Svennilson includes manufactures of iron and steel, most of which are excluded from the other classifications. The apparent agreement between the SITC and Tyszynski totals conceals an excess of £7·4 m. in Tyszynski under non-ferrous metals and an excess in the SITC of £6·4 m. under ferrous metals (mainly steel rails).

(e) *Chemicals*
The SITC group includes plastic materials, soap, perfumery and toilet preparations and essential oils, all of which are excluded from Class III 0 of the pre-1954 United Kingdom Trade Accounts. Tyszynski includes all of these except plastic materials.

(f) *Other items*
Tyszynski excludes arms and ammunition; Svennilson excludes cement and newsprint. Svennilson also excludes exports to the Channel Islands.

TABLE II

Exports of manufactures from leading countries in 1950 on alternative classifications

$ m.

		Engineering products	*Textiles*	*Metals*	*Chemicals*	*All other items*	*Totals*
UK	Tyszynski	2322·9	979·7	436·8	333·5	947·5	5020·4
	SITC	2174·5	1005·9	437·1	403·7	1080·9	5102·1
US	Tyszynski	3286·6	385·6	527·2	667·2	977·4	5843·0
	SITC*	2863·2	397·0	505·1	698·9	1031·6	5495·9
France	Tyszynski	521·1	518·0	320·0	202·7	445·0	2006·8
	SITC	441·5	500·1	339·1	220·6	483·9	1985·2
Germany	Tyszynski	495·0	91·8	301·3	213·9	338·1	1439·0
	SITC	472·4	95·2	287·8	220·9	383·5	1459·7
Belgium/	Tyszynski	139·2	267·7	427·6	139·3	217·3	1191·1
Luxembourg	SITC	155·2	272·1	432·5	135·0	281·0	1275·8
Sweden	Tyszynski	266·3	8·4	63·4	26·6	189·3	554·0
	SITC	251·1	9·5	65·0	23·5	232·3	581·4
Canada	Tyszynski	212·5	16·0	333·6	86·0	563·3	1211·4
	SITC	215·4	18·3	335·1	109·6	556·4	1234·8

* Excluding special category exports.

III

We may begin by studying the growth of world trade in manufactures in terms of the shares of the principal exporting countries. In Table III below are given the exports of each of the countries in Tyszynski's study except India (which does not make use of the SITC). These figures show the growth in each country's exports of manufactures from 1899 to 1950; and in the last columns are added the exports of each country in 1950, 1953 and 1954 under Section 5–8 of the SITC.[1] It is possible to derive from these figures a very rough index of the growth in the volume of trade in manufactures on Tyszynski's assumption[2] that we may deflate the total for 1913 by an index of the unit value of British exports and imports of manufactures and subsequent totals by an average of the indices for British and American exports of manufactures from 1913 to 1950. After 1950 it is possible to make use of the UN index of the unit value of manufactured exports. The resulting index of volume is shown at the bottom of Table III.

[1] I have added the provisional figures for 1960. Later tables, except Table II, have been left unaltered, but if brought up-to-date would show a continuation of the same trends.

[2] Tyszynski, op. cit., p. 282.

Table III

World Trade in Manufactures, 1899–1960

	1899	1913	1929	1937	1950	1950	1953	1954	1960
	£ m. (*Tyszynski*)					(*SITC*)			
UK	211	396	557	386	1,793	1,822	2,099	2,171	3,001
USA*	72	168	501	350	2,087	1,963	2,557	2,670	4,033
France	94	164	261	105	717	709	886	962	1,809
Germany†	145	355	512	403	527	521	1,307	1,579	3,620
Belgium	36	65	135	106	425	456	637	655	1,117
Italy	22	45	88	62	273	276	315	338	965
Sweden	6	17	43	45	198	207	258	296	579
Switzerland	26	42	69	52	293	(293)	392	400	618
Canada	2	9	80	86	432	440	669	670	899
Japan	10	32	96	129	245	(245)	372	496	1,286
Total	624	1,292	2,342	1,723	6,989	6,932	9,492	10,237	17,927
Value index	100	207	375	276	1,120	100	137	148	259
Unit value index	100	127	178	150	412	100	117	115	128
Volume index	100	163	211	184	272	100	117	128	183

* Excluding special category exports in the SITC totals for 1950–60.

† Including the whole area of the Reich in pre-war years, when the area of the Federal Republic accounted for some 70 per cent of total exports.

The changes in the shares of the leading exporters are more readily apparent when Table III is expressed in terms of percentages.

The volume index at the foot of Table III brings out the rapid growth in world trade in manufactures before the first world war and the sharp change of trend thereafter. After expanding by perhaps 60 per cent between 1899 and 1913, the volume of trade appears to have shown only a small net increase over the next quarter of a century. The initial recovery

Table IV

Share of leading exporters in world trade in manufactures, 1899–1960

	1899	1913	1929	1937	1950	1950	1953	1954	1960
UK	33·8	30·6	23·8	22·4	25·7	26·3	22·1	21·2	16·7
USA	11·5	13·0	21·4	20·3	29·9	28·3	26·9	26·1	22·5
France	15·1	12·7	11·1	6·1	10·3	10·2	9·3	9·4	10·1
Germany	23·2	27·5	21·9	23·4	7·5	7·5	13·8	15·4	20·2
Belgium, Italy, Sweden, Switz'land	14·4	13·1	14·3	15·4	17·0	17·8	16·9	16·5	18·3
Canada	0·3	0·7	3·4	5·0	6·2	6·3	7·0	6·5	5·0
Japan	1·6	2·5	4·1	7·5	3·5	3·5	3·9	4·8	7·2
	100·0	100·0	100·0	100·0	100·0	100·0	100·0	100·0	100·0

in the twenties carried trade in manufactures well past the previous peak of 1913 but in the ensuing slump there was a sharp contraction and only part of the loss had been regained before the outbreak of war in 1939. Tyszynski's figures suggest that the post-war expansion in trade in manufactures was already of the order of 50 per cent above the 1937 volume by 1950; and in the next four years a further expansion of over 25 per cent took place. If these estimates are accepted, world trade in manufactures is in 1955 well over twice as large by volume as in 1913 and three and a half times as large as at the beginning of the century. Moreover, it has been growing since 1950 at 7 per cent per annum, an extremely high rate of growth except under conditions of recovery from slump.

Table IV shows the decline of the United Kingdom's share of world trade in manufactures from about one-third at the beginning of the century to little more than one-fifth in 1937; the corresponding advance of the United States' share from under 12 per cent in 1899 to 30 per cent in 1950; the decline of France up to the second world war and her recovery since; the rise of Japan in the pre-war period; and the equally rapid emergence of Canada as a large industrial exporter.

The trends since 1950 are also interesting. The initial improvement in the British share in total trade has been followed by a sharp drop to a lower proportion than at any previous time. The United States' share, on the other hand, has fallen back less than one might expect, even when special category exports are omitted, and Canada's increased share has been fully maintained. Western Germany has come back swiftly into world markets and has been recapturing markets from other European producers, but she has still a long way to go before her share of the trade in manufactures reaches the pre-war proportion of undivided Germany. Until 1954 Japan had made comparatively little progress and in 1953 still ranked below Switzerland as an exporter of manufactures. Germany and Japan together supply just over 20 per cent of the world market, compared with 31 per cent in 1937 and 11 per cent in 1950; even in 1955, therefore, it is unlikely that a full adjustment has been made to the recovery of Germany and Japan as manufacturing nations.

The exporting countries in Tables III and IV account for a

high proportion of world trade in manufactures. If we accept Hilgerdt's estimates, they normally supplied 82 per cent of the total in the first twenty or thirty years of this century. His figures are as follows:

TABLE V

World Exports of Manufactured Goods

	1901–5	$ m. 1913	1926–29
Ten Leading exporters	3,261*	6,086*	10,186
World Total	3,990	7,450	12,400
Ratio	82	82	82

* Canada omitted. As will be seen from Table III, this omission is insignificant.

If the proportion in 1954 had remained at 82 per cent, world trade in manufactures in that year would have totalled about $35,000 m. This is a good deal higher than can be accounted for by adding together all the countries in OEEC, the United States, Canada and Japan. For this larger group of exporters, the total in 1954 was only $30,900 m. Calculations made by the Board of Trade suggest that other countries account for about 10 per cent of world trade in manufactures; on this basis, the total in 1954 may have come to about $34,300 m. which would imply a ratio for the ten countries included in Table III of 83·5 per cent rather than 82 per cent.

TABLE VI

World Exports of Manufactures, 1950–54

	1950	1951	$ m. 1952	1953	1954
United Kingdom	5,102	6,130	5,996	5,876	6,079
Germany	1,460	2,793	3,334	3,662	4,422
Other OEEC countries	6,704	9,777	9,197	8,944	9,659
USA	5,496	7,401	7,290	7,159	7,477
Canada	1,235	1,566	1,922	1,872	1,876
Japan	687	1,184	1,057	1,041	1,389
Total	20,684	28,851	28,804	28,554	30,902
Index of value	100	139	139	138	149
Unit value index*	100	117	121	117	115
Index of volume	100	119	115	118	130

* Index of average unit values for twelve leading exporters of manufactures, from UN *Monthly Bulletin of Statistics*.

It is possible to trace the growth in exports from the leading countries since 1950, making a rough assumption for those members of OEEC for which returns under SITC headings are not available for 1950.[1] The figures show a peak by volume in 1951, with a dip in the two following years and a rapid expansion in 1954 which appears to be still in progress in 1955. No less than 90 per cent of the net increase by value in world trade in manufactures between 1951 and 1954 was accounted for by the increase in German and Japanese exports. The fact that world markets were booming must have made it much easier for other exporting countries to adjust themselves to this increased competition.

IV

If we turn next to look at the *importers* of manufactured goods, we find far less adequate data. Hilgerdt's estimates for selected pre-war years are reproduced in Table VII for the ten countries that featured in earlier tables as leading exporters. For convenience (and to allow comparison with

[1] I.e. Switzerland (for which it is possible to use Tyszynski's figures), Greece, Turkey and Portugal. For Italy an estimate has been provided by the OEEC Secretariat.

TABLE VII

Imports and Exports of Manufactured Goods for 10 leading countries

$ m.

	Imports				*Exports*			
	1901–5	1913	1926–29	1954	1901–5	1913	1926–29	1954
UK*	455	603	1,082	1,904	1,172	2,029	2,683	6,079
US	279	475	1,064	3,323	320	721	2,027	7,477
France	182	344	336	1,012	520	875	1,356	2,704
Germany	183	338	512	1,215	800	1,615	2,001	4,422
Belgium	93	169	209	1,202	166	280	448	1,835
Italy	102	226	259	818	87	194	401	947
Sweden	49	76	187	1,051	28	68	178	829
Switzerland	82	134	209	695	127	192	305	1,120
Canada	117	309	627	2,708	—	—	336	1,876
Japan	54	97	241	325	41	102	451	1,389
Total	1,596	2,771	4,726	14,253	3,261	6,076	10,186	28,679
World Total	4,160	7,720	12,920	(35,700)†	3,990	7,450	12,400	(34,300)
Ratio (%)	38·4	35·9	36·6	(40·0)	81·7	81·7	82·1	(83·5)

* Including Ireland except in 1954.

† Assuming a margin of about 4 per cent between the recorded value of world exports (mainly f.o.b.) and imports (mainly c.i.f.). This is the margin implied in the figures for earlier years

Tyszynski's results) the exports of those countries in the same years are also reproduced. The SITC data for 1954 are shown in the final columns.

The countries listed in Table VII account for about 40 per cent of total imports of manufactures. Earlier in the century the proportion seems to have been considerably lower and to have shown no tendency to grow. This is at first sight a surprising result since it might be thought that the industrial countries would take a diminishing proportion of each other's exports of manufactures. One of the factors at work has been the decline in East–West trade; another has been the rapid increase in trade in manufactures (including components for assembly after importation) between Canada and the United States, the value of such trade reaching \$3·5 b. or over 10 per cent of world trade in manufactures in 1953; and a third circumstance has been the development of manufactures, such as aluminium and newsprint, which are also raw materials and freely traded between industrial countries.

Of the countries shown in Table VII, two (Canada and Sweden) import more manufactures than they export; three (Belgium, Italy and Switzerland) import over half the value of their exports; one (USA) imports about half as much as she exports (more than half in 1953, less than half in 1954); and the remaining four (UK, France, Germany and Japan) import less than half what they export. Japan shows the lowest ratio of imports to exports or, looked at the other way round, has the highest exports of manufactures in relation to her imports. The German ratio, which is now a little above the Japanese, has changed little since the late twenties, whereas the British and Japanese ratios of imports to exports have fallen and the French ratio has increased.

The most rapidly expanding markets for manufactures shown in Table VII are in Belgium, Sweden and Canada. These countries also show the most rapid rate of increase in exports of manufactures and it is probable that there is some connection between these circumstances: success in exporting must have enhanced importing power and at the same time must have added to import requirements.

The largest single market for manufactures is now the United States, with Canada second and the United Kingdom third. Even if the exchange of manufactures between the

United States and Canada is left out of account, the United States still takes first place and Canada falls only a little below the United Kingdom. Germany, Belgium, Sweden and France follow in that order.

If we add to the countries shown in Table VII the remaining members of the OEEC, we can account for a total on the import side of $18,278 m. (c.i.f.) in 1954 and on the export side of $30,902 m. The markets unaccounted for are concentrated largely in the outer sterling area and in Central and South America, these two groups of countries importing manufactures to the value of $8 m. in 1953 from Western Europe and the United States.

It is not possible, from earlier studies, to show how the market for manufactures in the primary producing countries has grown over the past half century. There is unfortunately no counterpart to Tyszynski's analysis from the side of imports. Svennilson, however, gives figures of the exports of manufactures from the United Kingdom, the United States, France and Germany to selected markets at dates between 1913 and 1950.[1] These data have been used to construct Table VIII. If we assume that the total share of these four exporters in imports of manufactures into the various markets did not change greatly between 1913 and 1950, the growth in

[1] Op. cit., pp. 296–8.

Table VIII

Exports from four industrial exporters to selected markets, 1913 and 1950

Market	*$ m.* *Exports of manufactures from*									
	UK		*US*		*France*		*Germany*		*All four exporters*	
	1913	1950	1913	1950	1913	1950	1913	1959	1913	1950
Argentine & Brazil	137·3	205·9	61·9	427·6	44·3	116·3	101·6	56·0	345·1	805·8
Turkey, French Morocco & Egypt	47·1	140·2	1·9	93·7	24·4	166·3	31·2	76·0	104·6	476·2
India and Pakistan	324·8	364·8	6·9	121·5	8·0	19·1	33·3	26·5	373·0	531·9
Australia	151·8	686·9	26·9	75·3	2·1	22·6	17·8	27·0	198·6	811·8
Total	661·0	1397·8	97·6	718·1	78·8	324·3	183·9	185·5	1021·3	2625·7

their exports provides a measure of the rate of expansion of these markets.[1]

The growth of the Indian market (which is rather understated because of the simultaneous rise of Japanese competition) was obviously comparatively slight in terms of current dollars; in real terms it must have contracted sharply. The South American markets show much the same symptoms. Even in Australia and the Near East, the increase is below the average for the industrial countries in Table VII. So far as it goes, therefore, Table VIII bears out the general conclusion, reached above, that the industrial countries have taken an increasing share of each other's exports of manufactures.

V

At this point it may be useful to analyse the network of world trade in manufactures. The latest year for which full figures are available in 1953 and the network in that year is shown below. For convenience, the flow of total exports, including primary products, is also shown (in brackets) underneath the corresponding flow of manufactures. The total amount of trade included in the diagram is $42,370 m. out of a total world trade in 1953 of about $75,000 m., the major omission being the exports of the sterling area and Latin American countries which came to about $16,000 m. The trade in manufactures accounted for is $27,230 m. out of a world total that was probably about $32,000 m.

In order to simplify matters, only four headings are shown: the United Kingdom, the United States, Canada, and OEEC countries other than the United Kingdom. Japan is omitted altogether (except under the heading 'Other Countries') and the trade of Canada, other than with Western Europe and the United States, is also not shown.

Each of the four exporters enjoys a decisive advantage within a special market: the United Kingdom in the sterling area; the United States in the Western Hemisphere; Canada in the United States; and OEEC countries in their trade with one another and with their overseas territories (which, with

[1] I am indebted to the Board of Trade for a calculation showing that imports of manufactures into Australia grew from $338 m. (c.i.f.) in 1913 to $1,212 m. in 1950, i.e. in a slightly lower proportion than exports (f.o.b.) to Australia from the four countries included in Table VIII.

Japan and Eastern Europe, make up a large part of 'Other Countries'). Thus the United Kingdom's exports of manufactures to the sterling area are double the combined exports of other OEEC countries and the United States; the United States in turn exports over four times as much to Canada and nearly twice as much to Central and South America as to the United Kingdom and the other OEEC countries; and the trade in manufactures that the latter countries carry on with one another is more than twice as great as their imports from the United States and the United Kingdom. Similarly, in the markets outside the sterling area, the Western Hemisphere and Western Europe, the continental OEEC countries account for about twice as much of the trade in manufactures as the United States and the United Kingdom.

A number of other conclusions emerge from the diagram. One is the subordinate position occupied by the United States in markets outside the Western Hemisphere. In European markets she sells much less than the United Kingdom and less than half as much as Germany. In the British market, her sales of manufactures in 1953 were not appreciably greater than Canada's. It is only in the miscellaneous group of countries, which includes Japan and the Philippines, that she has a larger share than the United Kingdom of non-American markets. It is possible that this situation reflects discrimination against American exports in non-dollar markets but it is unlikely that by 1953 discrimination was a principal determinant of the pattern of trade.

It is also of interest to compare the success of the United Kingdom and the other OEEC countries in exporting manufactures to the Western Hemisphere. Each sells about as much in the United States alone as in the whole of Central and South America; but in the Canadian market, only the United Kingdom sells on any scale. Even the United Kingdom is apparently less successful in meeting American competition in Canada than in Latin America.

Of the OEEC countries which are treated as a group, Germany is much the most important. In 1953, for example, her exports of manufactures to OEEC countries, excluding the United Kingdom, came to $1,910 m. or over one-third of 'intra-European' trade in manufactures. Her exports to all other countries came to $1,750 m. compared with exports

NETWORK OF WORLD TRADE IN MANUFACTURES, 1955

($ 000 m.)

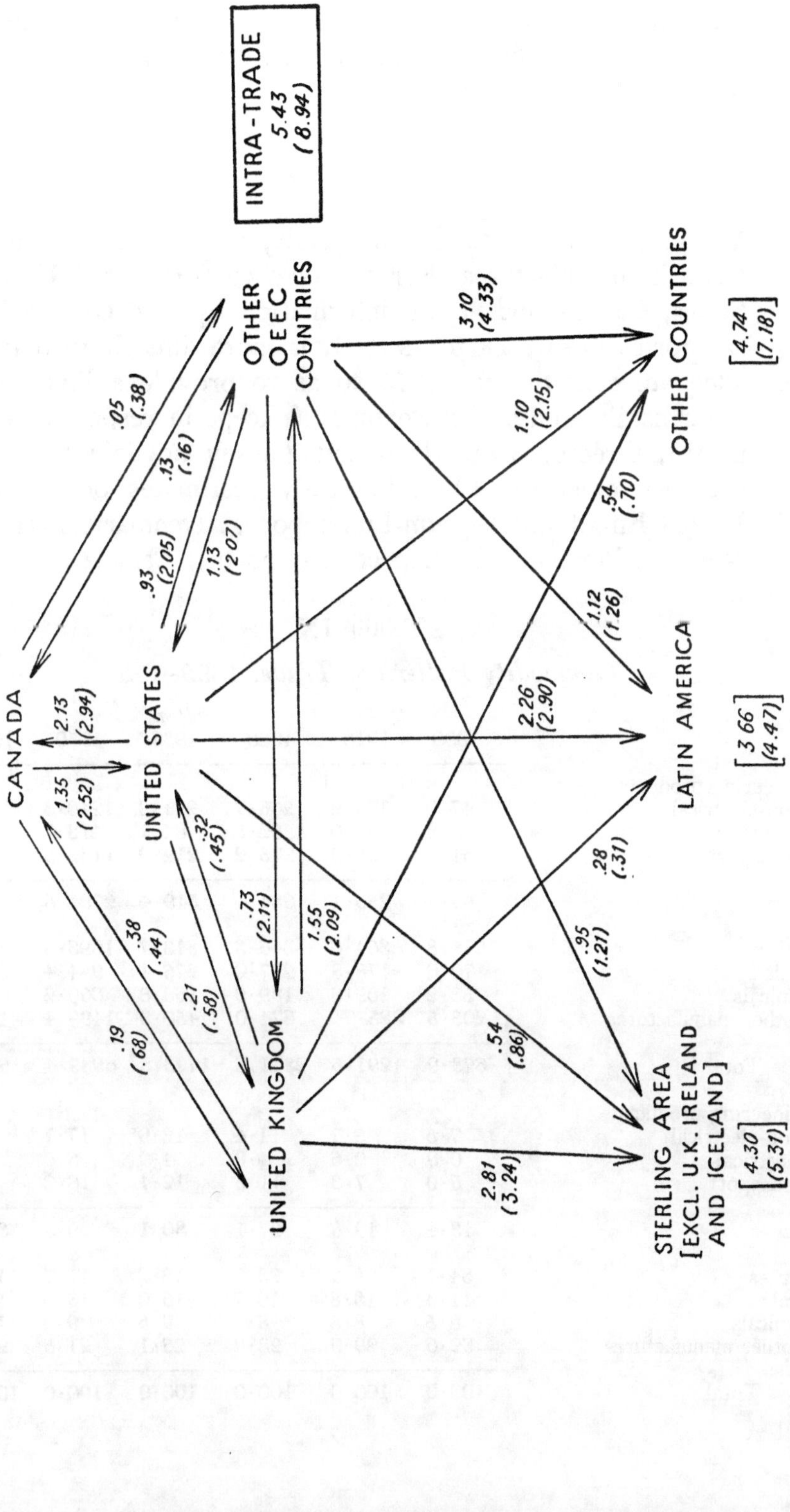

from the group of $7,180 m., so that in 1953 the German economy was more strongly oriented towards European markets for manufactures than was the economy of the rest of Western Europe.

VI

We may turn now to the commodity composition of world trade in manufactures. For all OEEC countries, the United States, Canada and Japan, information by SITC commodity categories goes back to 1951. It is more difficult to obtain adequate statistics for 1950 so as to provide a link with Tyszynski's study. For Portugal (except in respect of exports), Greece, Switzerland and Turkey no data by SITC category exist for 1950; for Italy (estimates only), the United Kingdom, Belgium-Luxembourg, Denmark, France, Norway, Portugal (in respect of exports), Canada and the

TABLE IX

Commodity Pattern of Trade, 1899–1953

	1899	1913	1929	£ *m.* 1937	1950	1950	1953
Engineering products:							
Non-electrical	47·0	125·2	266·7	221·8	1240·3		
Electrical	5·8	33·0	92·5	84·7	418·7		
Transport	31·0	94·8	275·2	212·9	1132·5		
	83·8	253·1	634·4	519·4	2791·5	2536	3749
Textiles	212·8	364·6	546·3	313·7	1093·9	1099	1132
Metals	70·6	178·8	297·0	276·1	944·4	9441	1322
Chemicals	53·2	109·3	189·9	163·8	660·2	717	984
All other manufactures	203·5	385·7	674·0	450·3	1499·4	1641	2305
Total	623·9	1291·5	2341·6	1723·3	6989·4	6934	9492
Engineering products:							
Non-electrical	7·5	9·7	11·4	12·9	17·7		
Electrical	0·9	2·6	4·0	4·9	6·0		
Transport	5·0	7·3	11·8	12·4	16·2		
	13·4	19·6	27·1	30·1	39·9	36·6	39·5
Textiles	34·1	28·2	23·2	18·2	15·7	15·8	11·9
Metals	11·3	13·8	12·7	16·0	13·5	13·6	13·9
Chemicals	8·5	8·5	8·1	9·5	9·4	10·3	10·4
All other manufactures	32·6	29·9	28·8	26·1	21·5	23·6	24·3
Total	100·0	100·0	100·0	100·0	100·0	100·0	100·0

United States there are figures by SITC Section and for selected SITC Divisions, but without geographical breakdown; for all the other members of OEEC, figures exist classified by Section, Division and, in some cases, Groups, and showing origin and destination as in 1951 and later years.[1]

Using the commodity groupings adopted in Table II and confining ourselves to the ten countries for which continuous figures are available, we can re-calculate Tyszynski's data so as to obtain the results shown in Table IX. The last two columns in the table make use of the data published under SITC headings.

The main change has been a shift away from textiles and towards engineering products. Metals and chemicals have shown a slight upward trend since 1899, although the change between 1937 and 1950 was the other way. The miscellaneous group of manufactures has shown a pronounced downward trend, especially since 1929. This group consists largely of consumer goods; and it is a fair generalization that international trade in manufactures has been moving away from consumer goods and towards capital goods while trade in manufactured materials has been relatively stable. It is unnecessary to labour this point as it has been made in some detail by Svennilson and emerges clearly from Tyszynski's article. If Tyszynski's figures are broken down, as he suggests,[2] into consumer goods, finished capital goods and manufactured materials, the result is as follows:

[1] I am grateful to Mr Milton Gilbert and the staff of the Statistics Division of OEEC for supplying me with the above information and with some of the data for 1950 and 1954 used in the article.

[2] Op. cit., p. 276, n. 3.

TABLE X

Composition of World Trade in Manufactures

	1899	1913	1929	1937	1950
Textiles	33·5	28·8	24·1	18·9	17·3
Other consumer goods*	26·8	23·1	20·5	18·9	15·1
Capital goods†	12·5	18·5	25·8	28·7	37·7
Manufactured materials of which:	27·2	29·6	29·6	33·5	29·9
iron and steel	6·0	7·7	7·8	9·9	8·1
other	21·2	21·9	21·8	23·6	21·8
	100·0	100·0	100·0	100·0	100·0

* Including 'not classified'.

† Including motor vehicles and other engineering products sold to final consumers.

Whereas in 1899 finished consumer goods formed 60 per cent of trade in manufactured goods, by 1950 the proportion had fallen to less than one-third; on the other hand, the proportion formed by capital goods (including motor vehicles) had risen from one-eighth to three-eighths. Manufactured materials other than iron and steel remained steady at a little over one-fifth of the total, while iron and steel showed some tendency to increase, rising over the whole period from 6 to 8 per cent of total trade in manufactures.

Next we may show how the main exporting countries have adapted their export trade to these trends. For this purpose it would be desirable to have figures of volume rather than value, since a transfer of resources to an expanding group of manufactures may be accompanied by a fall in their price and so be concealed in statistics of value. Nevertheless, even the value figures are a useful index of the speed of adjustment.

TABLE XI

Proportion of main categories to total exports of manufactures, 1899 *and* 1953

	Engineering Products		*Textiles*		*Metals and Chemicals*		*All Other Items*	
	1899	1953	1899	1953	1899	1953	1899	1953
UK	17·5	44·9	47·0	15·5	17·4	17·8	18·1	21·8
USA	27·9	54·2	7·9	6·6	34·3	20·2	29·8	19·0
France	5·7	25·7	35·8	18·6	13·6	32·5	44·8	23·2
Germany	8·9	45·7	20·6	5·9	20·7	25·5	49·8	22·9
Belgium, Italy, Sweden, Switzerland	8·9	25·3	42·6	15·8	19·3	29·7	29·3	29·1
Canada	30·2	18·5	7·5	0·9	9·7	36·0	52·6	44·6
Japan	0·2	18·1	58·4	36·1	21·5	21·0	19·8	24·8
Average	13·4	39·5	34·1	11·9	19·8	24·3	32·6	24·3

It is obvious from Table XI that every country has had to make radical changes in the commodity balance of its export trade and that, even now, there are wide differences in export structure between industrialized countries. Japan, for example, is as dependent on textiles as the whole group of industrial exporters were in 1899; and although engineering exports form an increasing proportion of her exports, the proportion in 1953 was no higher than the average for world trade in manufactures in 1913.

Over the past fifty years, the differences in export structure between the largest exporters appear to have narrowed. Engineering products now account for 45–55 per cent of the exports of manufactures of each of the three principal exporting countries. In textiles, also, the spread has narrowed, although the proportion that they form of British exports of manufactures remains well above the corresponding proportion for the United States and Germany. Metals and chemicals form a higher proportion of German, and a lower proportion of American, exports than formerly and the range between the highest and lowest proportion is much less. The miscellaneous group, which once formed nearly half Germany's exports of manufactures, now accounts for less than a quarter, and the proportion is very close to that for the other two countries.

The data in Tables IX and XI can also be looked at from the point of view of the distribution of trade between the exporting countries. The share of the principal exporters in each of the main categories of exports in 1899 and 1953 is set out in Table XII:

TABLE XII

Shares of leading exporters in main categories of exports of manufactures, 1899 *and* 1953

	Engineering Products		*Textiles*		*Metals and Chemicals*		*Other Manufactures*	
	1899	1953	1899	1953	1899	1953	1899	1953
UK	44·0	25·1	46·6	28·8	29·7	16·2	18·8	19·8
US	23·9	36·9	2·7	15·0	19·8	22·4	10·5	21·1
France	6·5	6·1	15·9	14·9	10·3	12·5	20·8	8·9
Germany	15·4	15·9	14·0	6·8	24·3	14·5	35·8	13·0
Belgium, Italy, Sweden and Switzerland	9·6	10·8	18·1	22·4	14·1	20·7	13·0	20·2
Canada	0·6	3·3	0·1	0·1	0·1	10·4	0·5	12·9
Japan	—	1·8	2·7	11·9	1·7	3·4	0·9	4·0
	100·0	100·0	100·0	100·0	100·0	100·0	100·0	100·0

It is curious that no country lost ground in all four of the categories in Table XII. The United Kingdom in 1953 had a rather higher proportion of world trade in the miscellaneous group; France, of the trade in metals and chemicals; Germany, of engineering products. Each of the remaining exporters gained a larger share of the market under each heading (except that Canada's exports of textiles remained negligible). No country, not even the United States, occupies the commanding position of the United Kingdom fifty years ago.

Of the four categories, engineering products show the most stable pattern, with North America and the United Kingdom sharing about two-thirds of the total trade at both dates, but in very different proportions. The countries of continental Europe appear to have preserved much the same share of the market over the period. The same is true, although not of each continental country, of base metals and chemicals, where the major changes have been the rise of Canada and the decline of Germany and the United Kingdom. By comparison, the changes in the pattern of trade in textiles and in the consumer goods that make up the greater part of 'Other manufactures' have been much larger it is almost exceptional for a country to have about the same proportion as at the beginning of the century of world trade in these two categories of exports.

The development of the commodity pattern over the past few years is analysed in Table XIII. This shows the changes that have taken place in the exports of the countries for which a total was given above in Table VI (i.e. OEEC countries, the United States, and Japan).

The changes, except in the miscellaneous group, have been strikingly in accord with the longer-term trends already dis-

TABLE XIII

Commodity Pattern of Trade, 1950–54

(\$ *m. and* %)

	1950	1951	1952	1953	1954
Engineering products	7392	9754	10888	11043	11795
%	35·9	33·8	37·8	38·7	38·2
Textiles	3251	4674	3437	3439	3723
%	15·8	16·2	11·9	12·0	12·0
Metals	2830	4034	3593	4005	4186
%	13·8	14·0	15·9	14·0	13·5
Chemicals	2189	3245	2855	3014	3627
%	10·6	11·2	9·9	10·6	11·7
Other manufactures	4909	7144	7029	7052	7571
%	23·8	24·8	24·4	24·7	24·5
Total	20573	28851	28804	28554	30902
%	100·0	100·0	100·0	100·0	100·0

cussed. Engineering products have risen from 35·9 per cent of the total in 1950 to 39·5 per cent in 1954.[1] Textiles, on the other hand, have fallen back from 15·8 per cent to 12·0 per cent—a fall that may be exaggerated because of the reaction from the high prices that textiles were fetching in 1951 after the outbreak of the Korean war. The other three groups show no clearly marked trend.

It would be possible to carry this analysis further and show how the competitive position of the leading exporters has changed within each commodity category but this would take us too far from the purpose of the present paper. The main points of interest are brought out in Table XIV which shows the changes from year to year in the share of the four principal exporting areas (US, UK, Germany and other OEEC countries) in the trade in each category of manufactures.[2]

[1] The percentages in Table XIII differ somewhat from those in Table XI because of the inclusion of a number of European countries not included in Table XI. The differences, however, are comparatively trivial.

[2] The residual in each case represents the share of Canada and Japan.

TABLE XIV

Share of principal exporting areas in world trade by main category of manufacture, 1950–54

	1950 %	1951 %	1952 %	1953 %	1954 %
Engineering products					
US	38·7	38·2	34·8	35·1	33·4
UK	29·4	25·5	24·8	23·9	23·3
Germany	6·4	9·7	13·4	15·2	17·3
Rest of OEEC	21·6	22·6	22·2	20·9	21·9
Textiles					
US	12·8	13·6	15·0	13·8	12·4
UK	30·6	28·2	27·3	26·5	24·5
Germany	2·9	4·5	6·0	6·3	7·0
Rest of OEEC	43·8	41·7	40·4	41·9	41·0
Metals					
US	17·8	16·4	18·0	15·6	16·0
UK	15·4	10·1	11·2	13·7	12·9
Germany	10·2	11·4	11·7	11·4	11·5
Rest of OEEC	40·2	45·4	40·3	42·9	42·3
Chemicals					
US	31·7	30·4	28·8	27·1	27·6
UK	17·9	15·9	18·0	16·5	15·7
Germany	10·2	13·1	12·6	15·8	16·6
Rest of OEEC	34·1	34·9	33·9	32·7	32·4
Other Manufactures					
US	20·9	19·5	19·0	19·3	18·5
UK	21·8	21·0	18·9	18·2	17·4
Germany	7·7	10·5	11·0	11·9	13·6
Rest of OEEC	35·7	35·8	36·6	35·2	34·4

In each group, the share of the United States and the United Kingdom was lower in 1954 than in 1950. The downward movement was general and progressive, with some exceptions, particularly in the early years and apart from the metals group, where the changes from year to year were somewhat erratic. The British share of the world market in engineering products fell sharply in 1951 and continued to fall, rather less conspicuously, in each subsequent year, the contraction by 1954 being quite as great as the parallel contraction of the British share of the world market in textiles. The German shares in each group of manufactures except metals display an almost undeviating rise that slows down perceptibly after 1952; even in metals there was some improvement in Germany's share of world trade between 1950 and 1954. The OEEC countries, other than the UK and Germany, seem to have held their own, as a group, in engineering products, metals and (after 1951) textiles, but they have been losing ground in chemicals and apparently also in other manufactures.

VII

Finally, we may turn to look at the commodity pattern of *imports* of manufactures by market area. Here we are confined largely to information relating to the past few years, although there are also some indications of the changes at work over a longer period in the data provided by Svennilson.

We may begin by examining the position in 1953. In that year, the exporting countries bought from one another about

Table XV

Exports and Imports of Manufactures by Main Categories in 1953

	OEEC countries, USA, Canada and Japan		
	Exports $ *m.*	*Imports* $ *m.*	*Ratio of Imports to Exports* %
Engineering products	11043	5528	50
Textiles	3439	1749	51
Metals	4005	3825	96
Chemicals	3014	1858	62
Other manufactures	7052	7052	66
	28554	17574	62

three-fifths of their total exports of manufactures.[1] The question naturally arises whether there is a marked difference between the type of manufacture that they buy in this way and the type that they export to other markets. To this question Table XV supplies at least part of the answer.

Table XV suggests that engineering products and textiles form a larger proportion of the trade in manufactures between industrial and other countries than of the trade that goes on between industrial countries. Base metals, on the other hand, would appear to be traded mainly between industrial countries. Chemicals seem to be of about the same importance in the two sets of markets. In general, industrial countries import a more miscellaneous group of consumer goods, with textiles forming a smaller component, and mix a larger proportion of base metals with their imports of finished capital goods.

We may check these conclusions by comparing the commodity composition of exports from the three main areas to one another (including, for this purpose, Canada) and to the various third markets (excluding Canada) shown in the network of trade in manufactures. The results of this comparison are set out in Table XVI.

It is apparent from Table XVI that engineering products do indeed form a larger proportion of trade with markets outside the continent of Europe and North America than of trade

[1] The ratio falls to under 50 per cent if the OEEC countries that are not large industrial exporters are excluded. (See Table VII.)

TABLE XVI

Commodity composition of trade in manufactures between major industrial areas and between those areas and third markets, 1953

	Engineering products		*Textiles*		*Metals*		*Chemicals*		*Other Manufactures*		*$ 000 m. Total*		
	Intra trade	*Third markets*	*Intra trade*	*Third markets*	*Intra trade*	*Third markets*	*Intra trade*	*Third markets*	*Intra trade*	*Third markets*	*Intra trade*	*Third markets*	*A… ma… ke…*
US	1·81	2·07	·14	·34	·34	·28	·34	·48	·65	·71	3·28	3·88	7·
UK	·92	1·72	·35	·36	·26	·29	·18	·32	·54	·74	2·25	3·63	5·
Other OEEC countries	2·14	1·85	·93	·72	1·48	·70	·84	·62	2·04	1·26	7·43	5·15	12·
Total	4·87	5·64	1·42	1·62	2·08	1·27	1·36	1·42	3·23	2·71	12·96	12·66	25·

within or between those continents. This is true also, but to a much smaller extent, of textiles. On the other hand, as emerged from Table XV, base metals enter more largely into trade between the industrial areas than into their trade with third markets; and the same is true, though less markedly, of trade in miscellaneous manufactures.

Table XVI also brings out the different market orientation of the three areas, already apparent in the network above. The British export trade depends particularly heavily on non-industrial markets and although its share of those markets is highest in textiles, it is in engineering products that dependence on 'third' markets is greatest in comparison with sales to other industrial countries. For the other OEEC countries it is in metals that they have the largest share of 'third' markets but again it is in engineering products that dependence on those markets is greatest.

On the whole, however, it is the resemblance rather than

TABLE XVII

Imports of Manufactures into leading industrial countries, 1953

	Engineering products	*Textiles*	*Metals*	*Chemicals*	*Other manufactures*	*$ m. Total*
UK	445	135	595	212	409	1796
US	355	315	1294	380	1425	3769
France	425	46	160	119	173	923
Germany	126	195	282	95	209	907
Belgium	390	86	197	121	339	1133
Italy	296	40	173	97	157	763
Sweden	317	145	144	92	195	893
Switzerland	196	72	106	72	162	608
Canada	1485	230	236	241	768	2960
Japan	161	15	31	69	43	319
Total	4196	1279	3218	1498	3880	14071
	%	%	%	%	%	%
UK	24·8	7·5	33·1	11·8	22·8	100
US	9·4	8·4	34·3	10·1	37·8	100
France	46·0	5·0	17·3	12·9	18·7	100
Germany	13·9	21·5	31·1	10·5	23·0	100
Belgium	34·4	7·6	17·4	10·7	29·9	100
Italy	38·8	5·2	22·7	12·7	20·6	100
Sweden	35·5	16·2	16·1	10·3	21·8	100
Switzerland	32·2	11·8	17·4	11·8	26·6	100
Canada	50·2	7·8	8·0	8·1	25·9	100
Japan	50·4	4·7	9·7	21·6	13·5	100
Total	29·8	9·1	22·9	10·6	27·6	100

the difference between the commodity pattern of exports to the two sets of markets that is most striking. There appears to be a strong tendency for the structure of a country's export trade to vary comparatively little from one group of markets to another.

To return to imports, Table XVII sets out the imports of manufactures of the ten leading exporters that have appeared in earlier tables.

The pattern of imports is a highly variable one; hardly any two countries are alike. The three largest industrial exporters, however, show some similarity, except that the United States has particularly low imports of engineering products and an unusually high proportion of imports of miscellaneous manufactures, while Germany's imports include a high proportion of textiles and the United Kingdom's of engineering products. There is also some similarity in import structure between the European countries other than Germany and the United Kingdom, the biggest scatter being in textiles. Chemicals once again show the most stable proportion of total trade in manufactures, forming from 10 to 13 per cent of total imports in eight of the ten countries.

CHAPTER 15

Organization for European Economic Co-operation[1]

I

THE fact that international economic co-operation has to be organized is nowadays taken for granted. It was not always so. When governments sought to reduce, rather than to extend, their control over economic affairs (particularly over international commerce and investment) they were content to straighten out occasional differences with their neighbours as they arose or to join with them for limited and specific purposes like postal regulations. International contacts were relatively intermittent and almost exclusively bilateral. With the growth of control over economic life, however, a more lasting association between governments has become necessary, both to harmonize their economic policies and to deal with world forces against which merely national measures are ineffective. Governments setting out to control forces with a wider sovereignty than their own must sooner or later seek the co-operation of their neighbours. The economic problems of an age of planning do not admit of a bilateral solution or of settlement *ad hoc*. Standing arrangements are necessary, with a central staff keeping the problems under constant review and organizing the consultations and negotiations to which they give rise.

It may be useful if I give some concrete idea of the scale of these arrangements as they now exist [in 1951] in OEEC—which is by no means the largest international organization. OEEC is, in fact, a continuing conference of eighteen countries,[2] honeycombed with committees, sub-committees and working parties of all kinds, engaged sometimes in multilateral negotiations on behalf of the governments represented,

[1] Paper read to the Manchester Statistical Society on February 13, 1952.

[2] Austria, Belgium and Luxembourg, Denmark, France, Germany, Greece, Iceland, Ireland, Italy, Netherlands, Norway, Portugal, Sweden, Switzerland, Trieste, Turkey and the United Kingdom.

sometimes in an exchange of views on highly technical subjects. There are about 2,000 formal meetings a year and an output of stencilled sheets issued through the secretariat (apart from what circulates in delegations or does not get further than typescript) of over 1,000 per week. The subjects covered range from the mechanization of small farms in Iceland and the marketing of fish in Trieste to the internal financial stability of member countries, the course of prices in international markets, or the Annual Report of the European Payments Union (EPU). The total size of the secretariat from messengers upwards is not far short of 1,000, but the main responsibility in the divisions engaged in drafting and research rests on about fifty officers. Member countries are represented by delegations varying in size from over a score to one man (who is also his country's ambassador to a number of countries including the USSR).

This is a formidable scale of activity and gives an air of extraordinary comprehensiveness. In fact, however, much of what is done is of interest only to a limited group of experts in each country and the issues that come before the top committees of the Organization include only a few in the field of general economic policy. There is never any difficulty in finding technical and procedural problems to occupy the Organization. Delegations rarely oppose any proposal for a study, whatever the subject. But this is not true of general economic problems. Governments show a good deal of hesitation in raising such problems and the initiative has repeatedly had to be taken by the secretariat.

II

Not only must there be organization. If there is to be economic co-operation, someone must take the initiative. Someone must raise the issues that endanger international harmony and draw attention to any fresh threats to disequilibrium. Can governments be relied on to do this? Must they rely on the secretariat? Or can some routine be worked out that ensures that such issues are automatically raised?

I see no reason to rely exclusively on governments. Their attention is concentrated on their own problems and they rarely become conscious that other countries are similarly affected until rather late in the day. Their first instinct is to take independent action, not to rush to OEEC for advice. Yet some of them do not relish allowing the initiative to pass to the secretariat. At the time when OEEC was set up, there was a marked disagreement between the 'British' view of a secretariat that merely took the minutes and ensured that there were enough chairs for everybody to sit on, and the 'Continental' view that the secretariat should play at least as active a rôle as any of the delegations. Experience has justified the 'Continental' view. On the occasions that really mattered, it has been as often as not the secretariat that canvassed the views of delegations and put a paper in front of them, in an effort to let Ministers have proposals that stood a reasonable chance of acceptance. There has been no sharp segregation such as may have been expected, between secretariat and delegations, but on the contrary a great deal of very active co-operation in which the contribution of each has not been easily distinguishable in the final outcome. The Secretary-General, in putting forward his views, can consult his colleagues in the delegations informally without having committed any government. He can put forward concrete proposals that take account of their probable reactions and yet can be withdrawn without damage to the prestige of any of them.

The adoption of a satisfactory routine can facilitate the prompt discussion of urgent economic problems. It is, for example, highly desirable that the Organization should study regularly the movement of a dozen key indices of economic activity and offer their comments on them. The Managing Board of the EPU is already required to review the economic and financial situation of member countries once a quarter. There is also an annual examination of the internal financial stability of member countries. Countries have been asked each year to submit a number of programmes indicating the expected movement in their imports, exports, production, consumption and so on. But major issues may arise, outside such a routine, while the various documents, which take several months to prepare and rapidly become out of date, are still being drafted. No formula can ensure that the threat of disequilibrium will be dispelled by arrangements laid down in advance, nor that proposals for action will be formulated automatically as a result of those arrangements. Someone has to be ready to take the initiative without waiting for all the evidence.

III

Why should any organization for economic co-operation limit its membership on a regional or continental basis? The fact of propinquity no longer dominates international relations. The Commonwealth, however far-flung, is as real a unit as any continent. And Europe, for political purposes, is now divided into two, if not three continents. The Western half, though continental in scope, is far from being either fixed in boundaries, united in its interests, or indifferent to its bonds with other parts of the world. It is certainly not an economic unity. More than one-half of its trade is conducted with the outside world. The largest trading country, the United Kingdom, carries on about three-quarters of its trade with other continents and undergoes a steady gravitational pull towards the Commonwealth and the United States. Between the major powers, there is no coincidence of interest springing from large scale interchange of goods and services: they are all industrial countries with similar industrial structures and in keen competition with one another within Europe and beyond. Of the total imports into the United Kingdom, France, Germany, Italy and Belgium in 1950, only one-sixth came from the other four countries in this group. The trade with the outside world consists largely in the export of manufactured goods in payment for imports of raw materials and foodstuffs; and in this trade the main countries compete with, rather than complement, one another.

If metropolitan areas alone are taken, only two countries draw less than a quarter of their imports from OEEC countries, but none draws more than three-quarters. If the monetary areas in EPU are taken, including the whole of the sterling area, for example, it is still true that no country draws as much as three-quarters of its imports from this larger area. The average works out at about two-fifths for the smaller area and nearly two-thirds for the larger. In terms of export markets, trade with other members of OEEC and within the EPU area makes a better showing, but for most countries remains a long way short of 100 per cent.

In the export and import trade of the major Western European countries, there is a strong family resemblance, combined with differences in detail. Manufactured goods, particularly machinery and vehicles, metal goods and textiles, account for a higher proportion of total exports, and food and raw materials of total imports. The trade of the smaller countries has generally a different structure, with net imports of manufactured goods and net exports of food and raw materials, but the totals are not large enough to offset the surpluses and deficits of the industrial countries and prevent a high degree of dependence on sources of supply and markets outside Europe.

The same picture emerges in relation to the movement of capital or labour from one country to another. Western European countries have developed countries overseas by international investment but have not sunk comparable sums in one another, nor are they likely to, without special prompting. Migration from one country to another is hedged about with restrictions and takes place on an extremely limited scale. Even the settlement of trade deficits and surpluses between European countries pre-supposes a satisfactory balance with the rest of the world and a currency with a wider acceptability than Western Europe alone.

All this is true. But it is beside the point. The countries represented in OEEC are all located in Western Europe. But they enjoy the close collaboration of the United States and Canada; and the goodwill of the British Commonwealth is to some extent assured through the membership of the United Kingdom. The vast bulk of the industrial potential of the globe has some voice in OEEC's deliberations. Japan and the USSR are the only major industrial countries with no power to participate. If the members of OEEC can harmonize their policies it will be no mean contribution to the larger task of world-wide harmonization.

Moreover there is a very practical advantage in a limited membership. Eighteen delegates can sit round a table and feel the pressure of a common sentiment. Eighty delegates are a mob and inevitably behave irresponsibly unless organized on party lines. The smaller the group, the less the need to make speeches, and the more the scope for direct argument. Through the use of sub-committes, and by delegating decisions to the most trusted personalities, it is possible to transact business promptly and efficiently without always voting down a minority. Co-operation in other words is closer, not only because there are fewer interests involved and a greater coincidence of common problems, but because the machinery admits of fuller discussion, and greater unanimity.

IV

What, next, is an international organization to *do*? It is all very well to have a club, just sufficiently exclusive, and with excellent service. But most clubs, at least when they were founded, responded to some evident need.

When OEEC came into existence, the main tasks of international economic co-operation centred around one or two relatively simple concepts. The primary aim of the member governments was to raise the standard of living to a satisfactory level without continuing external assistance and without large-scale unemployment. The standard of living was threatened by a series of shortages and by the tendency to inflation and a chronic adverse balance of payments in which these shortages expressed themselves. The first requirement was the expansion of production to the maximum possible extent. Coupled with this were other tasks: to overcome inflation; to break down barriers to trade and work out a satisfactory system of international payments; and to distribute as equitably as possible the scarce resources upon which recovery depended. The main bottlenecks in recovery could all be reduced to dollars, since more dollars meant power over scarce resources, whether in the form of imported materials or in the form of additional capital. It was inevitable, therefore, that the dollar problem should dominate the activities of any international economic organization. It was, in fact, the offer of dollar aid that was responsible for the creation of the OEEC; and the division of aid was the major task undertaken by the Organization in its early stages.

The setting up of the OEEC had been preceded in the summer of 1947 by a conference in Paris to which each of the participating countries submitted a kind of Four-Year Plan outlining, in terms of detailed programmes—of production, consumption, imports, exports, investments, etc.—how it proposed to achieve economic recovery. These programmes were aggregated so as to obtain a rough measure of the total external aid that they pre-supposed; and the total, after being whittled down, was put forward to the Economic Co-operation Administration (ECA) as a statement of the combined dollar deficit for the four-year period.

The OEEC came into existence more than six months after the conclusion of this conference. Its first task was to make recommendations to ECA on the distribution of aid between the members. The method by which these recommendations were formulated was important, not only because it proved successful but also because it provided an object-lesson for much of the subsequent work of the Organization. First of all, since the recommendations could only be made after an objective assessment of the economic position of all the claimants, and since such an assessment involved an elaborate study of a mass of figures, it was necessary to entrust the task to a few chosen persons, subject, of course, to later approval by the Council of the Organization. Four 'wise men' were appointed —the Chairmen of the Council, the Programmes Committee and the Trade Committee, and the Secretary-General of the Organization. By narrowing the number of persons in this way, it was possible to remove not only the atmosphere of a public meeting but also the sense of representing national interests, and to build up a common sense of responsibility in which individual judgment had freer play. The four 'wise men' became, for the occasion, international personalities, and so far from pushing the claims of their own countries, were obliged either to disinterest themselves in them or to put them lower than they would otherwise have dared.

Secondly, the criteria by which aid was divided were exclusively economic and quantitative. The detailed programmes of member countries were analysed so as to test their plausibility and self-consistency; to measure by one index or another their dependence on external aid; and to establish the claims of each country to such aid.

Thirdly, no real attempt was made, either during the division of aid or subsequently, to co-ordinate the programme of individual countries. Although OEEC has repeatedly invited countries to submit quantitative programmes of one kind or another, it has tended to proceed by way of criticism of individual programmes or by way of showing that the individual programmes could not add up since they were mutually inconsistent, leaving it to members to take action independently rather than forcing them to adhere to a common programme laid down in detail in Paris.

The first division of aid laid the basis for the second, which maintained the same proportions between countries as the first although the total was lower. Subsequent division have been made by ECA without discussion within the Organization.

Division of aid may still be the crux of economic co-operation. But if so, it cannot be undertaken by a purely civilian organization. For aid will now be afforded from different motives and be apportioned by different criteria. No longer can one think of aid as a blood-transfusion designed to nurse Western Europe back to economic health. Aid is now a subvention by one ally to another; its object is the creation of a larger military potential at an earlier date. The aid that is necessary can once again be assessed only after scrutiny of the programmes of the countries that are members of the alliance. But the programmes that take precedence now are the military programmes, and these programmes cannot be taken as fixed when their adequancy is one of the major points at issue. The two-fold problem of ensuring the best and fullest use for purposes of defence of existing man-power and industrial capacity and of securing an equitable sharing of the financial burden is one in which military and economic considerations are closely interwoven. It is a problem that does not readily admit of discussion by a wider group of countries than are committed to the military alliance. Other countries must feel the repercussions of the decisions taken; but since they decide their military programmes independently, and neither proffer aid nor are candidates for it, they cannot participate in the decisions and can have no standing in the discussions leading to them.

I lay stress on the division of aid because it has a wider significance than is commonly realized. In the first place, it has the quality of inescapability. In any administration the things that *have* to be decided take priority over the things that are important to decide, still more over the things that it would be desirable to decide. There is a greater realism, urgency, and bite to negotiations of any kind as soon as these negotiations *must* be brought to a head because a decision cannot be deferred or avoided. This is as true in international as in national affairs. A discussion of general policy may ooze away through the phrases of a question-begging resolution into the sluggishness and indifference of national administrations. But if there is money to be divided, a cut-and-dried decision as to who is to get it and how much is hard to avoid.

Secondly, the provision of aid in the form of a financial grant necessarily raises all the major issues of economic policy. Not for nothing does the budget take pride of place in the determination of a country's economic policy. A loan may be made on a more limited perspective of specific capital assets. But an outright grant is not likely to be governed by any narrow measure of deserts. Whether it is made to speed economic recovery or to sustain a greater outlay on defence, the grant is not likely to be settled without a full review of the general state of economic health in the recipient country. Both its national and international accounts will come within such a review and no one index, such as the balance of payments, the volume of unemployment, the budget surplus or deficit, will be treated as a sufficient measure of requirements. Aid cannot be given on the basis of some simple formula—such as economists keep working out in other contexts—but generally requires an elaborate analysis of available indices and declared policy. If the economic policies of allies—or, for that matter, of neighbours—are capable of harmonization, the division of economic aid offers the best prospect of achieving it.

The division that has to be made, however, is not one of money only. *Any* scarce resources may call for division. It may be necessary, for example, to assist the movement of labour from one country to another or to withdraw obstacles to it. Fuel and raw materials may be scarce and call for international allocation. So also may be military equipment or the components from which they are manufactured.

If the division of aid was the father of OEEC, the integration of Europe was certainly the mother. Alongside the severely practical problem of building recovery out of dollar aid, there was an ideological problem of piecing together the shattered fragments of continental economies into a more enduring unity. There was little in the first problem to designate a European grouping for the claimants to American aid beyond the convenience to America of treating with geographical neighbours through a single organization and the convenience to European countries of reviewing their common predicament in order to concert a common strategy of recovery. When aid came to an end, and when the dollar shortage was mastered, the *raison d'être* of OEEC could no longer be found in the common danger of economic disaster. Other threats remained—the common danger of aggression on the one side and inflation on the other—and other obstacles to recovery, other sources of disharmony, other limits to economic development. But they had not the compulsion to joint action of Marshall aid

The second problem on the other hand, lost none of its urgency. If economic integration was the aim, the strategy to be followed was not a step by step removal of dangers common to each economy but a step by step integration of them all. This had its practical side, too; the steps had to include the breaking down of barriers to trade and the building up of a satisfactory system of payments within Western Europe. But, underlying the practical lay the ideal: a longing for unity that overstepped purely economic limits. There was a desire for a more permanent association, variously conceived in terms of a Customs Union, federation, close reconomic integration, co-ordination of national plans, and so on. Sometimes this desire found expression in the idea of a common market: it was supposed that, by a closer integration of European economies the energies of European producers might yield the larger returns enjoyed by American producers in their wider market. Sometimes it emerged in a stress on collective action as a preliminary to national action, in a desire to achieve a permanent subordination of national to common European interests. It was this urge for integration that gave birth to the Schuman Plan for the steel industries of Europe, to the proposals of Stikker, Pella and Petsch, and to some at least of the negotiations for regional groupings in Benelux, Finebel and Ukiscan.

V

The essence of economic co-operation is to eliminate disharmonies and create institutions that will maintain a satisfactory international equilibrium. The main action must always be taken by individual governments rather than by governments in concert. But no individual government can operate on the whole situation so as to make the necessary adjustments smaller or more tolerable; the object of economic co-operation, therefore must be not merely to remove specific disharmonies of policy but to preserve a continuous position of equilibrium within which adjustments may be made.

It goes without saying that economic co-operation presupposes independence. The members of OEEC do not act in unison but pursue policies governed by their local circumstances. They jointly subscribe to the objective set out in the Convention, but may give different objectives different weight or have objectives of their own to which other members do not subscribe. The decisions that are taken are taken unanimously so that each of the 18 members has a right of veto. In practice, any member that seeks to exploit its nuisance value to excess can nearly always be shamed into agreement with the others. The right of appeal if a decision of the Council cannot be implemented without real hardship disposes countries to more conformity and to a readier acquiescence in decisions that they would hesitate to take independently. But the members are plainly a long way removed from that united Europe of which many of them dream. They have undertaken to seek a common solution to their problems, and to have regard in their national policies to the repercussions of those policies on other members. They have built up strong delegations, knowing one another's ways and standpoints. They have a joint staff, skilled in international administration, ably led and working in harmony with one another and with the national delegations. But the members retain freedom of action within the commitments that they have assumed. They regard themselves as forming a continuing conference at which they may raise any economic problem to which they attach importance, and are in no way an international government in embryo.

It is inevitable that this should be so. Union would require a deliberate surrender of sovereignty backed by popular opinion. The step-by-step technique of achieving unity cannot advance far so long as there is no assurance of constancy in the group that is in course of integration, and a very real possibility that governments might come to power hostile to the very attitudes and philosophy that should form the bonds of union. It is one thing to set up an international post-office, for example, but quite another to let the size of one's steel industry, or of one's army, be settled by governments that might be neutral, or even on the other side, in a struggle with a totalitarian power. At some point in economic co-operation within a loose group of governments, elected on very different programmes, and with very different electorates, it would be highly irresponsible to go further without going all the way to complete unity. The affairs of one country are necessarily mixed up in the affairs of its neighbours; but there are some directions in which it would be fatal to a country's independence to get too mixed up.

In the long run, European unity may be inevitable. But so long as people are not yet conscious that this is so, and have the right to choose their own government, economic policy has to be conducted on a different assumption. The extent to which co-operation is carried will not exceed the limits of national interests, generously interpreted.

Where OEEC is seeking to reach decisions, therefore, and not merely to compare notes, it is able to do so only on a limited footing. The problem of conducting the discussions of any 18 persons so as to obtain their unanimous assent even to a general proposition is difficult enough. It is infinitely more difficult to get them to bind themselves in advance to a common plan of action. In bilateral negotiations it is at least possible to narrow the issues in dispute and by testing the ground to discover whether the two sides can come to agreement without exceeding their instructions. But in the kind of multilateral negotiations that the machinery of OEEC gives rise to, even the issues may not be understood, or they may be different for different delegations; some delegations may be without instructions altogether; and the negotiations may have to be conducted in a large meeting at which over a hundred people are present.

One important corollary of this is that it is idle to think of economic co-operation within OEEC in terms of the preparation of detailed plans expressed in quantitative terms. Member countries have in the past been invited to submit their national programmes for periods varying up to four yeasr ahead, and these programmes have frequently been in great detail. They have included programmes for imports and exports by commodity and by market or source of origin; production of the main raw materials, foodstuffs and manufactured products; investment by main categories; consumption under various headings; but never finance, either in the form of budget details or of future banking policy.

The original reason for inviting those programmes to be submitted was two-fold: first to provide a background against which dollar aid could be allocated; and secondly to prepare a sketch of the measures necessary for full economic recovery and to assess the magnitudes involved. There was never any real prospect that these programmes would be fully co-ordinated, or that if they could be co-ordinated as they stood that they would still be valid at the end of the day. Member countries have found from hard experience that while it may be useful to prepare programmes of this kind in order to bring out the more remote consequences of immediate trends and to get an idea of the directions that policy should take, it would be foolish in the extreme to treat such programmes too literally and as expressing hard and fast targets. If this is true on the national level, it is even truer on the international.

The programmes that countries are now invited to submit tend to be more general and to relate to the movement of the main variables in the national accounts. These programmes presumably form the basis of decisions in NATO as to the sharing of the financial burden of rearmament. European countries, however, have, without exception, shown an increasing indisposition to submit figures extending more than a year or so into the future except by way of illustration of what might conceivably happen. They have tended to dwell more on the general direction that policy should take than on any quantitative indices of the results which they hope to secure by those policies.

A particularly striking illustration of the difficulties of co-ordinating national programmes is offered by the efforts that were made to co-ordinate investment programmes. Even in a country exercising rigorous control over investment, the preparation of an investment programme is a matter of considerable complexity and the adjustments made in the original estimates require long negotiations with different Government Departments and the exercise of strong pressure to keep the total within the agreed figure. In the OEEC, it was soon apparent that different countries exercised such a widely different degree of control, that the information that could be obtained was so inadequate, that the negotiations that would be involved were so formidable, and that the power to enforce any decisions taken was so limited, that a comprehensive co-ordination of investment programmes was quite out of the question and that even co-ordination of investment in particular directions could not accomplish a great deal. The most that could be done was to afford each country a general picture of the total size of the investment programmes of the members as a group and bring to its attention more forcibly the danger that it might be exceeding what was desirable in some particular direction.

Such international planning, therefore, as has taken place has been directed to humbler ends. The scrutiny of programmes has been more closely associated with the division of aid than with the preparation of joint targets; with no aid to be divided, the programmes that are worth examining are a great deal more general and linked more with the discussion of financial policy than with specific physical controls.

VI

One conception of economic co-operation that was given great prominence in the early days of OEEC was that of a Customs Union. Curiously enough, this lay at the very opposite extreme of economic thought to the preparation of a joint plan of action expressed in fully co-ordinated programmes. There was never much prospect that a Customs Union would be possible without a far closer political union and without the creation of a number of new international institutions. Countries were also unlikely to be prepared to accept the wholesale disturbance to their existing industrial structure that would follow from the withdrawal of protection, unless the process were spread over a very long period.

The idea underlying the proposals for a Customs Union was that of the creation of a common market in Europe in order to enable the member countries to reap some of the advantages of specialization enjoyed by the United States in its large unified market. Other proposals of a more modest character have been put forward in the past two years tending in the same direction. These proposals have been influenced not only by economic but also by political considerations. What began as a move towards European unity has been watered down first to a move towards closer economic integration, then to efforts to reduce somewhat the barriers to intra-European trade and, finally to the harmonization of economic policies. In each successive year there has been a different slogan: first, unification, then integration, then liberalization, then harmonization.

These slogans implied that it was more desirable or more urgent to strengthen the commercial links between European countries than between those countries and the outside world. Given the dollar shortage, this view could be defended on economic grounds without reference to wider political aspirations. An expansion in inter-European trade was an obvious step towards economic recovery; but not if it were made at the expense of trade within the outside world. It has always been accepted by the Organization that Europe's future hangs on its successful integration within a restored world community in which the lack of balance between North America and other countries has been removed.

The actual measures taken by the Organization in the field of trade and payments have been severely practical. The two key decisions have been to remove quantitative restrictions on an agreed proportion of imports from their countries and to set up the European Payments Union.

It was not until nearly the end of 1949 that the Organization adopted the first main resolution calling for greater liberation of trade. It is a mistake to assume, therefore—as is commonly done—that it was this drive towards liberalization that accounted for the rapid increase in intra-European trade in the period after 1947. It is almost impossible to establish the actual contribution made to the growth of intra-European trade either by the measures of liberalization taken at the end of 1949 or by those that have followed. It is not known, for example, what proportion of trade was already free of quota restrictions in 1949 or earlier, nor what proportion of the trade that was nominally subject to quota failed to reach the level at which existing quotas were fully taken up. It is difficult also to disentangle the influence of such special factors as the recovery of Germany from the specific measures taken by governments to reduce barriers to trade. It is even doubtful whether, if one segregates the multilateral element in the trade of member countries with one another, that element has gained in importance over the past few years in relation to the bilateral element.

Making all allowances, however, for what might have occurred in any event as a result of the growth of industrial and agricultural production and consequently of national incomes, the measures of liberalization that were taken did represent genuine pressure on all the member countries to proceed more rapidly than they otherwise would have done, to refrain from sliding backwards at the least excuse, and to put an end to discrimination between member countries in their import policy.

The original method adopted for liberalizing intra-European trade was to insist that all member countries should free from quantitative restrictions a minimum proportion of private imports as measured at some base date (in practice, 1948). This formula was ingenious, absurd, but effective. It has now been supplemented by the adoption of a common list of imports which each member undertakes to free from quota restrictions by some fixed date. There are two elements in the common list: the smaller part consists of those commodities which countries have already agreed to free, and the larger part consists of commodities on which countries have agreed to concentrate their efforts when they are removing trade restrictions. So far, the first element consists solely of textiles.

Countries that have difficulty in reaching the agreed minimum of liberalization have the right to justify failure *ex post facto* to the Organization. They are required to submit their case to a committee drawn by lot from a panel nominated by all the member countries, and the recommendations of this committee are reviewed by the Council of the Organization. This appeals procedure is of great interest and may, in the course of time, be further developed.

The recovery of European countries was probably less threatened by bilateral trade arrangements and quota restrictions than by payments difficulties. These difficulties took two forms: a country might be in general deficit and require credit in order to maintain imports until it could make the necessary internal adjustments; or it might find itself accumulating a surplus with some of its partners which it could not offset against a deficit with others. The second difficulty arose from the first, since, if the balance of payments of all countries was in equilibrium, there could be no real difficulty about offsetting surpluses and deficits. The essential problem, therefore, was to obtain the necessary international credit and feed it in, taking care to give debtors an incentive to return to equilibrium without excessive disruption to their economy. It was also necessary to avoid introducing incentives that would distort the pattern of trade and make fully multilateral arrangements more difficult to secure. The first of these requirements was met by the voting of Marshall Aid; the second was to some extent secured by the system of drawing rights under which countries were able to obtain Marshall dollars in return for accumulating a surplus with a debtor country.

The payments schemes negotiated in 1948 and 1949 had various blemishes and did not establish multilateral settlements within Europe. With the setting up of the European Payments Union in the middle of 1950 a great advance was made. A member country was enabled to ignore its surplus or deficit with other member countries and to treat its total deficit or surplus as the thing that mattered. It was also able to ignore any fluctuation from month to month and concentrate on its cumulative net surplus or deficit. Finally, the European Payments Union made provision for the grant of credit by the countries in surplus to the countries in deficit and offered the prospect of a workable scheme even when Marshall Aid ceased.

The fundamental problem of international economic co-operation—as indeed of domestic economic policy—is to find the right blend of compulsion and discretion of automatic, checks and correctives and scope for the exercise of human judgment and intelligence. From this point of view, the European Payments Union is skilfully devised. It imposes automatic penalties on those who are in deficit without denying them all prospect of special aid. It allows those who are in surplus to reap some reward but without leaving much incentive to remain in surplus. It rests on the good sense and strong-mindedness of the Managing Board and on the solidarity of the members of the Union. But it rests even more on the success of the members in avoiding a large deficit in their balances of payments. It was a bold step to set up the EPU while the total deficit of the member countries with the outside world was still of the order of at least a billion dollars a year. It was an even greater risk to do so at the outset of a rearmament boom when the terms of trade were moving strongly against the principal European countries. But, given what Europe had accomplished in the first years of Marshall Aid, it was a justifiable risk.

PART IV: ADMINISTRATION AND PLANNING

CHAPTER 16

On Being an Economic Adviser[1]

'. . . The valued file
Distinguishes the swift, the slow, the subtle.'
William Shakespeare

I

THERE was a time when the business of industry and of government was transacted without the cloud of expert witnesses that is now considered necessary. In the days before the war it was rare to find in government employment any professional economist or anyone who carried the label 'economic adviser'. It was not until the outbreak of war that economists began to find themselves sought after as advisers and a fashion was set which, after the war, became something of a fad. I propose to discuss the work of these mysterious personages, drawing on my own experience as an economic adviser.

When I look back on this experience and try to analyse it, I do not find it easy to reduce it to a faithful and intelligible picture. Like the businessman who is cross-examined by an economist on how he runs his business, or the aged man suddenly confronted by the White Knight, I have no difficulty in giving an account of my activities—indeed, a number of rather conflicting accounts. But like them, I find, to my consternation, that the account turns out to be one which I am hardly able to recognize and which sensible men may well regard as faintly absurd. The easiest course for me to take is

[1] From *Scottish Journal of Political Economy*, October 1955.

to present a mass of illustrative detail and abstain rigorously from generalization, since generalization requires long reflection and not just long experience. I shall try, however, to offer some generalizations and substantiate them without presuming much knowledge either of economic theory or of administrative practice and without entering into detail about the issues on which advice was required.

There are many different kinds of economic adviser, performing different functions and employed in all sorts of organizations. There are the advisers in the public service attached to government departments, foreign embassies, nationalized industries, and so on; there is the advisory work that goes on in commerce and industry, banking and finance; and there are the free-lance consultants who offer advice for a fee or, more commonly, issue it gratis in the public press. There are advisers who never emerge from the backroom and have their say entirely in private; and there are those, like the Council of Economic Advisers in the United States, whose advice may be published and, in due course, challenged by hostile critics. There are also top-level advisers who are sufficiently exalted to need no staff, top-level advisers who direct the work of a considerable staff, and the less exalted advisers who form the staff and advise the advisers.

This last classification merits some elaboration. The typical pre-war adviser was of the first type; he was a person of standing and distinction in his profession who was asked to act in a personal capacity as adviser to a large organization; or he was invited, as one who had already made his name as an economist, to join a panel of expert consultants. A well-known example is that of Sir Sydney Chapman, who, after serving with the Board of Trade during the First World War as head of the General Economic Department, was later appointed Economic Adviser. Another familiar (and illustrious) example is that of Sir Henry Clay, who became Economic Adviser to the Bank of England in 1931 and during the war was for a time, like Sir Sydney Chapman, Economic Adviser to the Board of Trade. Among the various advisory panels of economists which have been set up from time to time in this country the best-known are the Economic Advisory Council, a representative and unwieldy body that came into existence in 1930 and has not been heard of since 1939, and its successor, the Survey of Financial and Economic Plans, which expired in giving birth to the Economic Section of the Cabinet Office early in 1941. About the work of these two bodies little has been made public, but the general trend was obviously away from a highly distinguished group of outsiders, approving or composing occasional memoranda on set themes, to a paid staff, working full-time within the normal administrative machinery.

The second type of economic adviser, directing the work of a permanent staff of economists, is now increasingly common. Such an adviser may be the head of an economic intelligence division or of a market research department, he may be in charge of a planning staff, or he may combine administrative and advisory duties like the Economic Adviser to the Military Governor of the British Zone of Germany after the war. When administrative duties are added—or even when they are not—an adviser of this type may turn out to be someone who is not a professional economist at all, or has only a limited acquaintance with economic theory, but has a reputation for common sense and organizing capacity. He may, for example, be a business man who understands the ways of government, or an army officer with a staff training, or an editor who has successfully run a daily or weekly newspaper.

Although the duties of advisers of this type are superficially very heterogeneous it is surprising what a large element they have in common. Very much the same gifts of character, temperament, experience and intelligence are required whether the staff which the adviser directs is in the Treasury preparing briefs for the Chancellor, or in the Ministry of Aircraft Production planning the aircraft programme, or, for that matter, in the economic research department of a university. The work varies a great deal more than the bent that goes with it.

So much is this true that it is reasonable to ask whether an academic training in economics is indispensable to an economic adviser or whether it is not more important to find a man with the right gifts and trust him to work out the theory for himself. To a mature and experienced man with an eye for the ways of the world there is nothing very abstruse about economic theory: certainly not about those parts of economic theory that are truly operational and bear on the real dilemmas of policy. It is arguable that the economic theory that is taught always relates to the problems of an earlier decade or even an earlier generation and that it is left to administrators to recognize the new problems as they emerge, grapple with them and subdue them with such theoretical tools as they can fashion. All this may be so: there have been some brilliant late-comers to economics and some stimulating amateurs. Yet I must confess that when I look, not at the few exceptions, but at the mass, I find that my regard for economics as an intellectual discipline is quickly restored and that I should be loath to dispense with that discipline in anyone aspiring to be called 'economic adviser' except by way of courtesy.

My own experience has been largely as one of the myrmidons who form the staff of this second type of economic adviser, and who can indeed be classed as a separate, third, type. At one time, however, my work approximated fairly closely to that of the second type and at another it had some of the characteristics of the first. I propose to give you a concrete description of that work, first at the Board of Trade (where I acted as Economic Adviser from 1946 to 1949) and secondly with the OEEC in Paris (where I was Economic Adviser from 1949 and the end of 1950).

II

Before doing so, however, I must ensure that you have in your minds some picture of the inside of a large sprawling organization with large sprawling responsibilities, since it is precisely within such organizations that economic advisers are generally employed. Although I have used the term 'organization', even this, I fear, is a little misleading, since it is more common to find a large muddle tempered by a little organization than a large organization struggling to prevent an occasional muddle. This is inevitable. In a small firm everybody knows what is going on, and yet misunderstandings arise, slips go uncorrected, work of little value is given precedence over far more important work, and the management is constantly failing to detect and prevent waste of time and effort. How much more true this must be where the employees number thousands, the departments are many and specialized, decisions have to be taken in the dark and remote from the persons affected, and the need for speed collides with the need for consultation with all the interests affected. What then of a government department where, on top of all this, come the pressure of public opinion and the risk of parliamentary rebuke? In such an atmosphere policy swings between the opposite poles of caution and rashness: caution when action can be deferred or hedged, rashness when sudden decisions have to be taken; caution among the lowly who are inhibited by a full understanding of the obstacles to action of any kind: rashness among the exalted who have fewer inhibitions and are ignorant either of the real issues involved or of the probabilities governing the decision to be taken. The various divisions within the department, loosely geared together, uncertain of the limits of their responsibilities, losing and gaining staff almost every week, themselves dissolving from time to time into new divisions or subdivisions, and facing an avalanche of fresh problems on which to advise, fresh cases to decide, and fresh policies to apply, inevitably present to the newcomer the appearance of muddle.

Nor are appearances altogether deceptive. There *is* plenty of muddle, just as there is plenty of muddle in every army. But the muddles which come to the attention of the public are not necessarily those that really matter. The public may utterly condemn one department for some piece of trivial craziness while the Minister of another, far less efficient, department builds up a great reputation. It is usually possible to tell from the outside which departments are the most efficient but it is rarely possible without working in one to gauge the precise degree of remediable muddle from which it is suffering—and certainly quite impossible to alleviate the muddle by offering advice from outside.

You may ask yourself, as I did when asked to go to the Board of Trade, what an economic adviser could hope to accomplish in such an atmosphere. There was surely little that needed to be said to a large and versatile staff of skilled administrators by an economist who, in any event, had not taught economics for many years. I was told that I should be much more likely to influence policy if instead of writing paragraphs for *The Economist* I wrote minutes for the President. I was doubtful about this at the time and remain doubtful now. What did seem possible to me was that, as a result of nearly four years in the Ministry of Aircraft Production, I might know more about certain types of muddle than my future colleagues, and that these types of muddle might crop up in the Board of Trade. Most people seemed to treat the experience of the Ministry of Aircraft Production as proof of the ease with which our economy might be planned. I drew the opposite conclusion, and justified to myself the acceptance of the post of Economic Adviser on the grounds that I should be renewing the daily combat with chaos that was dignified by the title of 'planning' in the Ministry of Aircraft Production.

Here I may repeat to you three pieces of advice which I was given by the first permanent civil servant with whom I worked, Sir Piers Debenham. (I should add that he was a very unusual civil servant, even when one applies the high standard of unusualness necessary in the British Civil Service, and that he proved to be no more permanent than I was.) He laid down, first, that a man was no good as a civil servant until he had had three years' training in frustration—after that he found the right way to go about things instead of constantly knocking his head against brick walls; second, that no one bothered to decide *important* matters—what always received prior attention was what was *urgent*; third, that the first obligation of a civil servant was to keep his Minister out of scrapes. This bureaucratic testament I found hard to swallow at the time but it stood me in good stead later.

I found from experience, however, that one other maxim was even more important. This was that the civil service was the last home of private enterprise; it was most unusual to be told exactly what to do. No doubt some civil servants could content themselves with waiting for the files to arrive, but only if their duties were specific, continuing and publicized. A new arrival had usually to find work for himself, not hang around waiting for it; he had to take the initiative, discover for himself who did what and who needed help, and by launching a minute or commenting on an intercepted file, win acceptance as an 'authority' on the chosen subject. This was as true of economic advisers as of anyone else. It was rare for any division of the Board of Trade to send me a file out of the blue, but if I once showed an interest in some particular problem and wrote anything, however misinformed, on the subject, I could rely on a steady traffic in files, almost indefinitely, from the division concerned.

It was important to learn this lesson early, because the adviser who does not take the initiative readily is soon diverted to other work. A busy man who has an economist attached to his staff is often at a loss to see any difference between the economist and his colleagues; although he may feel vaguely that the economist should have some special function, he is not quite sure what that function is and has little time to work out special assignments for him. To have one more subordinate who is for ever asking, 'What do I do next?' and, still worse, to have no answer ready, is a bore and a burden, but to have someone who can single out the significant question, and the significant item of information, and thrust it forward uninvited is a godsend. The difference between a good economic adviser and a bad one is that the first keeps asking, 'Would it not be better to do this?' or 'Have you realized that?' while the second buries himself in the preparation of long and pointless memoranda that no one has time enough to study.

Unless he occupies a very exalted position in the official hierarchy, therefore, the economic adviser is apt to discover that he is very rarely asked for advice. His duties may be both trivial and ill-defined and he may easily find himself excluded from consultation on the very issues on which he feels qualified to offer an opinion. A government department when it recruits an economic adviser, particularly if he is a young man, always feels tempted to thrust on him the unappetizing responsibilities which every other member of the department shuns. He will be asked, for example, to write speeches for his Minister (who will generally have the good sense not to deliver them). He will be asked to look at all the more cranky suggestions that are sent in by members of the public or Members of Parliament. He will be asked to draft lengthy reports which are a standing responsibility of the department, but which senior officials are too busy to undertake. Added to all this, he may find that while he is an adviser, no one particularly wants to be advised. He may be left without access to the person in authority who ought to have the benefit of his advice.

It may seem odd to you that I should make this point. The layman generally assumes that an economic adviser is a very exalted person and that if he is attached to a department he advises the Minister. When I was at the Board of Trade I was often referred to by outsiders, quite mistakenly, as adviser to the President. This was obviously not only wrong in fact but quite wrong in terms of the normal working of the British administrative machine. The person in the Board of Trade who advises the President is the Permanent Secretary. If there is an Economic Adviser, it is his duty to pass any advice that he has to offer to the Permanent Secretary. There may be occasions when it is tempting to by-pass the Permanent Secretary and send something straight to the Minister. With one solitary exception, however, I made it a point of principle never to seek to minute the President or to advise him in any way other than through the Permanent Secretary, and I am certain that departure from this principle would be fatal to sound administration.

In a sense, nearly all the senior officials were economic advisers. If one stopped to think what they did and how one could measure their output it became apparent that it was their job to advise the President and that the more senior they were, the larger their output of advice on important matters. They might have other duties involving the articulation of a policy already accepted or the formulation of proposals to modify existing policies in the light of experience of their working, but they also expected to have the last word in the chain of advice that leads up to the President a great deal more often than the economic adviser.

III

I now turn to the work that I did at the Board of Trade. When I was on the point of leaving, my last task was to advise the Permanent Secretary on a successor, and I found it convenient for this purpose to put on paper a short description of my duties, so far as I could fathom them. I pointed out that these duties had varied a good deal over the three years in which I had been employed and that some of them, since they had no obvious association with the post, would not necessarily fall to my successor. I summarized them as follows, taking account of the way in which they appeared to be evolving at the time.

Speeches: I was called on by the Private Office (i.e. by the President's staff) to prepare verbatim speeches for the President. I was aware that the President always wrote his own speeches and in due course I was able to establish that he would be satisfied with a summary of a few draft passages, although he liked at times to have a full speech in order to see the general drift of the argument. More frequently, I was asked for additional points, corrections, tables, estimates, and so on. Sometimes the same duties had to be undertaken for the Government spokesman in economic debates in the House of Lords or for the Permanent Secretary (who was frequently invited to address the Imperial Staff College, an Export Conference, or some other body). The speeches that I wrote were usually on general economic issues: for example, on the Budget, the economic situation, the progress of industrial recovery, the export drive, and so on.

Briefs: I was frequently asked to brief the President on some subject of no direct interest to the Board of Trade (e.g. the extermination of rabbits, the supply of animal feeding-stuffs) or on a subject that touched several departments but none very deeply: (e.g. the long-term programme put forward to the OEEC in 1948 in connection with the Marshall Plan). I generally briefed the Permanent Secretary for meetings of standing inter-departmental committees of which he was a member.

Memoranda: I was sometimes asked to prepare a document for the President or the Secretary on some general subject, such as controls, raw material prices, and so on. A memorandum seems to be prepared by each successive Economic Adviser on the proposal for a Channel Tunnel and I recall with some regret that this was the work on which I was principally engaged in 1949 when the great debate on devaluation was in progress. Other memoranda, sometimes on problems of policy, sometimes based on research that I had undertaken, were prepared on my own initiative.

These memoranda would be sent to various people in the Board and sometimes to a few economists in other departments. They might be considered at a meeting of the Research Committee (which was useful if further research was required but not as a means of selling new ideas to the policy-makers); or they would (more usually) form the basis of a discussion at the Secretary's regular staff meetings; or they might be revised for submission to an inter-departmental committee, although this was rare unless the document had been prepared to order.

Committees: I represented the Board on one committee which was engaged in considering drafts of the *Economic Survey* and was also a member in my personal capacity of the committee that reviewed the investment programmes of the various departments. I was naturally drawn into various 'working parties' and 'study groups', but tried to keep attendance at such meetings to a minimum. Apart from formal duties, there was necessarily a great deal of inter-departmental discussion in which I became involved. For example, I generally acted on behalf of the Board in most of its dealings with the Economic Section of the Cabinet Office.

Twelfth Man: Occasionally I was used as a reserve for busy departments, either to go abroad or to help in the preparation of material for conferences. For example, I visited Canada in 1947 as a member of the Liesching Mission, because it happened to be difficult to find a member of the Board of Trade who was familiar with the problems and could be spared for the purpose. Similarly I went to India in 1949 when no one else was free to go.

Receptionist: Foreigners on a tour of Whitehall studying British economic problems, the technique of planning, and so on, frequently came to the Board of Trade and it was generally left to me to provide the answers. There were visitors from India, New Zealand, the United States, Germany, Persia and other countries, and they had a regular itinerary from one pundit on the doctrine, or practice, of planning to another. The pundits, I fear, were rather disillusioning and the visitors often left in some perplexity. For some reason, I never seemed to be visited by British economists, who appeared capable of making up their own minds about British economic problems and planning, or else did not think that the Board of Trade would have anything useful to say on the subject. Sometimes I was asked to talk to an American journalist, or to show a German politician how things were done in Britain. This generally meant a conducted tour through the Board, with a factory visit thrown in.

Expert Economist: Now and again I was asked, usually by the Secretary, for advice on a rather involved economic issue. My experience was that he had nearly always reached a satisfactory answer independently, so that my advice was more of the nature of confirmatory evidence.

The issues most likely to lead to a request for such advice were in the realms of wage and price policy and budgetary policy. (It was such questions that particularly occupied Sir Stafford Cripps while he was still at the Board.) More commonly I was approached by other members of the Department who were still under the illusion that there was some magic about economic theory more powerful than common sense. Sometimes I was able to help: generally because I had better or later information about their problem or because I was in a better position to judge how it related to what was going on elsewhere.

I happen to have a note of the subjects on which I wrote minutes during the month of July 1948 and the list is perhaps not unrepresentative. It shows only one side of the work of an economic adviser, the side that takes the form of written comment and analysis, but it does so in a very concrete way and for that reason may be worth quoting. It includes minutes on:

The long-term economic survey,
The long-term demand for steel,
The long-term demand for exports,
The balance of payments, 1948–52,
The monthly economic report,
Sterling area balances,
Trade with the colonies,
Exports of commercial vehicles,
Industrial productivity (four minutes in all),
Capital investment in 1949,
Industrial investment,
Government control of prices after nationalization,
The clothing ration,
The future of the Tudor,

Synthetic detergents,
Benzol,
Coking coal,
Vermiculite.

I should perhaps add that nearly all these minutes and memoranda, however long, had to be dictated and were not subsequently revised. Since coming back to academic life I have been struck by nothing so much as the entirely different tempo at which work is done. A paper on which a university professor spends a week has to be put together in Government service in a few hours, with nearly as much emphasis on lucidity, economy and order in its composition. Information has to be absorbed, views exchanged and decisions come to at a rapid pace that rarely slackens. All this forces thought. But it also encourages improvisation and forbids that more elaborate, precise and scholarly treatment of a subject that satisfies the academic temper. One has constantly to pluck apples from the tree of knowledge before they are ripe.

It will be apparent that, in my case at least, the Economic Adviser was no secluded oracle or venerable sage, to be consulted at rare intervals. He was instead an ordinary working member of the Department, drawing occasionally on his training in economic theory but far more commonly on experience and contacts built up over a long period. He was engaged in problems of economic planning in the broad sense: largely in the problems that assume quantitative form and are expressible in programmes.

We have all become a great deal more familiar with Government programmes since the war, but I doubt whether public understanding of them has made much progress. The essence of a programme is that it is an instrument of co-ordination. Programmes are designed to show everybody the direction in which policy is pointing and to stir administrative effort in that direction. This is true, for example, of export, import and investment programmes, just as it is, or used to be, true of the aircraft programme. My main function in the Board of Trade, since it was closely associated with those programmes, was thus a co-ordinating one. I had to keep myself fully informed on the circumstances bearing on departmental programmes and to do everything possible to see that that information was turned to account.

Since work of this kind inevitably involved constant use of figures I had to be something of a statistician, and I found that in some ways this was the most difficult and certainly the least understood part of the whole business. In my experience, very few senior officials in Britain and very few business men are happy in their sums. They have little need of highly-trained statisticians to redress this weakness, but they frequently need a colleague who can look at a table of figures and make the right deductions from it. An economic adviser who is incapable of this may have his uses but will generally be either superfluous or dangerous. A good economic adviser should understand what figures mean and how to use them.

The conclusion which I drew from my experience was that the most important qualification of an economic adviser was that he should be able to smell out what was going on, both inside his department and outside, and that he should be good at intellectual jigsaw puzzles. He ought to know the gossip and shop, and he ought to know how things fit together. These are, I imagine, the qualifications of a good staff officer; they are not the peculiar gift of professional economists, though a training in economics is an enormous advantage as a chart to the ramifications of economic policy.

I was, in fact, staff officer to the Secretary. A large organization like the Board of Trade does not co-ordinate itself automatically. Nor could the Secretary really secure effective co-ordination by referring everything to the divisions of the Board. There were too many issues not appropriate to a single division, and some not appropriate to any. It was those issues that were generally referred to the Economic Adviser. He was expected to keep an eye, not on the problems of individual divisions, but on the matters of major policy that were likely to emerge: a fuel shortage, raw material prices, deflation, controls, dollars and all that. He might also choose to interest himself in special problems, such as price policy in nationalized undertakings, methods of expanding steel supplies, and so on. Most of these interests, however, could be regarded as springing from idiosyncrasy. They would not necessarily be shared by other Economic Advisers, since they were of less immediate concern to the Board, or came within a single division of it, or were the primary responsibility of some other Government department.

I have dwelt on the need for an economic adviser of the staff-officer type to be young and nippy, out and about, lapping up gossip, and picking other men's brains. Perhaps I have overemphasized these things. In any organization, the main job of the economic adviser is to recognize the big issues, to think steadily about them, and to be ready with the right advice at the right time. An adviser who can do that job has generally no need to look for other work to occupy him. But the big issues arise out of lesser ones on which the adviser is inevitably consulted; he finds that if he is to gain a hearing on the big issues he may first have to establish some reputation on the lesser ones; and he may well find that the influence that he can exert is necessarily limited on the really big issues, on which many voices will be raised, while on issues that are in one sense secondary but potentially important he can be of much greater service because such issues are not recognized early enough or given the attention they deserve. If I may put the matter concretely: although I believe that my advice on devaluation was consistently right, pressed as strongly as possible and at exactly the right time, I do not flatter myself that it had any real influence on the course of events; on the other hand, I probably did have some influence on fuel policy and export policy because I knew a little about the technique of drawing up a programme while those who were trying to plan fuel and exports were comparatively unfamiliar with it.

IV

My experience at the Board of Trade may throw some light on the work of one kind of economic adviser. When I joined the OEEC in Paris I found myself engaged in work of another kind. I was no longer attached to an administrative hierarchy with a clear responsibility for framing and carrying out economic policy. I was, instead, at the head of an economic intelligence division within the secretariat of an international organization and my advice was offered primarily to the secretariat and only indirectly to the international delegations attached to the OEEC.

My duties in Paris were less varied and can be more briefly catalogued.

Preparation of Reports: The main business of the Economic Directorate was to prepare the annual report of the Organization and any further reports that appeared necessary. The annual report was of great importance for a number of reasons. In the first place, it summarized the views of the Organization on the need for Marshall Aid in the forthcoming year and on the progress that had been made over the past year. It was in a sense a statement of the OEEC case for use by ECA whenever the annual appropriation of Marshall Aid fell due. Apart from this, however, the report had an important function in giving some consistency of policy to the various activities of the Organization. These activities tended to be carried on throughout the year in isolation from one another and it was only during the preparation of the report that it was possible to review them as a whole and consider in what fresh direction the efforts of the Organization should be directed.

As time went on it became necessary to prepare other reports: for example, a quarterly report for use by the Managing Board of the European Payments Union. Sometimes, too, a document that was more of the nature of a manifesto than of a report had to be prepared, setting out the views of the Organization on some new turn of events, like the outbreak of war in Korea, or setting targets for coal, steel, housing, etc., for Western Europe as a whole.

All this meant keeping track of what was going on inside the Organization, partly with a view to making the composition of the report easier and partly in order to improve the co-ordination of the activities that were in progress.

Statistical Bulletins: It has been my experience in almost every organization of which I have been a member that the amount of muddle is inversely proportional to the excellence of the statistical services. I have watched the general level of administration improved time and again by measures for the proper assembly and presentation of statistical data. This has generally meant the preparation of a statistical bulletin, so that all the members of the organization could use the same figures and have ready access to them instead of keeping them tucked away in some forgotten corner of a file or circulating them on flimsy bits of paper in a form that made comparison with other figures circulating in the same way quite impossible.

For this reason I made it my business in Paris to set on foot the preparation of the two bulletins which are now published by the Organization, one relating to foreign trade statistics and the other to general economic statistics. These bulletins appeared to be doubly necessary after the institution of the European Payments Union, since the Managing Board required to have at its disposal some authoritative comparison of the development of the economies of the member countries.

Committees: The view taken in the OEEC of the functions of the Economic Directorate was that the less time the members of that Directorate spent in committees the better. This was a view with which I was in wholehearted agreement. But it was impossible to avoid a good deal of committee work, for example, in piloting the annual report of the Organization through an extremely critical committee of distinguished economists who were liable to treat each turn of phrase with the same attention that a lawyer would give to a clause in an international agreement. At a later stage, when an Economic Committee was set up, it was also inevitable that the economic adviser should serve on the committee and take responsibility for the drafts submitted to it.

Formulation of Policy: The General Secretary of the Organization naturally turned to the economic adviser for advice on the general trend of policy that should be recommended for study and approval by the member countries. On issues such as liberalization of trade, harmonization of economic policies, the institution of a European Payments Union, and so on, the economic adviser would be expected to give a lead and to work out in more detail any suggestions put forward by delegates from the member countries. The economic adviser would by the same token be called in to give his views on the future work of the Organization and particularly on what should happen to it after the completion of the Marshall Plan.

Staff Problems: I doubt whether it is generally realized how much of the time of the permanent secretary of a Government department or the general secretary of an international organization is spent on questions of staff. Even the economic adviser, as one of the senior officials in the secretariat, and as the head of a staff of some forty persons, inevitably spent a good deal of time on establishment questions. I should estimate that certainly 10 per cent, and as much as 20 per cent, of my time in Paris was taken up in this way; and I certainly did not reach as high a proportion as some of my colleagues.

Independent Expert: I spent a short time towards the end of my stay in Paris preparing a report on Germany in conjunction with Mr Jacobsson for submission to the Managing Board of the EPU. While this report had no necessary connection with my post as economic adviser, it seemed not unnatural for the EPU to turn to a member of the secretariat for guidance.

Apart from all these duties, I had naturally to organize the research work undertaken by my own staff, to give as much time as I could to the work which they were doing along lines parallel to my own, to keep in touch with the national delegations and exchange ideas with them and to see any economists who were visiting Paris, or myself pay a visit to economists in Geneva or elsewhere.

V

The first business of a good businessman, a good administrator or a good economic adviser is to make a thorough assessment of what is happening. He has to decide what the situation is, how it is changing, and how quickly it is changing. An economic adviser, however, usually differs from his colleagues in business or administration in that he stands outside the stream of action, commenting, warning and persuading but without himself deciding. He may do this officially, and for pay, as a member of some organization, unofficially and for pay, as a working journalist or lecturer, or unofficially and without pay as a habitual correspondent of the editor of some well-known newspaper.

In any of these circumstances, he is as much concerned to *sell* his advice as to offer it: he is up against a marketing problem. Indeed, it is this problem that tends to condition the organization of the adviser's staff. Marketing means maintaining close contact with those who seek advice; it means having the necessary standing, personality and professional competence to gain a hearing. But since there are only twenty-four hours in a day it becomes increasingly difficult to combine the work of formulating advice and selling it; of making an assessment and then putting it over; of picking up significant gossip and retailing it. The function of advising tends to disintegrate, the salesmen separating from the assessors, while the assessors of today, the improvisers, fed on yesterday's gossip, separate from the assessors of tomorrow, the planners, fed on a stingy diet of research.

In terms of the organization that existed in Whitehall in my time, the Chief Economic Adviser had to be skilled in getting the ear of the Chancellor rather than in producing some original idea of his own, and was inevitably guided by the professional economists in the Economic Section or by the expert administrators on the Central Economic Planning Staff. Alone among economic advisers, he was, so to speak, the head of a department, free to exercise his own judgment and to have the last word about what was put to the Chancellor by the planning staff.

In the United States the 'sales' function is complicated by the existence of Congressional committees before which an adviser may have to appear, and by the absence of executive control over Parliament such as the Cabinet exercises in this country. It is not enough in America to convince a Minister and leave him to handle Congress; the economic adviser may be dragged in to explain and defend the policies that he has recommended.

The problem of 'marketing' advice is by no means peculiar to economic advisers. It is, for example, one of the outstanding difficulties of technological research that a large staff of scientists may easily lose touch with other departments and with the general policy of the firm employing them and be unable to present their conclusions to the management in the right form or at the right time. Much of what I have said about economists in advisory positions applies *mutatis mutandis* to other experts and in particular to the head of a research department.

The responsibilities of economic advisers vary and so does the size of their staff. At the Board of Trade I had one assistant who undertook very useful research for me until, discouraged by my failure ever to find time to see her, she sought employment elsewhere. In Paris I had a staff of about forty. I am in no doubt which of these arrangements was more to my liking. I infinitely preferred the freedom that I enjoyed in the Board of Trade to seek information wherever I chose and, in a sense, call the whole department to my aid, to the task of maintaining a staff in full employment, and, seeking to compose internal squabblings, rid it of the weaker brethren and bring in reinforcements.

Yet I recognize that a staff is often indispensable—and sometimes quite a large one. A man who acts as head of the market research division, or of statistics and intelligence, or of the economic section of a large business or organization, has certain routine duties that could not be carried on single-handed. Such duties, however, are not, strictly speaking, those of an economic adviser. If the firm wanted to understand national policy or national trends it might either appoint such an adviser or ask some outsider to act as consultant. An outsider who was unfamiliar with what was going on inside the firm and with current proposals would be unlikely to offer the best advice. Hence a firm that wants to shape its course in the light of an adequate understanding of outside affairs would be well advised to rely on the advice of someone on its own staff, whether he was classed as an economic adviser or otherwise.

I had one considerable advantage throughout my 'career' as an economic adviser. I was known to be anxious to end that career as soon as possible. There could be no rivalry with my professional colleagues, no shadow on anyone's prospects of advancement. I went to Berlin in 1945 reluctantly and for not more than six months; I went to the Board of Trade reluctantly and for three to five years; I went to Paris with the utmost reluctance, first for six weeks, then for six months, and finally under heavy pressure for a maximum of twelve months. I was thus throughout in the extremely fortunate position of one whose departure is imminent but unwelcome, and although I did not deliberately trade on this, it was a circumstance that ruled out many possible difficulties and gave me greater independence. I can well imagine that the career of other economic advisers might prove a great deal less happy and untroubled.

If I had to sum up my impression of the work of an economic adviser in a single sentence I should describe it as either highly frustrating, or maddeningly humdrum, or furiously active, or all three at once.

CHAPTER 17

The Work of the Economic Development Institute[1]

In the Washington Zoo a sign appears on one of the cages in the monkey house reading, 'Stratospheric Monkeys'. The unfortunate creatures behind the bars were apparently propelled some years ago to unexampled heights and on their return to earth were no doubt submitted to lengthy examination by men of science curious to know how they had stood it all. It is in a similar rôle that I appear before you today. While I am not yet behind bars and you will, I hope, not be too exacting in your examination of me, I have none the less been employed on an experiment of some scientific interest that removed me, except at intervals, from the solid earth of a good university and carried me up to that thinner atmosphere where high economic policy is bombarded by rays of almost cosmic intelligence. You will recognize, as I proceed, the traumatic symptoms born of this experience and put down, in charity, any incoherence in my remarks to an excess of G.

The experiment to which I have referred is now well into its second year, and it is no longer necessary for me, as it was when I addressed you a year ago, to speak of the Economic Development Institute as a foetal thing, still in the womb of time. Surrounded even before its birth with fairy godmothers, some of them dressed like international bankers, and succoured for a year on a prepared diet of seminars, the Institute has not only been safely delivered but is almost ready to be weaned. You may wish to hear something of the progress of this offspring of the Bank and allow me, in presenting my clinical report as one of the gynaecologists and pediatricians in attendance, to adopt a rather more personal tone than is usually considered proper among medical men.

I should like to begin, as all good narratives begin, at the

[1] Talk to IBRD Professional Staff Meeting, December 1956.

beginning. The idea of the Institute goes back several years to the days when Mr Rosenstein-Rodan was a member of the staff of the Bank. As he left the Bank some time before I joined, I am not sure how far the Institute as it now exists corresponds with his original idea but there is no doubt that it germinated from the seed that he planted. There is also no doubt that the Institute came into being only after long hesitation and debate, and that, if the hesitations were overcome and the debate ended in favour of the venture, this was largely because of the steady support it received from the Bank official on whom the work of promoting and organizing it largely rested—Mr Demuth.

My own association with the Institute began in 1954 when I received a cable asking me to come at once to Washington and advise the Bank on the merits of various proposals for a new Institute about which I had then little or no knowledge. Would it be best, I was asked, to set up an Institute run almost as a branch of the Bank? Or would this deny to the staff the academic independence to which men of the right type would be bound to attach importance? Would it be preferable to award scholarships tenable at a university and leave the successful applicants to go where they chose—to Oxford, Paris or Chicago, for example? Would it be possible to come to some arrangement with a university in or near Washington, subcontracting the teaching and preserving the atmosphere of a university campus? Could it be taken for granted that men in senior positions would be released to study abroad? If so, for how long? Would they not be the victims of departmental intrigue before their return? How many spoke English or had the grounding in economic theory necessary to allow them to profit from a limited period of study? All this added up to one major issue: would the Institute, if established, attract the right sort of men for the minimum period worth considering?

I came to the conclusion that if the Institute were to succeed, it would have to be located in Washington and that it ought to work closely with the Bank. I came to this not very surprising conclusion on two main grounds: first, that the Institute would require, particularly in the early stages, the enthusiastic support of the Bank and that this support would not be forthcoming, or at least not sustained, if the two institutions were not within easy reach of one another; secondly, that since the main justification for the Institute lay in the Bank's unequalled experience in its dealings with the under-developed countries, that experience should be, as far as possible, on tap, through the participation in the work of the Institute of the men on the staff of the Bank who spent their time wrestling with concrete problems of development. This is a conclusion which I have been under no temptation to modify over the past two years. I am satisfied that if the Institute has any future at all, it is in Washington and as an appendage of the Bank.

The second conclusion that I formed was that the Institute ought to follow the model of an administrative staff college rather than of a postgraduate seminar. I was not quite sure, to tell the truth, what was done either at a staff college or a graduate seminar, having seen neither in operation up to that time. I had no doubt, however, that senior officials would not be much interested, as postgraduate students should be, in the finer points of economic theory, but would want to start from the concrete situations and practical problems facing them in their ordinary duties. This meant the adoption, as a method of instruction, of a case-study approach such as is usual in staff colleges but has rarely been attempted in the teaching of applied economics.

I coupled with this conclusion a much more doubtful one: that the physical planning of the Institute should follow the lines of the Administrative Staff College at Henley near London. I suggested that a large country house should be found for the members of the Institute a little way out of Washington, near enough to allow easy access to the Bank but far enough out to ensure peace and quiet and to allow adequate scope for outdoor recreation. I had in mind conditions that are not too difficult to fulfil in the countryside round London but, as we later found, are not at all easy to secure in the neighbourhood of Washington. In drawing up my specifications, I was influenced by a stay of nearly two months in 1953 at the Merrill Centre on Long Island, an earthly paradise if ever there was one, where gladioli grow by the acre and the lawns could swallow up a polo ground or two. Without pitching my demands quite as high—I would certainly have settled for half a polo ground—I was anxious that the atmosphere should be soothing and restful. The irony of this hope became apparent to me later.

All this took for granted that there should be an Institute. It was precisely on this point, however, that my doubts were most acute. The Institute might have nothing new to offer and might fail to attract the right kind of customers. Nevertheless, I returned a qualified affirmative to the question whether it was worth launching the venture. I thought that able men would come more readily to the Bank for training than to other institutions of higher academic standing. I thought also that it was desirable that there should be a bridge between the Bank and economists in academic work and that the Institute might constitute such a bridge. Finally, I thought that the Institute might become a genuine centre for the exchange of views on economic development: in which the experience of the Bank could be submitted to careful scrutiny, both by the participants from under-developed countries and by economists seeking to arrive at useful generalizations. It seemed to me that such a centre could be of advantage not only to the participants but to the Bank itself and to economists outside the Bank.

It was perhaps because I reported in such tentative terms that the final decision was to establish the Institute on an experimental footing for two years. Very wisely as it later appeared, we aimed at only 15 participants in the first, and 25 in the second, course. The limitation to 15 participants, taken, I believe, on the advice of Mr Willitts of the Rockefeller Foundation, proved to be close to the number of what we accepted as good nominations for the first course. We received, in all, about 40 nominations, but many of these fell clearly below the standard set by the Admissions Committee; others had to be excluded because we were unwilling to accept two candidates from any one member country; others whom we accepted were unable to come. We ended up with 14 participants, of whom one was a woman. For the second course, we accepted 25 candidates, but five subsequently withdrew and two others attended for the first month only, leaving only 18 participants for the rest of the course. To this number, one addition was made from the staff of the Bank—a welcome innovation which I hope the Bank will see no cause to abandon in later courses.

The first course, which began in January of this year (1956), was by no means an unqualified success. I am inclined, looking back, to attribute most of its inadequacies to errors of judgment in my original recommendations. The first of these relates to the accommodation provided, the second to the inadequacy of the social activity in which the participants could engage. I had conceived of the Institute as a dormitory and social centre, as a home and a club, as well as a centre of study and research. In practice, the Institute proved a poor substitute for a home and fulfilled little of the functions of a club.

I had supposed that a handful of men from senior posts in under-developed countries would find much to talk over and debate, that they would welcome one another's company, and that they would enter readily into a college atmosphere under one roof. I recognized that the one house that we had been able to find that came within reach of our specifications left a great deal to be desired; and we took corresponding pains over the interior decorations and furnishings. I did not reckon with the inevitable noise and bustle; with the shortcomings of the building, which obliged us to have tradesmen on the premises almost without intermission for month after month; with the strong feeling among the participants that something more was due to men of their seniority than a single room and a share of a bathroom; with their conflicting desires for more privacy and more company, more personal services and more scope for doing for themselves. Above all, I took too little account of the cumulative effect of six months' separation from wives and families in a strange city with few relaxations. Two of the participants had the added worry of sickness in their families and at least two others were largely preoccupied with their personal health. The more men in this state of mind were held together in a compact group, the more the atmosphere was liable to be poisoned by resentment and neurasthenia until the enthusiasm and energy of those who were reasonably content began to wilt from infection.

Before the end of the first course, it had already been arranged to move several of the participants to a neighbouring hotel. For the second course, it was decided that the participants should all be housed for the first month at the hotel, and that thereafter they should make their own housing arrangements, if they preferred to move elsewhere. It was also decided that the Institute would raise no objection if any participant elected to bring his wife and family with him. So far as I can judge, these changes have worked well and there has been a more evident contentment and disposition to study than during the first course. This has by itself contributed towards solving the second problem to which I have referred: that of providing adequate recreation and social activity.

Although a great deal of our time over the past year has been occupied with all the problems of organization inherent in the establishment of a new Institute, our main task was not one of organization. It would have availed us little if we had attracted first-rate nominations for the second course, housed and entertained the participants to their entire satisfaction, built up an excellent library, and made all the necessary administrative arrangements, if at the same time we had given no thought to what the participants should discuss and study. We shall be judged in the long run by the kind of curriculum that we offer, by the new ideas that we bring home to the participants, by the perspectives that we enable them to form. Since our purpose is educational, our success must be measured by what the participants learn from us or from one another. It was encumbent on us, therefore, to devise a curriculum that provided the maximum opportunity of learning the things of most significance.

This may sound simple, especially to those of you who think of the Bank as a storehouse of wisdom in which one can readily find the secrets of healthy development. The world is full of people eager to expound 'the simple truths and few' on which prosperity can be built; quite a few of our guest speakers—and, for that matter, quite a few of our participants—felt impelled to dilate on those truths in the face of increasing sales resistance or evident boredom in their audience. But the truth, as Oscar Wilde remarked, is rarely pure and never simple; if it were otherwise, six months would be altogether excessive to convey it to those whose minds were open, and completely unavailing for those whose minds were closed.

The drawing up of a curriculum was no easy task. First, there was the limitation of time: the time of the participants, who were in Washington for six months only; and the time of the staff, who had to acquaint themselves with the available literature, digest it, select appropriate reading assignments, and prepare to lead a discussion on the multifarious topics selected for inclusion in the course. Then there was the limitation of age; we were dealing, not with young students delighting in the exercise of intellectual curiosity, but with mature men, impatient of prolonged study and anxious to be shown the practical bearing on the affairs of their own country and their own government of the matters under discussion. There was no large faculty over whom they could be dispersed in accordance with their own interests, but a small staff whose combined experience of economic development was necessarily limited. The available textbooks were for the most part highly inappropriate and none approached economic development explicitly from the angle of the administrators for whom we had to prepare. Last, but not least, there were the limitations imposed by the learning process itself. Education, as everyone who has had to do with children is well aware, is a freakish business in which what is learned and what is taught rarely coincide and a whisper may be heard by those who are deaf to a shout. Who could say, in advance, how the imagination of an administrator, if any imagination remained, would respond? And yet education that does not quicken and train the imagination is likely to prove a fake and a waste of time.

As we bent ourselves to the preparation of a curriculum, we met an unending stream of suggestions for including fresh subjects, for enlarging, never for reducing, the dimensions of the course. We also found a general aversion from giving to the course a theoretical content, except perhaps for the benefit of those who lacked any grounding in economic theory. These two views to some extent cancelled one another; for we obviously could not decide what to omit and what to emphasize without some prior conception of the governing factors in development, that is, without some theory that would give shape to the course. We naturally did not want to adopt a doctrinaire view of economic development; nor did we want to compel anyone to accept the conclusions to which we might ourselves feel driven. But since our intellectual efforts, and the intellectual efforts of the participants, were inevitably directed towards understanding the complex forces governing development and the ways in which these forces might be controlled, we were equally inescapably involved in trying to formulate generalizations and theories in the light of which development could be planned.

I shall not attempt to do more than outline to you the curriculum which we now use. It is neither the exercise in case studies that I had at one time contemplated nor the course in the economics of development that would be appropriate in a postgraduate seminar. We spend most of the first month discussing the preparation of a development programme, its purpose and its limitations, the problems of forecasting involved, the administrative complexities to which it gives rise, the degree of co-ordination to which a democratic government may reasonably aspire. We then pass to a more detailed consideration of the various aspects of policy that need to be tied together in a development programme—monetary and fiscal policy, for example—and we study some of the wider economic considerations to which anyone framing such a programme should be alive. We emphasize the broad structural changes, social as well as economic, that development brings about, looking back over the historical record and trying to single out the strategic factors. We then go on to the planning of investment and capital formation, the organization of the capital market and the contribution that might be made by development banks and by foreign aid and foreign investment. Finally we turn to agricultural and industrial development and the means by which they can be assisted.

In all parts of the course, we use case studies to give concreteness to the general considerations that emerge from our discussions. For example, we had two meetings on the Indian Five Year Plan in order to illustrate how one kind of development programme was prepared and another meeting on the Bank's report on Nigeria to illustrate a different kind of development programme. We have had meetings on the origins of the industrial revolution in Britain in the eighteenth century and on the contrast between Chinese and Japanese experience in the latter part of the nineteenth century. We put ourselves in the position of the Staff Economic Committee in order to appraise the prospects of Ceylon, Guatemala and

Mexico. Later, we shall put ourselves in the position of the Staff Loan Committee in order to review some of the projects financed by the Bank in the past few years. These case studies nearly always give rise to a lively discussion and I hope that, in course of time, more and better cases will be prepared. Their value is always greatest where they provide a full-scale illustration of some important issue of principle (or theory) and where this issue can be fairly easily disentangled from a mass of historical detail, much of it largely irrelevant.

You will naturally want to know—and this is a question that I am constantly asked—how everything has gone: whether the participants have come up to expectations, what they have learned, what we on the staff have learned, whether the Institute, by some unspecified standard, has been a success. I find difficulty in answering some of these inquiries. Just as I should have difficulty in saying of a single year's teaching at my university that it was a success or a failure, so I feel some hesitation in offering an emphatic answer on behalf of those who have studied at the Institute. There is no simple way of calibrating our effectiveness; we can judge only from observation and from the opinions expressed to us by the participants themselves. These opinions, so far as they related to the curriculum, have been almost uniformly favourable; and they have been expressed with much more enthusiasm during the second course than during the first. Although there is still need for a great deal of further experimentation, I think that it can be claimed without presumption that the course is well adapted to the needs of those who take it and that it exercises a very real influence on their thinking.

We have relied heavily on discussion as a method of instruction and this has obvious limitations, especially when, as in the first course, the membership of the discussion group remains the same and there are wide differences, both in intellectual capacity and background, between the participants. There is a constant danger that some will talk far too much and some far too little so that it becomes impossible for the select few who can make their points succinctly and without irrelevance to maintain the thread of the discussion. There are other dangers: superficiality, because only the principal speaker is well versed in the subject; inconclusiveness that is interpreted as a sign, not of freedom from dogmatism but of uselessness; absence of controversy to give spice to the views expressed. We have certainly encountered all these dangers but kept remarkably free of others, notably the danger of political dispute. Since nearly all the participants have already undergone a prolonged period of training in an industrial country in Europe or America, they have a great deal in common in the general drift of their ideas and the differences in outlook between them have rarely been greater than when a group of administrators in the same country sit down together to discuss economic development.

I doubt whether many of the participants would confess to changing their minds during the course on points of view that they held strongly before it began; but all of them become conscious of factors in development of which they were previously unaware or to which they gave too little emphasis. Many of them want to pursue their own specialist studies; but the chief merit of the course is that it enables them to plot their special responsibilities on a map covering a much wider area.

During the first course, we were frequently assured by some of the participants that they would try to set up a similar course on their return home. Imitation may be the highest form of flattery; but we were not altogether reassured by this response and should have preferred to hear of some administrative change or policy proposal traceable to our discussions at the Institute. It is therefore a welcome sign that during the past three months there have been no fresh threats of imitation and a far more persistent effort to relate the course to lines of action that might be adopted or proposed by administrators in the exercise of their duties.

I now turn to the relationship between the Institute and the Bank. It was part of the original plan that the Institute should remain in close contact with the Bank and that it should draw heavily on the experience of the Bank in its courses of instruction. The Bank has in fact given powerful support to the Institute and this support has been of inestimable value throughout the past year. For most of the time, more than half the staff—if I may reduce Messrs Adler and Diamond to a mere vulgar fraction—came from the permanent staff of the Bank. If the proportion is now no more than one-half, it is still, by common consent, the better half. Then we have had over two dozen visitors from the Bank to talk to our seminar meetings and a further number to take part in them. The Bank has conducted information conferences for us; it has helped us with many time-consuming administrative problems; and it has made a great effort to create interest in the Institute in all member countries, mobilizing for this uphill work a tireless and optimistic cohort of photographers who seemed determined to put some sex appeal into development. To all those who have helped in one or other of these ways, I should like to express the thanks of the Institute. I should like also to thank our visitors from other agencies, such as the United Nations and International Monetary Fund, who gave their time voluntarily in order to lead discussions in the Institute; and the distinguished representatives of academic and public life who came as guest speakers.

We had hoped to tap the experience of the Bank not only through talks by staff members with first-hand experience of under-developed countries but also through the use of bank documents and files. I confess that here I felt some disappointment. I recognize that I have seen only a small proportion of what is available in the Bank; I gratefully acknowledge the minutes, excerpts and specific instances to which some of you have drawn my attention; I appreciate particularly the willingness of the Bank to make much of its mimeographed material freely available to the Institute. Yet I am by no means sure that our best written material consists of confidential bank documents rather than printed papers and articles freely available elsewhere. There are no doubt some lively stories in the archives; but there are still livelier stories that will probably never be printed. If one wants vivid illustrations it is usually much better to invite a guest speaker than to circulate a document; the document may provide a single illustration while the speaker recalls many.

Two types of document are of particular value to the Institute. One consists of the typical case study, presenting the facts of some actual situation that might fruitfully be debated; the other takes the form of a study of some problem of economic policy, seeking to arrive at useful generalizations and taking advantage of the data available in the Bank about the success or failure of the expedients adopted by member countries for dealing with it. The first type of document is common enough, the second is relatively rare. It is however, the second type of document that we are generally in search of, since it rests on a much broader base of experience than the first, which necessarily deals with circumstances that may not be typical or recurrent.

I hope that some of the participants in this or some later course will be asked to go through the Bank's files on a specific project and prepare a report such as would normally go to the Staff Loan Committee. This exercise would be of special value if it were possible to produce, for comparison, the actual report, based on the same data, that was prepared in the Bank. Again, if there existed in the Bank two documents on the same subject, one making the case for it and the other making the case against it, or one submitted by the would-be borrower and one prepared to justify a refusal to finance the project, these twin documents would provide useful working material either for a seminar or for testing the insight and judgment of an individual participant.

Many of you may be a little puzzled how the Bank comes to be mixed up in the educational business and feel that a 'school', however high-grade, is out of place in a bank. If the function of the Bank were no more than to make a series of loans for disconnected projects, on the same footing as the long-term loans made by private investment banks, the incongruity would be obvious. But the Bank lays claim to wider functions. It claims to assist the process of economic development by its advice and guidance and it tries to relate each project which it helps to finance to the whole investment effort of the borrowing country. These claims may strike the outsider as somewhat exaggerated if he looks only at the relatively trifling contribution made by the Bank's loans to capital formation in the member countries of the Bank. But in the under-developed countries, the Bank enjoys a prestige out of all proportion to the capital which it lends and not at all in disaccord with the Bank's pretensions as world adviser on economic development. If these pretensions are to be well founded, and if the Bank's lending continues to be guided by a philosophy of development, is it not of the highest importance that this philosophy should come under scrutiny and that the Bank's pragmatic approach to economic development should be supplemented by more systematic study?

May not the Institute, sitting a little independently of the Bank but with access to the information and experience accumulated within it, have an increasingly important part to play in the Bank's activities?

I have hesitated over the past year to make too much of this rôle of the Institute, partly because there was very little time to formulate comments or raise issues for the Bank's consideration, and partly because I thought it unwise to offer comment or criticism before the Institute had established itself, had reached well-grounded conclusions, and was sufficiently sure that differences of view would not automatically be resolved in favour of the Bank. There are, however, a number of suggestions which, had I one more hour, I should willingly develop. I think, for example, that it would do no harm to take another look at the process by which a country's creditworthiness is assessed; at the confidence reposed in estimates of future power requirements and the scepticism towards estimates of future gross national product, as if the one were more ascertainable than the other; at the inadequacy of the data on capital formation in the under-developed countries and the inflow of capital into these countries. I have the impression that the Bank is still too much wrapped up in individual projects and gives too little thought to alternative ways of assisting economic development. I am shocked when I observe the blessings of private enterprise rammed down Austria's throat while Yugoslavia, a few miles away, is allowed to learn for herself by experience, or inexperience. I am convinced that the Bank has much valuable data, for example, on the economics of constructional projects, that would be worth publishing and that a greater effort should be made to assemble this data in publishable form. I am convinced also that since development is primarily an educational process, the Bank is bound to become increasingly interested, if not actually involved, in educational problems.

Although much of what I have said has been in terms of the first person singular, the development of the Institute has been no personal affair. When the staff was not in seminar with the participants it was in almost continuous seminar with itself. We hammered out the curriculum together, wrestled as one man with the intellectual problems each part of it presented, reviewed jointly the day-to-day crop of administrative puzzles, swapped tales of woe and tales that were far from woeful, until it was hard for any of us, looking back, to single out our own part from that of our colleagues, or decide who first had thought of this or that. When I numbered, a year ago, among the most precious endowments of the Institute, those special contributions of our fairy godmother, a far-seeing bird and a jewel with a hard cutting edge,[1] I was still too little aware how much I had already learnt from them and how heavily I should have to lean on them. It has been my good fortune, and the good fortune of the Institute, to have had a staff as devoted, imaginative and congenial as it would be possible to wish for. I can wish my successor, Mr Hoffman, no greater blessing than that he should enjoy the atmosphere of harmony and good humour in which I have worked through the past eighteen months.

As this is the last occasion on which I shall be able to talk to you—always excepting those prolonged and convivial farewells in which no sentence is ever likely to reach completion—I should like to express my gratitude for the many kindnesses that have been shown me throughout the Bank during my stay in Washington. I came here with great diffidence and as a comparative stranger, and I found, as I was sure that I would find, a quite unexampled warmth of hospitality and readiness to help. I have profited enormously from the universal goodwill on which I was able to count and I shall continue to cherish the many friendships that I have formed. I have been greatly moved by the kindly efforts to overturn my preference for the fogs and frolics of Glasgow over the sun and sophistication of Washington. But, after all, those who have spent even a few moments in the stratosphere are not likely thereafter to be consistently rational and may need a long spell of convalescence and calm. I doubt whether I shall find it possible to stay away from Washington for ever; and there may even be some among you—who knows—who will be unable to stay away from Glasgow. If so, come and give me a refresher course on the Bank while I provide a course of native refreshments—on the house.

[1] My colleagues in the early days of the Institute were Mr J. H. Adler and Mr W. Diamond.

CHAPTER 18

A Visit to Moscow[1]

It would be absurd to suppose that a fortnight in Moscow could throw much light on the functioning of the Soviet economic system. An economist who spoke the language, knew the history, and was familiar with the nuances of current orthodoxy might have made some progress. For myself, I confess that what I learned was mainly on the negative side: not from what was said, but from what was not said; from the questions that were asked, more than from the answers that were given; from the observations that aroused no curiosity in Soviet economists rather than from their efforts to gratify mine. The questions with which I went remained largely unanswered, although I discussed them often enough. Yet they were the kind of questions that anyone who has been actively engaged in the preparation of programmes (or, in the Russian jargon, plans) would relish answering and could answer without disclosure of secret information.

For example, I was interested in knowing something of the investment programme. What was delegated to the firm or to the municipality and what had to be decided at the centre? Could a town decide to change over from trams to trolley-buses without securing the agreement of Gosplan? Could a firm expand its premises, out of accumulated funds and perhaps with its own labour, without getting the capital expenditure included in the five-year plan? How was the finance of the investment programme co-ordinated with other elements in the plan? Secondly, what of consumption? Were family budgets collected and trends in consumption analysed or were Gallup polls undertaken to test consumer preferences? Was production tailored to the consumers' requirements or were those requirements squeezed into the shape of current output by price changes, shop shortages and so on? Finally, how rigid was the plan? How often did it alter and how was it altered?

[1] From 'The Moscow Economic Conference', *Soviet Studies*, October 1952.

Who took the initiative in altering it? Who took the knock if things went wrong? Something had to give if there was a muddle. Under capitalism, it was employment that suffered; what was it under the five-year plan? And if we were to be told that there never was a muddle, we should know that there was in effect no plan either, economic planning being in practice an endless battle with change and the muddle that arises out of change.

Questions of this sort, however phrased, however concrete—or abstract—were generally met either with a circumstantial, textbook account of planning or with slogans. The first might do service in the lecture room and mesmerize students with its diagrams of the plan going down and the plan coming up; but it smacked too much of ceremony and too little of the real thing for an old hand at the game to be much impressed. The slogans were equally sacramental but were sooner exhausted. Three recurred, 'it's planned' (or 'it's in the plan'); 'this is a developing economy'; and 'everything is taken into account'.

Again and again we would ask questions relating to the short term, to the improvisations that are the stock-in-trade of the planner; back would come an answer that made sense only in relation to the long term, the paradise of the classical economist. I came to the conclusion that it was useless to go to the economists for an account of what was actually going on; their job was to preach the theory of the matter, to be Stalin's hot-gospellers, to say what was supposed to happen, not what did in fact happen. Their concern was with general strategy, not with the tactics and methods of the administrator. Their minds were riveted, as often happens in social philosophy, to the stiff models by which past thinkers demonstrated how the world goes round. The world has moved to a new orbit; but no one hastily discards a cherished model, and modifications are often dictated more by the need to keep it running than by obsolescence.

Let me add, in justice to the Soviet economists, that a collection of British academic economists might have done little better if cross-examined on the British investment programme, import licensing, purchase tax, and so forth. But they would, I think, have been more quick to recognize that the only satisfactory and meaningful answers must be in terms of administrative procedures with which they were unfamiliar.

I may illustrate in more detail what I have said above. We attempted on several occasions to get clear how the turnover tax was supposed to operate. The first was on the day of our arrival when, at about 3 a.m. on April 1st, our interpreter told us over a late meal that while we had been in the air, food prices in Russia had been reduced by government decree. At once we seized our opportunity. Did this mean that the turnover tax on food had been cut? Apparently not. Then was the Soviet farmer being paid less? The young man was appalled that such a thing should even be thought of. Perhaps the distributive margin had been reduced. No, that did not seem very plausible. By further cross-examination we elicited that, whatever the *short-term* device used, the fall in food prices was intended to re-align them with *long-term* agricultural costs, which slid down progressively throughout the year while cuts in food prices were made at intervals.

When the subject was next brought up, I tried to find out whether the turnover tax was employed to alleviate a scarcity and clear a surplus, or at least to bring about a calculated change in demand, much as our own purchase tax has sometimes been used. I took the example of television sets and asked whether it was the practice to begin by charging a high price, lowering it gradually as larger supplies became available. I was assured that scarcity would not be allowed to affect prices in this way and that to begin by charging a high price would mean that television sets were 'beyond the means of an average working man'. Now in point of fact television sets were at first marketed at 4,000 rubles. They had a small screen and were not technically a particularly good job. They proved unsaleable and stocks accumulated in the shops. The price was subsequently reduced, first to 3,000 and then 2,000 rubles. At 2,000 rubles television sets went 'under the counter'. Nevertheless the price was lowered to 1,000 rubles and the shortage increased. I find it difficult to reconcile these facts with the account previously given to us. This appeared to postulate a fairly fixed price for a new commodity, with a queue forming at that price and being gradually worked off. No doubt the queue exists now; but there was none earlier on. From later discussions with Soviet economists it seems fairly certain that the rate of turnover tax on individual commodities is changed from time to time, but rarely for short-period reasons.

A second illustration of the difficulty of getting at the facts from the economists was our attempt to establish whether family budgets were collected and how they were used. In particular we wanted to know whether such information was used in planning production. The Soviet economists were a little difficult to pin down on this, and referred us to a speech by Mikoyan with which none of us were familiar. I asked point-blank whether local statistical surveys were undertaken and family budgets collected and they replied that they were. From what I have since been told, I can well believe that this is so. Yet at the time I was left a little in doubt. For immediately afterwards, we were given a quite irrelevant disquisition, not on the constituent items in the budgets of individual peasant families but on the total budget of the collective farms as a group (on Consumption on Farms, as we should say). When the Soviet economists were asked whether some family budgets could not be published, the reply (that such information would be liable to misinterpretation and might be used against the Soviet Union) did not appear to relate to family budgets at all, but to some aggregate; for it was coupled with a rider that we all knew quite well why the Soviet made use of percentages while absolute figures were not disclosed—a curious point to make when it would be easy to express family budgets in percentage form.

In despair of arriving at an understanding of the Soviet economic system from talk with the economists, I tried to gain access to some of the Gosplan officials. This met with no success and I had to fall back on experience and observation.

The phenomena of economic planning are much more familiar to us now than in pre-war years and we have a clearer perception of the inter-connection of these phenomena. The driving force is usually the pressure of government demand, sometimes arising out of war requirements, sometimes out of heavy capital expenditure. This pressure, steadily exerted, eventually gives rise to inflation; but the inflation can be held in check by various devices, such as taxation, rationing, licensing, queues, overcrowding, and so on. At the same time bottlenecks come into existence. These threaten to disorganize production, distort the price structure (and so aggravate the inflation) and to delay the completion of key projects. The government is therefore obliged to institute controls over the scarce items, including labour and materials, as well as manufactured components. Gradually the 'planning' that started in one sector of the economy spreads to others and the economic system becomes co-ordinated less and less through the market and more and more through the controls. The controls are faced, however, with the double problem of keeping in step with one another and of adapting their plans to the vicissitudes of unforeseen events: in Britain, for example, a change in the terms of trade with foreign countries; in Russia an opening of the price scissors due to a bad harvest. This is the central problem of economic planning; and although Russian experience of it may be more than twice as long as ours and has (to say the least) diverged considerably from ours, we are not altogether lacking in understanding of the kind of difficulties that they are likely to meet.

In Russia, however, there are some interesting differences in the way in which the pressure of demand is controlled. The first, and major differences, lies in the rôle of wages. It is possible for the Soviet to hold wages fixed, irrespective of fluctuations in the cost of living, and to strike a wage bargain every year that relates payment to results. Given a rising level of output of consumer goods, the bargain need not be a hard one, since a social dividend can be declared in favour of most groups: the workers whose services are in greatest demand taking, no doubt, the lion's share. At other times, when real wages have to be cut, a greater measure of compulsion will enter and a still greater effort of propaganda will be needed if the planned level of industrial production is to be reached. Putting such a situation on one side, the Soviet authorities can afford to ignore any tendency to inflation from the side of wages as opposed to the side of demand. They can allow demand to press on supply to a degree that would be highly explosive in a capitalist country and can rarely be contemplated except in war-time.

A second difference, arising out of this, is that the Soviet authorities can manoeuvre for a falling price-level and yet maintain an inflationary pressure on production. Whether the price-level has in fact fallen over the past few years we do not know because there are no published index numbers and no foreigner in Moscow has gone to the trouble of collecting the necessary data. All that can be said is that the Soviet government has made a number of substantial reductions, mainly in food prices, in each successive spring since the currency reform; meat, for example, is now selling at about a quarter of its peak price at the end of the war. It would not be inconsistent with the recovery of agricultural production, the rapid expansion in industrial output, and the comparative stability on money wages, to suppose that prices were moving gradually downwards in order to let the larger flow of consumer goods find a market. Steady wages and falling prices would also be not inconsistent with the 'bourgeois thinking' of many western economists; and they would be in exact accord with the economic philosophy of the late Sir Stafford Cripps.

One further difference, which has attracted more attention, lies in the reliance on planning from the centre the production programmes of the main factories. It is difficult to be certain how far, in such planning, Soviet techniques really do differ from those that we used in the war, or from those employed now by the nationalized industries. It would appear that the Budget plays a subsidiary part, as it did here during the war years, and that financial controls are subordinate to administrative controls, as is natural where the needs of the consumer take second place to those of the government. I should be inclined to suppose that the key to an understanding of Soviet economic planning lies in its association with industrialization on the one hand and inflationary pressure on the other: it functions through the tapping of a large reservoir of agricultural labour, its canalization into a limited sector of industry which the government is determined to expand, and the absence of any market limitations to production in other sectors. Perhaps that is something of an over-simplification; but it appears to me to contain the gist of the matter.

Where there is inflationary pressure there are usually shop shortages. In Moscow, however, this symptom was not prominent and queues were comparatively rare. Food was abundant and unrationed. Even the price-cut that came into force on April 1st did not seem to have created any significant shortages although it was said to have brought about a perceptible increase in spending. On the other hand, good clothes were scarce and dear and queues formed readily wherever they were put on sale. There were also shortages of durable goods, such as watches and television sets. The delivery date for a private motor car was about three months. I was reminded of the four stages in the recovery of Western Germany: one year for the Germans to fill their stomachs, one to replenish their wardrobes, one to stock up their homes, and, thereafter, the export drive. The Soviet is some way into the second stage; there is still plenty of consumer demand to absorb what is put on the market.

A second symptom of inflation, particularly under 'planning', is hoarding. Wherever factories are held to a rigid programme, they will hoard everything they can—labour, materials, and even finished goods—so as to be able to guarantee delivery to schedule. A Russian engineer to whom I put this point was scandalized and indignantly denied that Soviet factories hoarded anything. But from other sources I gathered that the inference was, in fact, well-founded. The Chinese delegates made no bones about their own drive against hoarding of materials. They agreed that there was a constant tug-of-war between the central departments, battling with shortages, and the factories, determined to hold as large a stock as possible so as to keep their production from being disorganized. Yet it needed no first-hand corroboration to know that hoarding goes on in Russia. How else could a factory beat its programme by 20 or even 50 per cent? And how else could a motor car factory claim to change over to a new model without loss of production? The history of economic planning is very largely the history of stocks, which register the ebb and flow of demand and supply just as prices are supposed to in a market economy; it was surprising, therefore, how rarely economists and engineers showed any understanding of the rôle of stocks.

In conditions of full employment, such as are usual when there is inflationary pressure, there is generally a high labour turnover and a weakening of normal incentives. Of the first symptom, there was little evidence in Moscow. At the Moskvich motor car factory, employing some 6,000 workers, we were given a figure for labour turnover (from all causes) of 120 per month. There is some evidence that in the years immediately following the war, labour turnover in Moscow was considerably higher. The current low rate is probably due much less to any formal regulations governing dismissal and recruitment through a system of labour books than to the housing shortage. The houses that have been built since the war in Moscow have been put up for the factories rather than for the City Soviet and this gives the factories a powerful weapon to induce their workers to stay. It is likely also that the rapid increase in earnings with length of service exercises a similar immobilizing influence.

Although there is a ban on the movement of labour to Moscow, there is no doubt that it is still continuing and that the population is growing rapidly. A number of the arrangements in Moscow were explained to us in terms of the peasants living there who had only recently left the countryside and had not yet become accustomed to urban life. In the motor-car factory referred to above, there were over a hundred workers who had recently arrived from collective farms and had not yet had time to join the trade union. The presence of these workers was said to account for some of the posters in the factories aimed at reducing accidents.

The weakening of incentive was also not particularly in evidence. The Stakhanovite Movement and much of the publicity in the factories and factory clubs (Palaces of Culture and Rest) were aimed at heightening the incentive to effort. There were portraits of Stakhanovites prominently displayed; a much higher rate of pay was offered to Stakhanovites; and special shifts were worked from time to time under some propaganda label, such as 'Fight for Peace'. A good deal of emphasis, however, was clearly being placed on economy of raw material, rather than on higher output.

I was able to form some assessment of what was involved in the term 'Stakhanovite' in the course of a visit to the motor-car factory already referred to. Over one worker in three in this factory was a Stakhanovite and the factory was scheduled as a Stakhanovite Plant. To a layman, it looked like an oldish British engineering factory, with a rather inferior layout, and it did not appear that the workers were exerting themselves very differently from the workers in a similar British plant. I checked this impression with a trade unionist who had experience of such factories and he gave it as his view that they were in fact working rather less hard. I heard it suggested—

not in relation to this factory—that it would probably be true to say that about half the workers in a Russian factory were putting their backs into their jobs. Some large British factories would regard such a proportion as by no means unsatisfactory.

I also heard it suggested that it had become customary in Moscow for those workers who had any opportunity of doing so to add to their earnings 'on the side'. These earnings added up to something quite large and were a normal feature of the functioning of the economy, although less important now than in the days of rationing. Journalists engaged in free-lancing, doctors carried on a private practice, plumbers would come quickly only if they had reason to expect a good tip, taxi drivers would turn off the meter when they had a fare, and so on.

Taxation in the USSR serves its classical purpose of raising funds to meet the needs of government and is not complicated, as in 'bourgeois society', by egalitarian sentiment. The government does not seek to reduce class differences, since in theory there are none. Class is conceived of solely in terms of the ownership of the means of production, not of wealth or political power. There is no nonsense about regressive taxation; the turnover tax brings in over half the national revenue. There is no concern that interest rates are excessive; the rate on Government Bonds is 3 per cent and on Savings Deposits, left for a minimum of six months, 5 per cent. There are no death duties, no taxes on savings, no prohibitive levies on excess profits. One is almost tempted to think that the Soviet economy in its attitude to profit and to wealth is much nearer to nineteenth-century capitalism than to the twentieth-century welfare state.

We asked whether they were not afraid that inheritance might give rise to a new wealthy class. This question amused them and their answers were instructive. They pooh-poohed the idea that people might use inherited wealth in order to relax or cease from work, saying that in the Soviet Union everybody liked work too much to want to be a parasite. They pointed out that there could be no private ownership of the means of production and that there could therefore be no exploitation in the Marxist sense. Other communists to whom we talked referred us to Marx's chapter on Primitive Accumulation, from which it is a reasonable deduction that Marx would not have taken very seriously the danger that thrift could establish a capitalist class. They also reminded us that currency reform and other measures could soon deal with a growth of money or Government Bonds in the hands of private persons.

I believe that it is here that one finds the main clue to the communist outlook. For them the essence of capitalism is private profit; and the necessary consequence of a system of private profit is war and unemployment. It is this that makes them discount any professions of friendship by capitalist countries, distrust the intentions of the Goverments of those countries and look to their own defence by any means, fair or foul, that lie to hand. They feel in danger, not from the measures devised by particular statesmen, but from the inevitable operation of an economic system.

It would be comic to find men so much in the grip of a fantastic logic, if so much did not hang on bringing them to contemplate other assumptions. They are not prepared to think of an evolution of the capitalist system: the system was analysed for all time by Karl Marx and can only be conceived of as altering in conformity with the laws governing its motion that he put forward. The fact that these laws were absurd and that capitalist society has evolved rapidly does not interest them because, having one religion, they are not anxious to embrace another.

All this was impressed on me time and time again in conversation with communists of various nationalities in Moscow. An Austrian communist babbled to me about centres of power in capitalist society as if private industry had some secret hold on the Government—so much a travesty of life in Whitehall that one could only laugh out loud; he felt no necessity to examine the centres of power in communist society, or to consider the hypothesis that there might be no *centres* of power at all. A Canadian communist was fearful of the intentions of the US steel makers, as if they had some special influence on American foreign policy. (It was this same man—a journalist whose profession it was to observe things accurately and without bias—who assured me that the standard of living in Russia was already higher than in the United Kingdom and that in 10–20 years, it would be as high as in the United States.) A young Russian asked me how much unemployment was needed to run *the* capitalist system. Another Russian—a man of obvious intelligence and wide experience—interrupted me when I was discussing the problem of securing a satisfactory link between the laboratory and the production line, to say that under capitalism, economic development was naturally controlled by private profit. He seemed a good deal surprised—and it was one of the few occasions on which I saw a Soviet economist register real interest—when I told him that on the average fifteen shillings in the pound of the profits made by a firm in British industry went to the Government and that I should be very happy to think that private incentives now exercised any real influence on the pace and direction of economic development in the United Kingdom. I suggested to him that in contradistinction to the USSR, British firms had far less interest in the making of a large profit than had the British Government.

All those to whom I spoke appeared to have a passion for systematizing economic and social forces far beyond the limits of ordinary observation and to want the simplicity of a label to attach to each system once their minds had embraced it. I had a long discussion (in French) with a communist in VOKS, who, when I spoke of the differences between one capitalist country and another, and between twentieth-century and nineteenth-century capitalism, asked me to give our present economic system a name. When I refused to provide a label he pointed out that a single word was sufficient for all mankind, viz. humanity; and in desperation I gave him as the only label I could think of: 'The Welfare State'. Unfortunately I could not translate this into French and had to write it down for him, so that he was probably no further on, even with those mysterious hieroglyphics in front of him.

I must confess that the calibre of the older economists was a little disappointing. I was not surprised to hear that there had been complaints that social and economic research was lagging in the USSR behind technical research. I can recall no powerful analytical minds able to fight their way out of an old system of thought. Those whom I met seemed far more at home in the field of applied economics than in the field of theory. I suspect that the abler economists often gravitated to Gosplan rather than to academic appointments. In some ways I was more attracted to the younger interpreters who expressed themselves more freely and had views of their own. One young man lamented the mass of reading that he had still to do: this included 2,000 pages of Marx, 1,000 pages of Lenin and 7,000 pages of selected texts. (I was rather surprised to find that although he was a graduate he had still to read Book 3 of *Das Kapital.*) I asked him what foreign economists he had read, but although he was familiar with the name of Keynes, he had clearly read little or nothing by any bourgeois economist since the time of Marx. He was making a special study of the United States, but the only book that he had read by an American economist had been issued by the Labour Research Department of America and—I hope quite pardonably—I had never heard of it. Such acquaintance as these graduate students had with foreign economic thought was apparently acquired from lectures on 'bourgeois economics', supplemented by an occasional perusal of articles in *The Economist* or *The Times.*

The questions which were asked of us by the economists were significant. The younger men—the interpreters—generally asked political questions: What did the British think of the Americans? What attitude did Britain take towards a United Europe? How did people feel about the rearmament of Germany? And so on. The questions put to us by the economists at a special round table discussion may be worth quoting in full.

The first question related to the British balance of payments and what Britain was likely to do about it. A later question related to devaluation and whether it had been of any help to us. We were also asked about Britain's trade with the East and its importance to her. In answering this latter question, I laid emphasis on the *indirect* gain to Britain from an extension in the area of trade both as a contribution to relieving the pressure of dollar shortage and as a means of softening the force of Japanese and German competition. I laid stress, however, on the comparative insignificance of British trade with Eastern Europe. This surprised the Soviet economists, who appeared to think that at least our trade with China was of considerable dimensions (instead of less than 1 per cent of our total trade). Even when the meeting was over they reverted to the subject, asking us to make sure that we had not formed a mistaken impression based on wrong figures. In putting questions relating to British trade, the Soviet economists showed some familiarity with recent events: they quoted, for example, the successive import cuts that had been announced by the Chancellor and also mentioned an estimate of £700–£800 m. for the export of capital from Britain since the end of the war.

Several questions were asked about what was done in Britain to 'plan the work of private enterprise'. I gave a sketchy explanation of how controls functioned in Britain, and Peter Wiles put it to them that nationalization was commonly regarded in Britain as a sure way of escaping government control. One question related to high profits and the possibilities of squeezing them. I suggested that the relevant comparison was between distributed profits and wage earnings and that this ratio had fallen far below what it was before the war. Another questioner asked us why prices were still rising. We pointed out that wholesale prices were not rising, but had fallen heavily and that even retail prices would now be steady or falling, but for the withdrawal of part of the food subsidies. Mrs Robinson threw in that in the British economy prices rose as wages rose and with full employment wages showed a tendency to rise progressively; in this there was a fundamental difference between the British and Soviet economic systems. One of the last questions, which was also dealt with by Mrs Robinson, was why we had forsaken Adam Smith for Lord Keynes.

It is difficult to sum up a general impression of the standard of living. On the one side, there was no rationing, communal facilities for entertainment and recreation were good, the social services were highly developed; on the other, there was appalling overcrowding, clothes were expensive and lacking in style and finish, and real wages were far below the level in Britain (as far as I could judge, about half). There was little sign either of acute poverty or of affluence. The atmosphere was, not surprisingly, proletarian, and reminded me far more of a Lanarkshire mining town than of a great capital city.

The men in executive positions seemed competent, level-headed and of a practical turn of mind. Nowhere, however, was there much of the self-criticism natural to healthy government. Only once did I talk to a Russian who was prepared to poke fun at any side of Soviet life. Self-assurance tended to be carried to the point at which it became self-complacency.

This was most obvious in the younger generation. I asked one young man whether he would favour student exchanges between Russia and Britain. He asked me if I wanted a frank answer and I encouraged him to give one. He then said that he thought that the Soviet students would have nothing to learn. It was the same young man who was studying the US economy without having read a single book by any US economist of repute.

CHAPTER 19

Programmes as Instruments of Co-ordination[1]

I

PROGRAMMES are an administrative device which may or may not have an economic purpose. In a development programme the purpose is obviously economic, but in the world of entertainment where, so far as I know, published programmes were first used, the purpose is almost entirely organizational.[1] A concert programme, for example, advertises what is to be played, by whom, in what sequence and at what times. It serves both to organize the performance itself and at the same time as a means of communication between the performers and the concert-going public, just as a railway timetable, which is another kind of programme, simultaneously organizes railway services and informs the travelling public what trains are running, so that they in turn can make appropriate arrangements.

The programmes that I shall be discussing are rarely addressed to the consuming public. Some of them—for example, the development programme of an under-developed country—may have the same advertising function as a concert programme and be intended to fill the consumer with hopes of future enjoyment. But the principal function of the programmes that I shall discuss, whether they are used by an individual firm, by Government departments in war-time, or by the central planning organization of a communist country, is to serve as an instrument for the co-ordination of productive activities.

This function is most obvious at the level of the individual firm and in the type of programme that is the most frequently used by firms, namely a production programme. In any large organization where many workers have to be assigned fresh tasks every day, it becomes cumbersome to make decisions

[1] Abbreviated version of a lecture delivered at the Institut Universitaire d'Etudes Européennes, Turin, January 1961, and published in *Scottish Journal of Political Economy*, June 1961.

on each occasion with reference to a plan of work laid down in advance. Inputs of materials and components as well as of labour have to be adjusted to the outputs eventually required; and the longer the interval between input and output and the greater the variety of materials and components incorporated in the finished product, the more difficult it is to place orders without a production programme. Such a programme, when drawn up, covers a fixed period of time, and shows the outputs of various commodities which it is planned to produce during that time. This allows all operations to be phased and co-ordinated in relation to the outputs to be produced. It also reveals any shortages in labour and materials that are likely to arise and any future bottlenecks in capacity. For this reason it provides a basis for the recruitment of labour, and for inventory control, ordering of materials, and new investment in additional capacity.

Production programmes illustrate the three principal characteristics of a programme in the sense in which I shall use the term. First of all, they are quantitative in character: they are statistical time series relating to the future, not the past. The quantities, although expressed as amounts, are in fact rates of flow over time and differ in this respect from the quantities that normally figure in contracts—a difference that very often produces friction between those who administer programmes and those who administer contracts. Secondly, these quantities are usually in some sense allocative: that is, the different rates at any point in time add up to a fixed total which the programme sub-divides between competing uses. Thirdly, the quantities tend to be specified in physical rather than financial terms. It would be possible to extend the term 'programme' to cover similar financial statements, but the more usual expression is 'budget'. A budget is a programme drawn up by a consumer. At the national level, in a country with a consumer rather than a producer bias, the central budget is not only the spending programme of the government but can indeed act as a substitute for a development programme.

There are many programmes with the characteristics that I have listed. In addition to a production programme, a firm may have a buying programme and a sales programme extending over the same, or perhaps a rather different, period of time. Then it may have an investment programme to co-ordinate capital expenditure. At the national level there may be a host of programmes: for imports and exports; for different raw materials; for military aircraft; investment programmes; training programmes, and so on. Sometimes, to confuse matters, the term 'budget' is used: as in speaking of a steel or a man-power budget. Sometimes all kinds of other terms are introduced: for example, 'plan', 'projection', 'target', 'perspective'.

The use of these different terms derives from two circumstances. The first is that some so-called programmes are no more than calculations intended to help decision-taking while others embody the decisions themselves. I am concerned only with the second type of plan or programme: but I do not wish to detract from the importance of working out the consequences of economic decisions in parts of the economy not under the control of the programming authority. A programme should be an effort of imagination as well as a plan of action.

The second circumstance that gives rise to terminological confusion is that different programmes have not only different purposes but different time-horizons. A firm's investment programme, for example, is likely to cover a longer period of time than its production programme and may bear less and less the aspect of a programme the further ahead it extends. The production programme for the next three months may be a firm plan of production while the investment programme for the year after next may be no more than a target at which it seems reasonable to aim, or a sketch of what might be done if no major change in circumstances occurred.

These differences in time-span arise also at the national level. Communist countries, for example, often divide responsibility for short-term, medium-term and long-term planning between separate units. The first presumably relates to annual output plans, the second to plans for increasing capacity over periods of up to five years or so, and the third to those larger changes in the economic framework that can be brought about in the long run through better education, more research, and so on, as well as to those structural changes that may be necessary in order to adapt the economy to long-term economic trends. At the one extreme is the severely practical problem of organizing current output while at the other is what is now described by communist writers as 'perspective planning'.

Obviously, if one takes a long enough span of time one needs imagination and very little else in order to plan; and the plans, while they may come to exercise great influence like all the best fiction, will be dreams rather than programmes of action—'guess-plans' to use Stalin's derogatory description of them. On the other hand, if one takes a very short span of time it is very easy to end up with a programme that does not control events but is controlled by them. The programme may be constantly amended, not in order to give effect to new decisions, but to conform to the expected course of output over a period too short for fresh decisions to make much difference. The time-horizon of a programme ought, therefore, to be long enough to serve as an indicator of action, not a mere forecast of what has passed beyond decision; and it ought at the same time not to be so long that it extends to a period about which no decisions need yet be taken.

II

Programmes serve five distinct functions:

(i) They register decisions. Any decisions to change production can only become operative when it is reflected in the programme amendment.

(ii) They communicate decisions. They are a simple, unambiguous[1] and economical way of telling everyone what operations have to be carried out, whether they participated in the preparation of the programme or not.

(iii) They clarify and force decisions. In the course of drawing up a programme it is necessary to agree on what is to be inserted and what is to be excluded. This agreement is possible only if decisions have been made on the policies to be pursued and the success likely to attend these policies, the programme being a kind of summary of the policies and a way of giving effect to them. The programme also forces

[1] Not entirely unambiguous. My experience is that those who take programmes too literally can be a greater danger to good organization than those who add an excessive amount of salt.

attention on any obstacles to its fulfilment, and so helps to bring about earlier decisions for overcoming them. Eventually, it becomes the focus of all decisions affecting production.

(iv) They provide a measure of the success of earlier decisions. If the carrying out of these decisions leads to the fulfilment of the programme, the firm can take pride in a piece of successful planning. On the other hand, any divergence from a programme showing what a firm planned should happen can usually be interpreted as a failure to plan correctly. Efficiency in planning is not the same thing as efficiency in production but it is an element in it and there is a high correlation between the two.

(v) They allow decisions to be delegated. They not only communicate the decisions of a higher to a subordinate authority but provide an instrument of delegation to it. They constitute the marching orders of the subordinate authority in those fields where it is possible to lay down a general strategy; and they are at the same time a basis for the review of the subordinate authority's performance.

These functions are fulfilled by production programmes at whatever level they are used. An economic development programme, for example, is also a register of decisions, a method of communicating decisions, a focus of decision-making, a method of delegating decisions and a measure of the success of the plans which it embodies.

Each function has important corollaries on which I propose to touch briefly.

(i) For example, no firm imagines that once a programme has been worked out it must be maintained inviolate or that those who prepared it can go on holiday for a stretch. This follows at once from the first of the functions that a programme performs: it is a register of decisions. As a register, it cannot be closed so long as fresh decisions may become necessary, since it has to be constantly amended with each new decision. This is true of all programmes: what matters is not the programme but the effort of foresight that goes to its preparation, and the continuous process of amendment by which it is kept up-to-date. The idea that you need only prepare a plan once every five years is complete nonsense. A fixed plan is not only worthless, but dangerous: all planning that makes contact with the real world is re-planning. The activity of planning is far more important than the end-product, the plan; and the activity consists fundamentally in trying to secure, not just that decisions are taken in a different way, but that different decisions are taken. This cannot be achieved by treating programmes like the phoenix, as if they should take wing every five years or so from their own ashes; it can be achieved only if they are kept continuously alive by amendment and are used, as I have suggested above, as the focus of decision.

(ii) Nevertheless, new programmes do get issued from time to time and the fiction is often maintained that intermediate amendments are comparatively trivial and of no significance to the public. To give publicity to amendments blurs the image of a resolute management following confidently the path it has chosen. On the other hand, a new programme may not only confirm this image but is justified by the second of the functions which I have mentioned—the need to communicate decisions. A new programme gives amendments fresh authority by codifying them and tidies them up so that they cannot be overlooked or treated as stopgaps unrelated to the rest of the programme. Just as the railways are obliged to issue a new timetable periodically, although the timetable is changing all the time, so any planning organization likes to start afresh from a new fixed point at regular intervals and use the opportunity to review the programme as a whole.

(iii) A programme is a focus, not a substitute, for decision-making. It is a mistake to suppose that nothing ever gets decided or 'planned' until there is a programme. Just as it is nonsense to equate planning with the publication of a quinquennial programme, so it is nonsense to think that a programme settles everything and that no sensible decisions can be taken without one. It furnishes no more than a systematic way of trying to co-ordinate decisions and improve on unco-ordinated decisions. Although unco-ordinated decisions may be bad or costly so also may co-ordinated decisions: there is no magic about a programme that transforms the quality of decisions beyond the virtue that co-ordination lends.

I make this point because some people are puzzled how

one ever *begins* to prepare a programme[1] when the truth is, in a sense, that one never *begins*. One starts from a world that is already moving, not one that has to be set in motion. There are nearly always plenty of plans and the problem is chiefly one of choosing between them, giving scope to the more promising and trying to ensure that what is left is, as far as possible, self-consistent. No doubt one can travel away from a world where initiative is dispersed and there are many programmes towards a world in which, in principle (but never in practice), there is only one all-embracing programme for the entire economy. There is also a formal difference, and sometimes more than a formal difference, between programmes for publicly and privately operated enterprises. But it is only if one starts out from sheer administrative chaos—as did happen in the USSR after the civil war—that programmes take shape out of nothing instead of out of existing programmes.

(iv) The fourth function of a programme, to provide a measure of the success of earlier decisions, means that the programmes to which firms work under capitalism can never be purely physical. Since the crucial test of success is one of profit or loss there must always be, in addition, a financial constraint. Sometimes this constraint makes itself felt only in the longer run when a drop in profits or an outright loss forces a change in programme. Sometimes the constraint is made more immediately effective through a system of budgetary control and standard costing. Implicitly or explicitly, there is a financial programme alongside the physical one. Moreover it is the financial programme that takes precedence. The physical programme has an economic purpose and the final test of its success is not just whether it is fulfilled but whether when fulfilled it yields a balance of advantage to the firm. The values in which this advantage is measured are the values of the market and are consequently external to the firm. The programmes of the firm have, therefore, constantly to be adjusted by reference to external indicators unless the firm is to be involved in financial losses.

(v) These external indicators take the form of prices and costs. The significance of market indicators varies with the type of market in which they are determined; but the more

[1] The same bewilderment was common during the war when the layman drsetta to talk about the preparation of aircraft programmes.

free the market is, the more they give expression to the values of the ultimate consumers and producers in whose interests the economic system is supposed to function. Where prices and costs do have this significance, even approximately, the activities of firms can be co-ordinated from without by market mechanisms and the need to co-ordinate from within through programmes is correspondingly reduced. To put the matter the other way round, the existence of market indicators allows a much greater power of delegation and dispersion of initiative because subordinates can make use of an objective criterion of success in their decision-making.

That this is true at the national level is well recognized. The state is content to leave private firms a large measure of independence because it is confident that market forces will orient their planning to the public advantage. But exactly the same is true within large firms operating several branches. The fact that these branches can be given a simple objective such as the need to show a profit and can use external indicators to guide their reactions makes it much easier to allow them considerable autonomy. Moreover, just as the firm may seek to maintain some degree of control over its constituent units by supervision of selected programmes the same is true of the state, which may content itself with reviewing those economic aggregates such as investment and consumption, imports and exports, electric generating *capacity*, and so on, which it adjudges of critical importance to the uninterrupted growth of the economy.

Programmes, therefore, furnish a convenient instrument of delegation—the last of the functions already listed. Indeed, in some situations where market indicators do not exist, there is practically no other basis of delegation, except in the most general terms, and the programme then provides an unqualified measure of successful performance. As I shall show later, it is precisely when there is no market, or when market indicators are superseded or distrusted or enfeebled by excessive pressure of demand, that programmes come to dominate administrative action.

I need hardly insist that there is no value in a programme if it does not influence action. There is no point in taking decisions unless they are carried into effect—and programmes are simply a tool for decision-making. This may seem obvious enough in a firm where programmes are usually based on or backed by orders already received or confidently expected and contracts already placed or about to be placed, so that the links between programmes and their execution are necessarily close. But at the national level the links between what is planned and what actually happens are often distinctly tenuous.

III

That programmes assist good organization and can enhance productive efficiency goes without saying. It is not surprising, therefore, that many countries as well as firms make extensive use of programmes and that they sometimes become the basis for running an entire economy. In communist countries one sometimes gets the impression that the government thinks of itself as a large joint stock company whose shareholders are the next generation. The economy is organized much like a very large firm and the resemblance is particularly evident in the use that is made of programmes as an instrument in economic decision-making. There are, however, differences in the way in which the programmes are prepared—for example in the influence exercised by market forces. The attitude of the government is not only that of a producer rather than a consumer but it is that of a producer who calls the tune and can, within limits, tell the consumer what he is to be allowed. In other economies where development programmes are used, the consumer occupies a stronger position and market forces are not so consistently over-ridden. There are also many countries that make little or no use of programmes just as there are many firms that have no production programmes. This suggests that whatever the advantages of programmes they do not lie uniformly on one side and that there may be serious limitations to their use.

The nature of these limitations has already been explored by economists in two different branches of economic theory which are rarely brought into association with one another. In the theory of the firm, they have stressed the difficulty of maintaining administrative efficiency in large and complex organizations: if size at some stage of growth becomes a competitive handicap, then there is correspondingly less scope for programmes which are a palliative but not a cure for the inconveniences of size. In the theory of value, economists have approached the problem from the outside instead of the inside and have demonstrated the importance of an external frame of reference in maintaining the economic efficiency of productive units. This external frame of reference is provided by a free market in which the plans of producers can be linked with those of consumers. Market forces, by causing both producers and consumers to vary their plans, are an effective—but not necessarily ideal—method of co-ordinating production activity and directing that activity towards the satisfaction of consumers' wants. The market mechanism operates whatever the form of organization used by producing units and tends to eliminate those forms of organization that fail to withstand competition. Thus the use made of programmes by individual firms is limited by the need to prevail in competition for a market with other firms that do not make use of programmes; while at the national level, the market by enabling production to be co-ordinated through the price-mechanism provides a substitute for the centralized programme that might otherwise be employed.

These are not, I hope, matters that I need elaborate and qualify. For present purposes, all that I wish to establish is that the market is a solvent of complex forms of economic organization, that the more use is made of the market the less need there is for development programmes and that, conversely, the greater the effort to plan and organize an economy from the centre the more difficult it is to enjoy decentralization through the market. Carried to their logical conclusion, production programmes co-ordinated at the centre could transform the entire economy into one large firm. On the other hand, carried to its logical conclusion, the price-mechanism is capable of eliminating the administrative structure that we call a firm and substituting for it a series of *ad hoc* bargains between individual producers. We recognize at once the absurdity of trying to make the market do duty for all the organization that goes on within a firm; but do we recognize the equal absurdity of trying to organize for the benefit of consumers without allowing market forces to operate?

The limits to the use of programmes in substitution for

market forces do not arise simply from size. Economists are now a great deal more sceptical than they used to be whether any loss in efficiency need result as a firm grows in size. It used to be argued that there was an optimum size of firm and that beyond this optimum, managerial efficiency deteriorated. Nowadays it is more common to argue that while there may be a limit on the *rate of growth* of a firm without loss of efficiency, firms can adapt their administrative structure as they grow and that, while their costs may show little reduction they are unlikely to show any increase.[1] If this is so, it would seem to follow that all the firms in an economy could be amalgamated and run by the state as in a communist society, without any sacrifice in administrative efficiency.

This is not, however, a corollary that I find it possible to accept. One cannot discuss the efficiency of a productive unit without reference to its purpose and this purpose must embrace the satisfaction of the consumers' wants. However efficient a central planning organization, how can the programmes which it devises be as sensitive an instrument as the market for giving the consumer what he wants?

I do not say: 'for co-ordinating production'. It is certainly arguable that production can be organized efficiently in a single large unit: every army, after all, has to get along without using a market to decentralize decision-making. Nor do I assume that the consumer should always get what he wants: it may be more important to change the structure of the economy so that the next generation of consumers will get more. But if the problem is how to maintain efficiency *in meeting the demands of consumers*, can a firm grow until it swallows up all other firms without losing touch with those demands?

It does not seem to me sufficient justification to say that where there is a divorce between government and consumer priorities, there must be programmes that guarantee precedence to the government. Everybody recognizes that such a divorce can exist: that there may be a conflict between what consumers will buy on the market, if permitted, what they will vote for through their government representatives, if

[1] See, for example, E. T. Penrose, *Theory of the Growth of the Firm* (Oxford, 1960); P. S. Florence, *The Logic of British and American Industry* (London, 1953), and R. B. Heflebower, 'Observations on Decentralization in Large Enterprises', *Journal of Industrial Economics*, November 1960.

they have any, and what the government, with their agreement or otherwise, is prepared to allow them. Everybody would agree that the government would be justified in imposing its own priorities if it could establish that consumers were short-sighted or ignorant, or if it were trying, with the agreement of the electorate, to improve the social and economic framework within which consumers and producers form their private plans. But the government has other ways of making its will prevail. It can tax or borrow, and range itself alongside the consumer in the market instead of trying to supersede market valuations through programmes. The budget offers it an alternative, less drastic, instrument of planning the economic system.

Even those who see no necessary decline in efficiency with size agree that there are some types of economic activity in which small firms predominate. The reasons for this predominance, and for the concomitant absence of production programmes in these small firms, include two which seem to me of special relevance. First of all, where it is necessary to follow the market closely and give customers personal attention, supplying products exactly adapted to their requirements, it is difficult to manage a firm of any size and equally difficult to make use of a production programme. The same is true, secondly, where changes—particularly changes in market conditions—are rapid and unforeseeable so that production decisions have to be taken frequently and quickly. The use of a production programme assumes on the one hand that the producer can to some extent call the tune and on the other hand that his time-horizon is not limited to the immediate future.

Now these are two highly important limitations. A longer time-horizon—to begin with the second—is one of the more important elements of novelty when administrative action comes to be based on programmes rather than on *ad hoc* methods of co-ordination. A greater effort is made to foresee surpluses and shortages, to predict exact delivery dates, to secure consistency between the more remote and the more immediate consequences of current decisions, to study the need for action before it actually arises. An important merit of a development programme is that it operates to exact a similar effort of foresight and extend the span of time that is brought under review; it does so not only for those who are preparing it but for the public on whose behalf it is prepared. If, however, a firm or a country is obliged to live from hand to mouth under conditions of rapid change that would make a programme out-of-date by the time it was prepared, the possibility of taking and adhering to a long view does not exist. A stable programme requires some stability in the circumstances to which it relates; a highly unstable programme is likely to be worse than none at all.

The other limitation arises out of the fact that a firm has to sell what it produces. If it has to hunt around for markets it cannot plan its production without running considerable risks. Since all production is in advance of consumption some of these risks are inescapable, and if production is to be efficient other risks have to be assumed in the shape of heavy capital commitments. But the risks are obviously much less in a seller's market than in a buyer's market; and it is probably significant that in Britain at least the rise of production programmes took place in the seller's markets of war and post-war years. Firms were able to count on large contracts that kept them working to capacity. The limiting factor in their activities became production rather than sales and they had therefore every incentive to plan the use of their capacity for a long period ahead so as to obtain the maximum output. If, however, there are no long order books and customers will not wait for delivery, output may have to move from its pre-established path to meet new and unexpected requirements, programmes begin to lose their firmness and planning relapses into improvization.

These limitations to the use of programmes in a firm—the need to offer the customer what he will buy and the need to take advantage of changing circumstances—still apply at the national level.

It is conceivable that the first limitation might completely lose its force. The government of any country is usually itself a large buyer of finished goods. If, to take an extreme case, it were *sole* buyer and consumers merely took what they were given without grumbling, it would be impossible to organize production until the government had made up its mind what it wanted. No one else would have any say in the matter and there would be no alternative indicators to which business enterprises could turn in order to decide what to produce. Naturally when one talks of the government making up its mind, it is no single mind that has to be made up but the minds of a great many people in positions of authority who may disagree with one another. However erratic the process of decision-taking may be; however frequently decisions are reversed and action is countermanded; however long it may take to bring inter-departmental consultation to a head and wrest a decision from vacillating officials; if the government masquerades as the sole consumer of final output, there is no short-cut by which its requirements can be established. The government alone can tell what the government will do. Once it has decided, it need not make use of any market or other mechanisms to state its requirements. It need merely proceed directly to draw up production programmes in agreement with whatever business units it maintains. These programmes will simultaneously give expression to government demand and to the possibilities of supply over the period to which the programmes relate. Demand and supply will be equated by administrative action without reference to any system of prices. The market limitation on programmes disappears for the simple reason that the market disappears.

Now although this is an extreme case it is not so very far removed from a variety of circumstances in which programmes are used extensively by governments. In war-time, for example, the government employs a high proportion of the available man-power either in the armed forces or producing equipment for them; and although civilian requirements remain large and are procured through the market, government requirements take precedence whenever there is any conflict of priorities. As Professor Devons has pointed out, the government tries to behave like a single consumer with a single set of priorities derived from the strategy by which it proposes to conduct the war. Civilian needs take their place within this strategy but are subordinated to it and it is the war strategy that governs production not the spending of consumers. Firms making against government orders need not necessarily use production programmes or they may construct their own programmes from the orders in hand; but as war-time organization improves there is an extension of programming and a greater effort to bring the priorities in the programmes into line with priorities decided upon centrally.

The same kind of reasoning can be applied where a great structural upheaval is in progress—associated, for example, with industrialization—and the restructuring of the economy is accorded (willingly or unwillingly) absolute priority over the immediate satisfaction of consumers' wants. If the government elects to impose its own priorities and treat the transformation of the economy like a military operation, it is likely to have to clothe its priorities in the form of production programmes and apply compulsion similar to conscription and direction of labour on the one hand and rationing and licensing of consumers on the other.

The extent to which it can use programmes, however, must depend upon how far it is itself the consumer of final output or in direct control of producing units. If there is a large private sector, as in non-communist countries, the government's power to control it is necessarily limited. The government may attempt to 'administer' civilian markets by limiting supplies, regulating demand, fixing prices, imposing taxes and so on, or by more drastic measures such as requisitioning, direction of labour, and so on. But the efficiency of these controls is as limited as the abilities and incorruptibility of those who administer them; and the programmes drawn up by the government may remain ineffective because market forces prove too strong.

The second limitation is the fact of change. A world free from change would be a world of routine in which there would be no need for organization because everything would have become perfectly organized, no need for managers because there would be no fresh decisions to take, and no need for programmes because everything would already proceed in a fixed sequence and at fixed times. Programmes are also out of place in a world of very rapid change in which foresight becomes impossible. In such a world it is unwise to lay down a fixed path because the one thing that one can be sure of is that it will be necessary to leave it. One has to make some working assumptions, remain prepared to change them, and improvize to the best of one's abilities.

Now consider the implications of rapid change in a centrally planned economy. If it is insisted that all programmes must be fixed centrally then it is necessary for the central planning staff to obtain information of the changes affecting each programme; to engage in all the necessary consultations in order to amend the programmes; to review the repercussions of these amendments on inter-related programmes and amend them too; to promulgate all the amendments; and to see to it that the process is completed so quickly that no fresh change makes the whole set of amendments out-of-date before effect can be given to them. Needless to say, for any but the smallest and simplest type of economy this adds up to a complete impossibility.

Given this impossibility, the central planning staff has to limit the number of programmes in which it interests itself directly. During the war, the Programmes Department of the Ministry in which I worked deliberately restricted itself to about a dozen items, knowing that any attempt to keep track of a larger number would distract the key members of the staff from their major task or would make it necessary to recruit a larger staff than could be readily co-ordinated by the informal but effective methods we employed. In the same way, I gather that in most communist countries the central planning organization has in recent years come to limit the number of commodities for which it prepares programmes. In Czechoslovakia, for example, the number has been reduced from 1,500 to about 200 and in the USSR from 5,000 to a few hundreds. This leaves the work of preparing programmes for other less important commodities to subordinate organizations: in war-time Britain, to the production as opposed to the planning department of the Ministry or to the principal contractors to the Ministry; in communist countries, to the planning authorities of individual states or regions or to trusts and other trade organizations.

But as soon as such delegation is accepted as a necessity it is no longer possible to ensure that programmes are coordinated, and it becomes necessary, the further the delegation is carried, to find substitutes for the market indicators which enable a large private firm, faced with a similar problem, to delegate planning authority to its branches and subsidiaries.

Nor is a limitation in the items programmed centrally the end of the matter. Each of the weaknesses that comprehensive planning encounters also afflicts the central planning of individual items. First, there is the problem of information. When changes occur, how can the central planner know all that is in the mind of the man on the spot where the change is taking place? How can he convey all that is in his own mind? As a central planner he may be confident that he knows what the government wants better than the producing unit; at the same time, the manager of the producing unit knows far better what the government can have. But if demand and supply—as we may think of them both—are far apart, are administrative methods well adapted to bringing them together? For real co-ordination, each should know the range of alternatives open to the other, and the terms on which one alternative might be substituted for another. When there is a market to react to, this kind of dialogue does occur between each buyer and seller and market prices. But in the absence of a market, the dialogue has to become a tête-à-tête not the long-distance telephone conversation that is all that may be possible.

Programmes can be operated centrally only if information not previously available is collected. This information, most of it statistical in character, *takes time* to collect, is often difficult to interpret, and has a different coverage at one time than it has at another. Thus there is a constant danger that the information available will give a misleading picture of the current situation, that a wrong construction will be put on the limited data supplied, and that the data will be the more useful for dealing with last year's problems than this year's. The fact that the data are statistical means also that those who run a centrally planned economy may give excessive weight to quantitative considerations and are likely to include a disproportionate number of people who have specialized in handling statistics (as opposed, for example, to handling people).

A further limitation arises out of the need for continual consultation. Here again there are problems of time and of communication. The central planner's sole advantage over other people is that he has access to information about what is happening right across the economy and about what the government proposes to do. But to make use of this access takes time. His stock of information is a rapidly deteriorating asset unless he makes a heavy investment in the study of current documents and in consultation with his colleagues. However hard he tries, he cannot know everything relevant to the decisions that he is called upon to make. Whenever an amendment to programmes becomes necessary, he may discuss the proposed amendment with those of his colleagues who are affected but neither he nor they can see the full implications, however much time they give to considering them. For the need to specialize in their own field limits their vision and their knowledge. It can easily happen that the colleague most concerned is not even told because no one was aware that he was about to come forward with an amendment that would make nonsense of the change under discussion.

In an economy which is not centrally planned these limitations are made effective by financial sanctions. If programmes are not altered quickly, when demand changes, the goods produced cannot be sold. But these sanctions need not operate in a communist country, even where the goods are made for a civilian market. It is a matter of principle in those countries to keep demand slightly ahead of supply—i.e. to maintain a seller's market—so that at any time there are bound to be some shop-shortages and an incentive to take what can be had rather than wait indefinitely for what is not to be had. It is partly because of the seller's market that the emphasis can be thrown so strongly on to production: there is every incentive to plan the use of capacity for long periods ahead if there is no difficulty in marketing the output.

The price of production programmes in these circumstances, given the inherent imperfections of planning, is thus exactly like the price of a long-term contract—the necessity to assure a market even when the output may be unsaleable. The assurance need not, of course, have an unlimited span: after a time, capacity can be changed over to more acceptable goods and junk produced in the meantime can be unloaded at a loss. But the output lost during the changeover may be heavy and the loss on the sale or scrapping of junk even heavier. It may, for example, take as much as six months before production of an item no longer wanted can be brought to a stop. I know very little of the experience of communist countries in such circumstances but I have very lively recollections of the shifts to which the British Ministry of Aircraft Production went to during the last war in order to keep a productive unit in operation: factories scheduled to go over to Typhoons continued to turn out Hurricanes by the score long after there was any apparent use for them.

IV

The fundamental problem of planning is thus to find the optimum degree of decentralization. In centrally planned economies the risks are run on the side of over-centralization because the mechanisms that are favoured—co-ordination through programmes—lend themselves to centralization. In the industrial countries of the west the risks are run on the side of excessive decentralization because the mechanisms that are favoured—co-ordination through market forces—promote decentralization. In the first type of economy the planners are prominent, few and powerful, while the second type of economy, being full of well-managed business enterprises, suffers from too many planners rather than too few. Its methods of co-ordination tend to be much less direct and to make much more use of the central government's budget, which operates as the principal instrument for regulating the pressure of demand and controlling the balance between the principal sectors of the economy. The government tries to co-ordinate its spending plans with the spending plans of other consumers, leaving producers to draw up their own programmes to meet the resulting market requirements. It may also seek to influence the rate of capital accumulation, the balance of payments, the distribution of industry and so on. But in its efforts to co-ordinate production it usually intervenes on the side of demand rather than supply, using financial means impinging on the budget rather than physical controls giving effect to programmes.

CHAPTER 20

Economic Schizophrenia[1]

ECONOMISTS have been in the habit of drawing a sharp line of division between producers and consumers. Each is represented as a unit of control over resources, intent upon maximizing the return on those resources either in the form of profit or of utility. Profit and utility are set in sharp juxtaposition to one another and both categories are purged as far as possible of the discontinuities and inconsistencies that make human behaviour so ungeometric. Sometimes a time dimension has been introduced because short and long run considerations may conflict; sometimes a probability dimension has been analysed as a bow to the uncertainties by which choice is usually surrounded. But producers and consumers have generally remained, in the writings of modern economists, the creatures of a series of equations, raw material for an electronic computer rather than the wayward and unpredictable creatures of everyday life.

Moreover, of the two ghostly puppets who inhabit the textbooks, it is the producer who is allowed to rattle his chains the loudest. He is a character who can be looked at with a proper suspicion both because he may act out of character and fail to maximize anything observable and because his presumed passion for maximizing profit may set up a kind of Hegelian tension within the economy by simultaneously obstructing and assisting social progress. The consumer, on the other hand, is too exalted to be seen naked. Since he is sovereign, his wish is law and that is the end of the matter. Almost the only aspect of the consumer's behaviour in which it is seemly to show curiosity and cite the facts of common observation is in respect of saving and spending. The discovery that saving is limited by the need to keep up with the Joneses ranks as one of the few intrusions of sociology into the economics of consumption.

[1] From *Scottish Journal of Political Economy*, February 1958.

The bloodlessness of the economic man, whether producer or consumer, has been a common complaint against the subject, especially from those who felt that money was an inadequate object of human ambition. Economists have generally countered that they knew what they were about even if their readers did not. All that they succeeded in establishing was the usefulness of an abstraction; on the other hand, they entirely failed to see the danger of the abstraction. If producers are merely an unknown quantity in a complicated equation, they can easily be superseded by other unknown quantities in a more simplified equation. If consumers are all-powerful ciphers, they can be treated as ciphers and shorn of their power. The more the operation of maximizing is reduced to a mathematical process, the more the individual producer or consumer appears inadequate or, indeed, redundant. Either the process is automatic and so requires no managerial skill at all, or it involves too many unknowns for the individual human mind to grapple with them successfully.

Economists have abstracted in their equations from the effort of planning. They have eliminated from economic behaviour the element of management and administration that is embedded in it and have then felt obliged to reintroduce it in the form of state action. Economic behaviour does not consist exclusively in responding to price incentives, in exchanging this for that, in market-oriented activity, but embraces much that goes on *within* the firms that produce and *within* the households that consume. In the market there is an obvious antithesis between firms and households; but the antithesis disappears when the two are looked at as administrative units. If, following Aristotle, economists had sought first to understand the activities of the household and then studied the firm as a special type of household, they would have been less seriously in error. They would certainly have done fuller justice to the activity which we call management.

Economists have also failed to do justice in the theory of demand to precisely those elements of realism on which they are accustomed to insist in the theory of production. Just as there are internal and external economies on the side of supply, so a change in consumption itself affects the valuations of other consumers. Consumption is inevitably a social activity and choice takes place under social pressures that interact with economic change. It is impossible to make sense of the activities of a firm in isolation from its market and all the productive facilities on which it draws; similarly, it is impossible to make sense of the activities of a consumer in isolation from the market circumstances that condition his choice and the customs, habits and beliefs by which he is surrounded. The producer's activities are exploratory; so, in a deeper sense, are the consumer's. Each fresh purchase has to be fitted, not just into an existing pattern of consumption, but into an emerging way of life. There are overhead elements on the side of demand at least as prominently as on the side of supply. The discontinuities and indivisibilities that play havoc with marginal cost theory are equally damaging to marginal utility.

The antithesis between producers and consumers has also prevented economists from conveying an adequate picture of the relationship between the two. If firms are set in sharp contrast to households, and their output is assumed to govern the standard of living, the whole maximizing process is distorted. Economists and their readers, mindful of the ultimate identity of production and consumption, come to use as the touchstone of success in an economy the volume of production which it achieves—very often, the volume of *industrial* production alone. They slur over the costly effort of marketing by which production is adapted to the pattern of consumer wants and rarely speculate on the correlative changes within households that go to determine whether an increased flow of goods and services from firms is of net benefit to the community. If one could measure consumption directly, it might quite well exhibit a falling trend or show no more than a gentle rise, while the available indices of production (and especially industrial production) were increasingly comparatively steeply. The very idea of trying to measure consumption from the consumer's side will strike many economists as fantastic; and although the task could not be carried out with precision, it is extraordinary how little thought the subject now receives, and how frequently in international comparisons, entirely inappropriate measures are quoted without reservation. In the USSR, for example, no less than 70 per cent of the output of manufactures consists of producer goods: the movement of the index of industrial production may not correspond in any way, therefore, with movements in the consumption of manufactures. There is not even a necessary presumption that consumption will one day reflect the steep climb in industrial output.

If we turn from the USSR to the USA we find phenomena of a different kind. We are assured that one-quarter of the national income consists of the unpaid services performed by housewives within the household; on this quarter, economists are almost completely silent, and on the trend in the ratio they are largely ignorant. We are told also that the American worker has at his disposal a larger stock of capital at home than in the factory where he is employed. What attention is given to capital accumulation in this very private sector? Is it not, in fact, a close approximation to the truth to regard the average American home as a small factory, highly equipped with labour-saving devices, where the housewife puts in a very long working week and her husband a rather shorter one? Of course, the tea-breaks are longer and there is some absenteeism. The money that changes hands does not altogether conform to the general conception of wages except when the younger members of the household require some incentive to co-operate; but it would be possible to cite payments on the farm and sometimes even in the factory that are not materially different. There are wage grumbles, labour trouble and even, on occasion, strikes. The household-factory may be run efficiently or inefficiently and the margin that separates the best and the worst is very wide. When more horse-power is needed in the kitchen or the workshop, the familiar problem of finance for re-equipment emerges and if there is not enough to plough back from last year's earnings, recourse may be had to the capital market, including that large sector of it that specializes in financing consumers rather than producers.

Does this seem far-fetched? Then look at the practical consequences of the opposite view. If a factory needs more capital and borrows for the purpose, it can buy equipment free of tax, is given an initial allowance or even an investment allowance, and is egged on by public opinion, the trade unions and its own workpeople. Its investment is intended to increase the flow of goods for final consumption. But let the householder decide to short-circuit the process and invest on his own account and see what happens. Almost all the goods with which he can re-equip are subject to a stiff tax; if he looks elsewhere for capital, he is snubbed and told that the country cannot afford it; and every agency that might help him to buy on credit is put on its guard against his anti-social behaviour. The set of factories run by producers—in effect, as sub-contractors to households—are given every advantage while the set of factories that we call households—in effect, the main contractors—get kicked for their initiative.

Economists continue to analyse investment as if it were exclusively an activity of producers. They recognize, rather reluctantly, that houses are a particularly important form of investment that cannot easily be left aside in any study of capital formation. They recognize also the growing importance of consumers' durables other than housing. But it is doubtful whether they appreciate just how large a slice of capital formation is represented by such durables; the contrast between the space given to the analysis of investment in producers' machinery and the space devoted to consumers' machinery is extremely striking and quite without justification. The time has come to treat investment by consumers on the same footing as investment by producers, to measure its size, the fluctuations to which it is subject, the sources from which it is financed, and so on. We know next to nothing about the run-down in consumers' capital during the war and its re-building since the war; yet without such knowledge how can we hope to establish satisfactorily what now governs private savings (in excess of what is directly invested in durable goods)?

Let us take another example. A great deal of the time of households is occupied in those negotiations with sub-contractors which we call shopping and in visits to their establishments which involve travelling. When it is desired to increase production, as in war-time, nothing is simpler than to do so by reducing the marketing effort that firms expend with a view to making things easier for the households that buy from them. Consumers can be deprived of delivery services, obliged to queue or to go short of what they want, put into uniform and offered standard goods. At the same time, productivity undergoes a sharp but spurious increase and consumers whose 'basic requirements' are met can be assured that, in spite of a tremendous economy in man-power, they are no worse off 'in real terms'. From this point of view, productivity is maximized by enrolling all consumers in a vast army in which consumption is 'rationalized'; the economies that are customarily associated with large-scale operation are achieved by creating units of consumption to correspond with the largest possible units of production. But if we set out to measure consumption as the consumer measures it, we are likely to reach a different conclusion. We have to deduct from what he gets all that he no longer gets; and the fact that this cannot be exactly measured does not make it any the less important.

Reflection on this example shows how entangled production is with consumption. If we try to establish what final consumption is once the exertions and inconveniences to which the consumer is submitted have been eliminated, we are chasing a will o' the wisp. The consumer cannot divide his life by a line on one side of which is consumption and on the other production. He may like or dislike the effort of shopping; he may dislike it and yet dislike it less when the whole community is obliged to shop harder for what it wants; or he may like it, but only when the effort of shopping is not complicated by queues. It may be possible to single out some acts of consumption and regard them as always pleasurable but a drain on the limited resources of the community. Other forms of consumer behaviour may economize the resources of the community and be anything but pleasurable. But a great deal of what the consumer does, at any standard of living above the minimum, does not fall neatly into either of these categories.

Exactly the same is true of production. No one is likely to detest every minute that he spends at work without making an effort to find another job. On the other hand, there can be few people who so love their work that they grudge every minute spent away from it. The fact that 'work' is paid for does not necessarily make it less satisfying than work that is not paid for. In the act of producing, a man does not cease to be a consumer any more than, in the act of consuming, he remains a producer.

This brings us back to an earlier proposition: that the activities of the firm have much in common with the activities of the household, and that economists would go less astray in analysing the former if they began from the latter. The most obvious illustration of this arises in relation to the behaviour of entrepreneurs. An entrepreneur is assumed by some economists to aim at maximizing his profits while others make allowance for the diminishing marginal utility of the income that those profits will afford him. The proper distinction is surely between those businesses where the proprietor himself decides the scale and type of operations in which the firm shall engage and those in which the proprietor takes the profit and has no other interest in the business. The first type of proprietor is exactly like any other wage-earning producer, except in respect of the satisfaction that he derives from owning and running a business; he is a consumer as well as a producer, free to decide whether he will work overtime in his factory or in his garden, whether he can aim at a high but uncertain income rather than a low and stable income without rising an unbearable disturbance in his pattern of consumption, whether the taxes that he will pay on additional income make it not worth the earning, and so on. His decisions can be understood by the same process of reasoning as the decisions of a miner or a docker whether to accept or reject opportunities of additional income.

On the other hand, the second type of proprietor is not a producer at all in this sense. He is simply a property-owner and he may be represented, with due qualifications, as interested primarily in the highest net return he can obtain. This does not mean that the businesses in which he invests are themselves conducted so as to yield the maximum return, either to their proprietors in dividends or in the net profits out of which dividend and other payments are made. Those who take the decisions are usually a different group of people who may be guided by the interests of the proprietors or may, within limits, disregard them, but whose motives cannot be analysed in terms of the normal behaviour of consumers/producers.

Yet even the activities of this group, whose interests in the profits of the enterprise they run are inevitably complex, can be understood more satisfactorily if viewed alongside the activities of the average household. The housewife has to run a household in the net income of which she has a substantial but by no means exclusive interest. She has to cope with a refractory group and seek to maintain a peaceful and co-operative relationship. She has to consider the wisdom of supplementing the family income by working outside the household, or by taking into the household work previously done for it outside. There are problems of location: the possibility of finding better opportunities of work for the older members of the household and better opportunities of education and training for the younger. There are, as we have seen, problems of investment. Above all, there is a task of management in which the activities of each member of the household have to be organized so as to engage their energies with the minimum of friction.

Nor is it likely that any trends visible in household management will fail to leave their mark in factory management or vice versa. The discipline of the Victorian household had its counterpart in the strict discipline of the Victorian business. On the other hand, the greater freedom of women in industry has been accompanied by greater equality in the home. Machines make their way more freely into households because they have already made their way into factories. The network of loans and investments in industry is paralleled by a similar network between households. There is scope for a fuller analysis of the interactions between habits of consumption and production, of the overflow in either direction of the changes at work in factory and household.

If the sharp antithesis between consumption and production were done away with, we should gain not only a deeper insight into our society but a less mystical view of things. So long as firms are regarded as the creatures of mysterious forces that the ordinary man cannot understand, so long will these forces be regarded as evil and requiring stringent control. But the more they are seen as approximating to the households in which every man lives, the more intelligible they will seem and the less hostility will their independence of one another occasion.

For Product Safety Concerns and Information please contact our EU representative GPSR@taylorandfrancis.com
Taylor & Francis Verlag GmbH, Kaufingerstraße 24, 80331 München, Germany

www.ingramcontent.com/pod-product-compliance
Lightning Source LLC
LaVergne TN
LVHW011111300926
849160LV00008B/345

* 9 7 8 0 4 1 5 8 4 7 5 9 9 *